Household Ecology

Household Ecology

ECONOMIC CHANGE AND DOMESTIC LIFE
AMONG THE KEKCHI MAYA IN BELIZE

RICHARD R. WILK

The University of Arizona Press

Tucson & London

The University of Arizona Press

Copyright © 1991
The Arizona Board of Regents
All Rights Reserved

∞ This book is printed on acid-free, archival-quality paper.
Manufactured in the United States of America

96   95   94   93   92   91   6   5   4   3   2   1

Library of Congress Cataloging-in-Publication Data

Wilk, Richard R.
    Household ecology : economic change and domestic life among the
Kekchi Maya in Belize / Richard R. Wilk.
        p.   cm.—(Arizona studies in human ecology)
    Includes bibliographical references and index.
    ISBN 0-8165-1214-0 (acid-free paper)
    1. Kekchi Indians—Economic conditions.   2. Kekchi Indians—
Social conditions.   3. Indians of Central America—Belize—Economic
conditions.   4. Indians of Central America—Belize—Social
conditions.   I. Title.   II. Series.
F1465.2.K5W55   1991
304.2′089974—dc20   91-16197
                                                               CIP

British Library Cataloguing-in-Publication Data
A catalogue record for this book is available from the British Library.

Contents

Figures

Tables

Preface

The far southern end of Belize, known as the Toledo District, is a distant and primitive place to the residents of Belize City, itself no great metropolis. Although Toledo is only 161 kilometers by air from the city, the long overland road is rough and sometimes impassable during the rainy season. Luxuries and amenities are few in Toledo, and its administrative center, Punta Gorda, is considered the worst posting in the civil service and police. It is rare to find a Belizean who has braved the ruts, potholes, and biting flies of the southern highway to visit Toledo, unless forced to go on business.

Toledo, in short, is an undeveloped hinterland; its inhabitants are considered conservative and traditional, isolates from the economic and political affairs of the rest of the country who preserve old ways of life. It is therefore a natural place for an anthropologist to go, and few people in Belize or in my graduate program were surprised at my choosing Toledo for my dissertation fieldwork.

FINDING THE KEKCHI

Choosing one of Toledo's five ethnic groups to work with was relatively straightforward. The Garifuna (Black Caribs) on the coast live in towns and migrate regularly to the United States for work. Some seem more modern in their dress, education, and outlook than the average rural citizen of the States. The Garifuna also had already been studied by other anthropologists, and one Garifuna was then getting a Ph.D. in anthropology. The East Indians who lived along the southern highway seemed completely deculturated. They no longer spoke Hindi, belonged to evangelical or Methodist churches, and preserved little that could be called traditional except for curry and *chapati* (flat bread). Of the two Maya Indian groups, the Mopan seemed already quite modern; many spoke English and drove trucks. Their increasing participation in

Belizean culture had been quite capably described in a recent dissertation (Gregory 1972).

For *real* tradition, I was told, the only choice were the Kekchi.[1] Some
of their villages are right on the main highway and are relatively modern, but there are still many communities scattered through the rain
forest along muddy footpaths, villages where people are monolingual
and have little contact with the outside world. They are isolated from
the modern cash economy, practice subsistence farming using the ancient technique of slash and burn, and still hunt and gather much of
their food.

Here was the ideal culture in which to study the impact of modernization on traditional agriculture, kinship, and households. I could begin in one of the more isolated villages and then compare it with other
communities where cash crops, consumer goods, missionaries, health
care, and education were having a modernizing effect. In March 1979,
after short visits to some of the more accessible northern villages, I left
Punta Gorda in a huge dugout canoe to go down the coast and up the
Temash River toward the most isolated and traditional village in the
district.

The trip upriver, past miles of uninhabited rain forest, reminded me of
the famous journey in *Heart of Darkness* (which I had just read)—a
voyage through time as well as space. With increasing distance from the
meager comforts of Punta Gorda, the conversation of my Kekchi com-
panions acquired new importance; the feeling of having left the modern
world behind was overwhelming (though not entirely unpleasant). That
night at Crique Sarco, I stayed with a missionary family who told me
tales of how isolated they were and of how the Indians were bound by
tradition. They saw themselves as pioneers, carving out a small enclave
of civilized medical care and education in a dark forest of ignorance.

The next day, nine hours' walking (including three hours of being
lost and two of detour) brought me to Otoxha. Located on a small rise
at the fork of two streams, it is one of the oldest Maya settlements in
Toledo. About 40 families were living there in small pole-and-thatch
houses scattered across a square kilometer of forest. Footpaths radiated
outward to the houses from a quiet grassy clearing, where there is a
Catholic church (visited by a priest six or seven times a year), a *cabildo*
(meetinghouse and jail), and a primary school. These outposts of national society were built of local materials from the bush; the schoolteachers were teen-aged Mopan Maya from another village who had
been to high school in Punta Gorda.

Differences between Otoxha and the northern roadside villages are obvious and striking. I had, of course, expected them from reading about Indian cultures of Mesoamerica. Almost no consumer goods were available, and people were ardently curious about those I carried. Almost everything that people consumed or used was grown, made, or gathered in the village. I was impressed with how few material possessions people had—besides an ax, machete, and a kerosene lamp or two, people depended on home-crafted baskets, handwoven bags, pottery, and stone metates. Even shotguns and metal corn mills were rare in Otoxha. Women wore traditional cotton skirts they bought or bartered from traveling Kekchi traders from the Guatemalan highlands, and they went topless most of the time. Men's clothes had more patches than original cloth. Almost everyone was monolingual in Kekchi.

Other signs that this village was more traditional than those I had seen before took longer to notice. Colorful fiestas, with ceremonial drinking and elaborately costumed dances, took place once or twice a year. The civil-religious *cargo* system of rotating offices seemed strong and elaborate. There was a functioning indigenous judicial system in which village elders arrived at consensus judgments. Talk of witchcraft was common, and sorcery appeared to act as a social control.

Later I heard about religious rituals that sounded ancient. Offerings were made to saints in caves, and incense was burned for the spirits of the hills, valleys, and streams. Many aspects of life seemed ritualized, from the little home altars with their wreaths of seed corn to the elaborate festive meals that followed work parties. People seemed to know very little of the outside world—they asked naive questions about the United States and tended to lump together and mix up all foreigners. For some time people feared I was a German or a Mennonite missionary.

Because I was there to study the effects of agricultural change on household organization, the most important thing to me about Otoxha was the lack of cash crop production or serious population pressure on land. It looked like a control case, a traditional baseline to which I could compare the more developed areas. As I expected, in Otoxha I found that kinship and household relationships were merged with a community network of cooperation. All the village men belonged to communal work groups (*faginas*) that cleared, planted, and harvested fields in rotation. Women cooperated with kin and fictive kin in child care and daily food preparation. Other traditional forms of village cooperation seemed to dominate village life: the fagina that maintained the village green and public trails; the groups that built and maintained the church; others that met to build houses, thatch roofs, and bury the dead.

Individual households and families seemed submerged in this community network. They had their own cornfields and pigpens, but most food producing and processing was by groups that were larger than a single household. A gift economy—foods and possessions constantly being given or loaned without much reckoning of balance—prevailed among Otoxha's households. At the same time, many kinship practices that were dying out in the north were still thriving: premarital bride service; nonchurch weddings; and even a case of polygyny.

As my teachers and reading had led me to expect, the gender-based division of labor in Otoxha seemed fuzzier than that I had seen in the more acculturated areas. Women were silent in public meetings (except trials), but their informal influence in the community was formidable. They did agricultural work much more than in the north, where women had little to do with farming and seemed to have less political voice or economic power.

So I reached the traditional society I had hoped for and set about finding the worm in the apple. The small enclave of Otoxha was under siege. Already the missionaries had made some converts in the village and had built a new church. And the new converts refused to participate in the village labor groups, breaking down community solidarity. A recent increase in alcohol use, I was told, had led to frequent public fights, more witchcraft accusations, and further decline in village cohesion.

Some villagers were experimenting with cash crops, even though it could take days to get a sack of rice to market. People, especially the young, wanted imported goods—radios, perfume, kitchen implements, and shotguns, for example. Sometimes they spent their money on baby formula, soft drinks, sunglasses, running shoes, and other items of no practical value.

Patterns of family and household organization seemed to be changing too, although I was unclear about what direction they were taking. But I expected to see a breakdown of the ties between households and an increasing isolation of the family, paralleling the erosion of the community. Parents complained that their children were no longer willing to contribute to the household economy. Inequality between families was increasing, I was told, as some households were more involved in the cash economy than others. Communal work groups were no longer as important, and men were becoming reluctant to assume the burden of traditional village government offices. Some years nobody wanted the highest position of alcalde. Village factionalism was getting more serious.

Compounding all these changes was the educational system—a joint church-state primary school with two teachers—which was implanting all kinds of new ideas and desires into children, perhaps encouraging them to leave for the city. Worse, British military units often passed through the village while patrolling the nearby border with Guatemala. They could not help but increase the pace of cultural change.

It seemed that I was just in time. Otoxha was only just starting the long slide into cultural homogenization. As new roads inched farther south, as the government increased its presence in the area, as missionaries became more active, a cash and commodity economy got more firmly implanted, and foreign agrobusinesses acquired more land, the Kekchi would be acculturated. The future, at best, would see them, like other rural Belizeans, as a semiproletariat, working seasonally for low wages on foreign farms (which were then being established in northern Toledo) while maintaining a small and marginal family subsistence farm or migrating elsewhere in search of higher wages.

Culturally, the prospects for the survival of a distinctly Kekchi way of life seem grim. New religions are swamping the old traditions that had been accommodated by Catholicism. Imported goods are replacing traditional crafts. As a previous ethnographer said, "The old customs are dying in the face of the technologically superior creole influence and there is nothing genuine, to use Sapir's terminology, to replace them. There is only the empty tinsel of American industry that the creoles have so feverishly embraced. One can only hope that the Kekchi will meet the challenge to change as successfully as the Maya of northern British Honduras and Yucatan seem to" (Rambo 1962 : 47).

RECONSTRUCTING TRADITIONAL SOCIETY

Otoxha was a difficult fieldwork setting. Not least of my problems was the lack of food; nobody would sell me so much as an egg. My host family was fast tiring of me and I of them, since they were involving me in a factional fight within the village. With the rainy season, and the possibility of being trapped for a month or two by rising rivers, fast approaching, I decided to return to town and rethink my research design. In the relative comfort of Punta Gorda I decided to work in a less remote village that could be reached by four-wheel-drive vehicle, a place where the process of change that I wanted to study was further along. In May I moved to Aguacate village and stayed there for 10 months. From there I also worked in Santa Theresa, a less developed village accessible on foot, and later spent two months in Indian Creek, a more developed community on the main highway.

As my fieldwork progressed, I studied the adoption of cash crops and corresponding changes in households, kinship, and community organization. Data on the productivity and organization of labor in the different communities helped me see how development caused change in social structure. It was disconcerting, though, to find that these changes were not always destructive. The traditional institutions were in many cases gaining strength and importance in the more developed areas. Was this some kind of cultural revitalization, the maintenance of an old form with a new function? Or was there a basic defect in the theories that had led me to expect something different?

More problems appeared when, after leaving Aguacate, I spent a month digging through the National Archives in Belmopan. I found that while Toledo had always been a backwater of the national economy, it had been through several distinct periods of economic investment, followed by stretches of recession and administrative neglect. There were, for example, large and active logging settlements and plantations in the Otoxha area in the 1890s. I found evidence that Mopan and Kekchi farmers had sold large quantities of corn and beans to the British government during World War I. After that, there was a logging boom, and a palm oil extraction factory employed over 900 laborers. The beginning of the Great Depression drastically cut the cash income and purchasing power of many Indians, but for others selling bananas to the Standard Fruit Company provided a large and steady income for several more years.

There were times when reams of official documents on Toledo were filed: surveys of population, agriculture, and resources; detailed descriptions of the Indians and their way of life and migrations; schemes for attracting investment capital; descriptions of road construction projects; plans for improving education. Then there would be years, even decades of silence—a few records of declining numbers of children in the schools and petitions for help from villages. Some Kekchi actually returned to Guatemala during these periods. The quiet 1940s and the active early 1950s, the quiet 1960s and the active 1970s: each time a bout of development began, the records gave the impression that this was the first time such a thing had happened in the area. Each new set of administrators echoed their predecessors, portraying Toledo as virtually undeveloped, a primeval forest full of untouched, primitive Indians.

So what appears to be a slowly developing frontier today had been a developing, or even developed, frontier in the past. What looked like directional change was actually cyclic. Areas that are the most isolated and traditional today had once been the most developed and modern, and vice versa. Otoxha once sent its children to a modern school with English teachers, and some villagers worked in a steam-powered mill. Eighty years ago you could get within an hour's walk of the village by regular passenger service on a modern launch. What today are the most modern villages, with electricity and running water, 50 years ago were the most isolated, places where white people were almost unknown.

And what of the cultural antecedents of those traditional Indians? Most Belizeans assume that because the Kekchi immigrated from Guatemala in the 1890s, they must have been in a pristine aboriginal state before they came. The conventional sources say that up to migration the Guatemalan Kekchi were virtually untouched and unacculturated (see, e.g., Villa Rojas 1967). They had even been spared the worst of the Spanish conquest, having been peacefully subdued by the Dominicans under Las Casas. The Kekchi had come to Belize as plantation laborers, but their employers had quickly gone bankrupt and the Indians had simply returned to the forest and their traditional ways. Thus, traditions were preserved and continuity with the past maintained (Romney 1959:110–15).

But the idea of continuity from pre-Hispanic times to the present rests on some very suspect foundations. Even allowing that the Dominicans did no more than appropriate the native political and economic system, and allow the Kekchi to continue as before, this protection was gone with Guatemala's independence from Spain in 1821. The Kekchi soon lost most of their land and were subject to coerced labor service (see Chapter 4). By the 1880s, when emigration to Belize began, the Kekchi homeland of the Alta Verapaz was a German colony in which Indians were virtual serfs on coffee plantations. A German ethnographer, a relative of coffee planters, described the Kekchi as having "a primitive way of life, free and independent, very little influenced by modern civilization" (Sapper 1926:190). But closer reading of historical sources suggests that the Kekchi have, in fact, endured cultural disruptions, drastic economic changes, religious proselytizing, political domination, forced migration, and loss of basic economic resources repeatedly and continually for over 400 years! How can one then observe a custom in 1928 (Thompson 1930b), or 1960 (Rambo 1962), or 1978, and assume that it is a survival from prehistoric times without making a giant leap of faith? And what preconceptions is that leap based upon?

What, for example, of the antiquity of Kekchi slash-and-burn agriculture? Let us remember that the Kekchi migrated into underpopulated lowland Belize from the densely settled highlands of Guatemala. Could not long-fallow swiddening be a recent adaptation to the new abundance of land? Early colonial documents say the Kekchi used intensive fixed-plot horticulture or infield-outfield mixed systems, (Viana, Gallego & Cadena 1955; Reina & Hill 1980; Marcus 1982) rather than slash and burn. William E. Carter (1969) studied recent Kekchi migrants to the lowlands from Guatemala who were still learning swidden agriculture. And recent archaeological work questions the assumption that swidden agriculture was the norm in pre-Hispanic times anywhere in the Maya area (Harrison & Turner 1978; Flannery 1982). Similarly, hunting and gathering do not necessarily denote a traditional lifeway. These activities are common among all rural people in Belize, not just Indians. Hunting was probably much less common in the highland homeland where both guns and game were scarcer. And some of the wild plants that the Kekchi gather are for sale, not home consumption.

The erosion of traditional crafts and their replacement by purchased materials has not been a gradual or even directional process. The Kekchi have had and used axes, machetes, metal cooking implements, china dishes, imported foods, kerosene lamps, cosmetics, and many other imported items for hundreds of years, when they could afford them. Women's traditional garb includes machine-made cloth and imported yarns. Metal hand mills have been used to grind corn for tortillas for many years, although stone metates (made in factories) are used to finish the grinding and give a distinctive flavor and texture. Highland Kekchi traveling merchants (*cobaneros*) sell cheap factory products (some of which look traditional, as metates do) all over southern Belize and eastern Guatemala, always for cash and in a modern and very businesslike fashion. Whether or not a Kekchi family owns imported goods—be they traditional cloth, or modern wristwatches—depends on how much money the family has to spend, not on how traditional or modern the household is.

What of the survival of Kekchi religion within the structure of the Catholic church? Like the antiquity of the civil-religious *cofradía* system, the survival of ancient religions is mostly an illusion. The Kekchi are as devout as any other Catholic people in the Third World. Their belief in spirits of the forest, hills, and streams, in hairy monsters and forest gnomes, is nothing like the institutionalized and hierarchical state religions of pre-Hispanic times (see Fox 1981). They are more directly comparable to the spirits, witches, and ghosts that have appeared to rural Christians in Europe and the United States (and have not always disappeared with "progress"). The cofradía system is a surprisingly recent introduction that bears limited resemblance to pre-Hispanic social or political forms (Chance & Taylor 1985). It has about 150 years' depth in Kekchi culture and so can hardly be considered more traditional than the U.S. Constitution, which may predate it.

If neither religion, material culture, political organization, nor agriculture provide direct links with the traditional Indian past, what of the basic Kekchi social fabric—the household, the kinship network, and the labor-exchange group? As I will show, there is not much continuity there either. Kekchi households form, ally with each other, break up, and move from place to place in response to changing markets, political and legal regulation, land availability, and the prospects for education and medical care. In all they seem little constrained by tradition, although some organizing principles provide continuity. What appears most traditional—the extended family household—is actually a recent innovation. Similarly, the large labor-exchange groups, which appear to be vestiges of some ancient precapitalist communal solidarity, are adaptations to capitalism that ensure survival in a precarious economic niche. Even the traditional pattern of gender-based division of labor may be an artifact of labor conditions over the last 80 years.

I did know something about world systems theory and peripheral capitalism when I went into the field in 1978. I had been well exposed to critiques of modernization theory, had read about how deeply Indians have been involved in market production for hundreds of years, and had dutifully demolished Redfield's folk-urban continuum in a class assignment. But knowing that the Otoxha Kekchi were no more traditional than those living in Belize City did not lead directly to better understanding of what I actually saw. Even while synthesizing my notes and data into a dissertation over the next two years, I wrote as if the southern Kekchi were precapitalist or subsistence farmers while those in the north were more heavily involved in a cash economy or more exposed to external economic, cultural, and political pressures. These terms allowed me to continue analyzing directional change, and to describe the impact of greater market participation on a subsistence economy, without using the words *traditional* or *modern* very often. But the dissertation remains a study of modernization that would not seriously upset Redfield, even if it concludes that modernization strengthens instead of weakens the extended family.

Between 1980, when my dissertation was finished, and the present revision of that material, I have been able to reexamine and penetrate some of the fallacies that underlie the image of "traditional society in the throes of modernization" that I have caricatured above. The fundamental shift in my perspective on the Kekchi during that time has required me to rewrite and revise every aspect of my original work. In this book, not a single page remains unchanged from my dissertation though I have used most of the same basic data on household organization and agricultural production.

My goal during fieldwork was to study modernization at the household level. My focus remains the household, but it is here the vehicle for a critique of the evolutionary and schematic models of cultural change that flow from both modernization and dependency theory. Households are creative responses, culturally constructed systems rooted in local history, local understandings, and local communities. By showing how households adapt to very localized economic and ecological settings, I argue that the transformation of the rural economy and of Maya culture proceeds through the conjunction of global and local processes. But in this conjunction people cannot be reduced to passive actors, responding to the world system in a determined way. They retain a voice and a creative role, shaping the direction of their own future. My basic agenda is to show that the household is the best social unit, the best analytical level through which to study these active strategies and the conjunction of local and global processes of change.

Acknowledgments

My academic debts are too large to repay and too many to list. Monetary support for my original field research was provided by the National Science Foundation (BNS 7814205), the Wenner Gren Foundation (3312), and the Graduate College of the University of Arizona. The University of California, Santa Cruz, provided a faculty research grant for analysis of census materials. The U.S. Agency for International Development gave me some paid time off from work in 1984 to continue my archival research in Belize. New Mexico State University allowed me to use their facilities to write and prepare the final manuscript for the book. I must also thank my parents, Max and Barbara Wilk, and my grandparents Eva Wilk and Edith and Irwin Balensweig for financial support that tided me over between grants.

In Belize my research was aided by literally hundreds of people. Most prominent in Toledo was Don Owen-Lewis, who taught me my first words of Kekchi and continues to educate me about the area and its people. The Aguacate villagers were patient and forbearing, and I depended constantly on their kind hospitality. The alcalde, Tomás Rash, helped me get settled in the community, and the Cucul family were especially friendly. Many people in Santa Theresa, Indian Creek, San Antonio, Blue Creek, and San Pedro educated and guided me, giving freely of their time and attention. I was assisted also by various government agencies, including the Marketing Board, the Agriculture Department (I particularly thank Louis Frutas), and the Lands Office in Toledo. The Department of Archaeology, especially the commissioner, Harriot W. Topsey, was consistently helpful and supportive of my work. The kind assistance of the staffs of the Public Records Office in Belize City and the National Archives in Belmopan made my work in their records possible. I also owe debts of various kinds to Pedro Cucul, Lou Nicolait, Laura Kosakowsky, Jerry Parham, Charles Wright, Ricardo Montero, Jim McDonald, Tom Juring, and the late William Mesmer.

The greatest influence on my intellectual growth while planning, researching, writing, and rewriting this book has been Robert McC. Netting. As a teacher, role model, mentor, and colleague, he has always provided the best possible combination of scholarly guidance and friendship. The other teachers, students, colleagues, and friends who have helped me along the way, contributing to my growth as a person and scholar, are too numerous to mention individually. To all, many thanks.

The one person who has made the greatest contribution of all is my friend, colleague, and wife, Anne Pyburn. Without her, there would be no book.

Household Ecology

1 Introduction

Why is it so hard to see through the modernization paradigm? Why are we so driven by the assumption that there is a directional and evolutionary cultural progression from traditional to modern that parallels an economic change from an isolated indigenous system to one that is open and attached to world capitalism? We can read Wolf on the "people without history," delve into Frank's essay on how the "Indian problem" was created by colonial society, and see how artificial traditional culture can be in Hobsbawm and Ranger's *The Invention of Tradition*. But it is almost impossible to understand ethnographic or economic data on change in the Third World without returning to these very concepts.

One reason this is so lies within the tradition of the discipline of anthropology. Boasian anthropology's mission, in part, was to rescue primitive cultures before they died out. This in turn led to studies of change under the rubric of acculturation, directional change in which traditional societies adopted traits from modern ones. It is not hard to see the implicit evolutionary scheme, as well as the empathy for the doomed, that underlies such ideas.

Most Euroamerican anthropologists are still taught that other cultures can inform us about the past and that learning from them is a worthwhile enterprise. But there are difficult contradictions between any concept of progress and the values of cultural relativism that are not addressed by mere preservationism. Fabian (1983:11–31) believes that anthropology places the object of study in another time scale entirely, in a mythical, representational, timeless time where change is suspended. He argues that only by creating this distance has anthropology found a safe object, that the distance of the self from the traditional and primitive is the essence of the discipline.

These ideals remain pervasive within modern anthropology and development studies, even among those who explicitly reject the idea that traditional cultures represent survivals from bygone eras. World systems

theory, which attempts to show that all cultures are modern, all integrated into a single ongoing system, fails to transcend the traditional-
modern paradigm when it works with individual cases. While Fabian's
argument may be exaggerated, he is right that we see the world through
an unconscious temporal map, even when we do not want to. Where he
may be wrong is in limiting his argument to anthropology and in implying that anthropologists are responsible for spreading this misper-
ception to other academic disciplines (Fabian 1983:144–61). Other disciplines that study the Third World, culture change, and the economy
of the world system also make evolutionary assumptions about traditional cultures, often in more-blatant and less-informed terms than anthropologists use. The concept of progress—evolutionary change from
primitive to modern—is a pervasive folk model in U. S. culture. It hin-
ders even the most astute historical analysis through its very language
and perceptions. How is it that people can "look traditional" even
when garbed in modern clothes?

All people define themselves in opposition to the other. At the same
time they look to that other for things they feel they have lost. A combination of nostalgia and arrogant superiority results.[1] These twin emotions are clear in modern Belizean Creole attitudes to the Indians; they
lie behind a political policy that offers both paternalistic assistance and
a disregard for the Indians' stated needs and desires. The relatively
well-off and modern Maya of northern Belize look to their past to re-
gain some sense of community and self, as well as for a political identity in a multiethnic state (Wilk 1986), while the Peace Corps volunteer
goes to the traditional village expecting to find all kinds of virtues that
are lacking in U.S. culture—a sense of community, deeply held religious beliefs, and a feeling of belonging.

But these desires create a boundary and a barrier.[2] The people on the
other side of the boundary also believe that there are desirable things
lying beyond it, things such as decent medical care, access to land and
goods, educational advancement, wealth, and excitement. Being traditional, to those who are so defined, means having an identity at least
partially determined by opposition to a dominating, and usually exploiting, culture (Hawkins 1984). Being someone's other also defines a
self. The division between traditional and modern is more than a paradigm in the mind of the visiting anthropologist, more than a way of
forming an opinion about foreign aid for a factory worker in Michigan,
and more than an attitude taken by a nurse from Belize City on a visit
to the Indians in the jungle to teach the benefits of modern medicine. It
is also the expectation and the frustration of those Kekchi when the

nurse teats them like children. People on both sides of the shared line between traditional and modern see things they want; neither side is always willing or able to move across the boundary.

While the terminology with which we describe progress and development is value-laden and tainted with misguided evolutionary assumptions, it preserves some useful concepts. Beneath the belief that others are just like ourselves at an earlier stage of development lies a perception that cannot be denied. The idea of development may obscure history, it may raise false hopes of progress and make a mockery of people's exploitation, but it also says something very real about the last 500 years of human history. However we may interpret or explain it, thousands of more or less autonomous economic, political, and cultural units all over the world have lost their autonomy and have entered into relationships that link them together. A wide variety of systems have been affected in a bewildering number of ways. The process has had a wildly uneven historical trajectory, fast at some times and stopped at others. Whether we call this a capitalist system or not, with the benefit of hindsight we can see that its arrival in any locale was a definite historical turning point. It is not wrong to speak of a precapitalist and a postcapitalist era for most of the Third World. The problem is to keep this hard-edged judgment of time from taking on the connotations of such terms as *capitalist/modern* and *precapitalist/traditional*. For these connotations are the cutting edge of ethnocentrism.

When we reject the modernization paradigm it is hard to maintain our sense of direction. We are left with a peculiar sort of task: a study of tradition and modernization without either concept. We must study change in retrospect, denying any inevitable evolutionary direction. We must find a way to look at change in a comparative perspective without collapsing the changes into categories that keep us from understanding them. Vocabulary and concepts become enemies, lying in wait to twist the analysis into familiar channels and grooves that draw us away from significant questions that are difficult to answer.

THE PROBLEM OF HISTORY AND THE KEKCHI MAYA

Penetrating the mask of modernization requires us to examine the assumptions we begin with in any study of another society. Today I have challenged my earlier assumptions, and those contradictions and reevaluations provide the groundwork for this book. I have briefly listed below the assumptions I held in 1978, followed by the reevaluation I have since made.

- The culture and social organization of the Kekchi (i.e., the presumed traditional people) are more continuous with the past than the culture of Euroamericans (i.e., the self-designated modern). In fact, what appears traditional is often a recent innovation, sometimes a direct response to modern culture.
- The Kekchi were isolated from the outside world and from a global economy for many years, and that isolation is just beginning to end. In fact, the Kekchi have been deeply and intimately involved with the world economy for over 400 years, although often in a subservient and exploited position. Isolation can be a product, rather than a cause, of underdevelopment.
- Kekchi material poverty is a result of their disdain for Western imported goods, and of a system in which gifts, rather than commodities, are valued and circulated in a moral economy. In fact, material poverty for the Kekchi, as for anyone else, results directly from a lack of money and an inability to obtain it through control of its sources. While money and goods circulate in distinct ways within the community, these are best understood as means of survival in an economically marginal and dominated position, rather than as picturesque remnants of a precapitalist era of gift giving. To claim that the Kekchi are poor because of their culture can easily lead us to blame them for their poverty.
- The development of the Kekchi economy, and the incorporation of Kekchi culture into world culture, is a progressive and irreversible process that will lead to a loss of identity and a substitution of national culture. In fact, the Kekchi have been through many periods of greater and lesser dependence upon, and submersion in, economic systems they do not control, without any discernible loss of identity or distinctiveness. What is happening now has happened before. If anything, Kekchi ethnicity has been better defined, even exaggerated, over many years of economic domination and discrimination.
- A cohesive corporate community is an inherent characteristic of traditional Indian culture, an expression of something basic and time-honored in their lives. In fact, even the original conception of the closed corporate community emphasized that community solidarity was a means of resistance and adaptation to the pressures of the colonial economy (Wolf 1957). Nevertheless, it is common to assume that close ties of interdependence between families and a high degree of sharing and reciprocity within the community are markers of traditional society, subject to erosion through modernization. As Wolf suggested, these characteristics are more a product of modernization than a precursor of it.

- Traditional ecological and productive systems can be equated with subsistence production, while modern production means wage labor or cash cropping. In fact, almost every agricultural system includes both subsistence production and exchange of both products and labor. The Kekchi have by all accounts not had a "pure" subsistence lifeway for well over 2,000 years, and, for at least 400 years, many have worked off the farm part-time.
- The cohesive, multifunctional, family-based extended household is traditional, and its functions and structural complexity have been eroded by participation in the modern economy. In fact, for the Kekchi, as for much of the rest of the world, the grand family is a chimera. There is nothing about participation in wage labor, cash crop production, or state institutions that is inherently destructive to large and complex households, or to wider networks of kin.

Once we take away all these basic tenets, not much is left of the idea of modernization, except such abstractions as greater "structural differentiation" and increased application of scientific knowledge (Smelser 1967: 30–31). At the same time, change is clearly taking place in the Third World, evolutionary change that does appear to have common threads and a common direction. The task I have set for myself here is to discuss cultural and social change outside the framework of diffusion or acculturation. A more difficult objective is to generalize about that change and to define its direction without using the muddled paradigm of modernization.

Wolf addressed this same task in *Europe and the People Without History* (1982), looking at the growth of a world economic system as a linked series of events with an underlying evolutionary dynamic, rather than as the expression of a global trend of the expansion of the modern at the expense of the traditional. But his approach tends to lump phenomena together under convenient labels. In maintaining the grand sweep and scope of a world history, Wolf ends up talking about "capital," "tribes," "lineages," "chiefdoms," and "modes of production," and cannot help but ascribe intention, motivation, and coherence to these analytical abstractions. Through coercion or unequal exchange, one mode affects another, one political organization destroys or absorbs another. The strength of anthropology, its ability to break down abstract forces into real social units with their own dynamics and real human actors with understandable motives, is submerged.

An antidote is to maintain a focus on a social unit that is closer to the ground, in which changes are comprehended by reference to the motives and actions of individual human beings. While social change viewed from the distance of history can be envisioned as abstract forces acting upon each other, change that is observable in daily life is generated by patterns of individual and group decisions. The household unit has become recognized as the most important and informative level of analysis for understanding how individual and group action leads to structural transformation on a larger scale (see Arcury 1984; Martin 1984; Netting, Wilk & Arnould 1984; Wilk 1987). By focusing on the household we can see how changes in a wider economic and social environment affect individual decisions about social life. Of course, such groups as lineages, communities, and kindreds that have a corporate existence can make decisions about how to deal with a change in land legislation, or a new market for village produce, or even a new tax. But in all those cases the final decisions about how to respond usually rest with individuals and with households.

It is commonplace in U.S. society and in others to perceive that cultural change strikes first and hardest in the family and household. And nowhere is the mythology of progress from traditional to modern more firmly rooted than in U.S. political culture. The very idea of family change is dripping with cultural associations and prejudices that require us to look very hard at every assumption before proceeding to look at cases. Here is an example of why this is so necessary:

> Our laws, the attitude of government officials, our policies and programs, all reflect the national attitude towards the family. Our economic policy can weaken the family; our public pronouncements can undermine it; our cultural community can develop a prejudice against family life. If these things happen, the family cannot be expected to survive, much less thrive.
>
> The family is the engine that drives civilization. Throughout history, those cultures that have failed to found their rules and attitudes of society on the central importance of the family unit have decayed and disintegrated.

The quotation is from the chairman of the board of United Families of America, conservative former senator Jeremiah Denton (1982: cover).

OUTLINE OF THE BOOK

Chapter 2 will take up the theme of the household in social evolution. I examine the early social theorists, both conservative and radical, who used the household and family in their historical analyses and in constructing their political programs. They could not separate their view of domestic life from their evolutionary premises and so were blinded to empirical fact. Present-day academic studies of the household are still mired in the same evolutionary morass. Attempts at evolutionary classifications of the household, linking it to types of society or types of economy, are simplistic and often wrong.

At the end of Chapter 2, I suggest that a historically sensitive cultural-ecological approach provides a practical alternative to evolutionary-typological household studies. But this requires redefining our basic analytical categories, a task taken up in Chapter 3, which discusses the use and abuse of the term *household* and draws on other empirical studies to suggest appropriate methodologies.

Despite this extended theoretical introduction, the core of this book is a case study. I contend that Kekchi households adapt to local economic and ecological situations, not global ones. This argument is supported by showing that household organization varies between communities, within individual communities, and over time. I explain this variability as the result of different systems of production and consumption. These systems, in turn, result from the spatial and temporal patterning of access to markets, population pressure on land resources, ecological variation, and the social organization of productive labor in agriculture.

Because I place so much weight on temporal and spatial variability in the Kekchi environment, I devote Chapters 4 and 5 to Kekchi history and cultural geography, sketching the history of the Kekchi from the time of the conquest and detailing the causes of their migration to southern Belize. In Chapter 4 I focus mainly on changes in economy, settlement, and social organization, and the many cycles of economic development and underdevelopment that have shaped the Kekchi adaptation, fitting them into the cultural landscape of southern Belize and briefly discussing other ethnic groups that live in the area. In Chapter 5 I concentrate on geography and the ecological basis of modern systems of production.

Chapters 6 and 7 contain a basic description of Kekchi productive systems, including agriculture, livestock, and hunting and gathering. I have extracted material from my fieldwork that relates directly to the issues of productive decision making at the household level. I pay particular attention to the division of labor, to the formation of labor groups of different kinds, the ownership of land and other property, and the elements of risk and productivity that shape decisions. In these chapters it becomes clear that very detailed local knowledge is necessary to understand the economic and social bases of the domestic economy. It is particularly important to look at the variability in the ways different households meet economic and ecological challenges.

While the descriptions of production in Chapters 6 and 7 are relatively static, in Chapter 8's discussion of agricultural change I aim at the dynamics of the system, looking at consumption and consumer goods to argue that social and economic inequality—between households, genders, and age groups—is a fundamental and causative aspect of changes in Kekchi production. And as the systems of production change, they place new constraints on, and afford new opportunities for, households.

The challenges of new forms of production, and of expanded production, are met by adjustments and changes in the social organization of labor. In Chapter 9 I discuss the various forms of labor groups and cooperative production in Kekchi society and show how these productive groups relate—or fail to relate—to households. Through contrasts between three villages, I show that households engaged in large-scale cash crop production use different social means of motivating and organizing labor than those engaged in subsistence farming. In particular, expanded production leads to the emergence of the household as the main cooperative work group.

The structural changes that occur in households as they accommodate to and invent new systems of production are examined in Chapter 10. Instead of discussing these changes schematically, as if one type of household turns into another type, I focus on the residence decisions made by individuals at various stages of their lives, and on the economic consequences of those decisions. While the political organization of Kekchi communities is mostly beyond the scope of this book, at the end of Chapter 10 I place individual household decision making in a wider context of kin group and village.

In the last chapter we move back from the specific to the general. What relevance does the Kekchi case hold for a broader understanding of rural life in Latin America? I believe that the Kekchi provide an object lesson in the ways in which continuity is constructed through tradition, at the same time that dynamic structural and economic changes are made. The household, it seems, is both a microcosm of this transformation and its main vehicle. And the path it travels is not paved by abstract forces in the world system, nor does it follow a rigid evolutionary or historical direction, but is instead cleared by real people making everyday decisions.

2 Households and Social Evolution

Whatever the cause, the last 2,000 years have seen similar transformations in many different societies. But an ethnocentric evolutionary ideology, a belief in the superiority of one social system over others, has clouded our understanding of events. What justifies that sense of superiority is a concept of change and historical sequence, of the new and better supplanting the old. And the complement of superiority, a consequence of the distance it creates, is a sense of nostalgia, of a loss that mirrors what has been gained.

TRADITIONAL APPROACHES TO TRADITION

It is commonplace to link Herbert Spencer's ethnocentric and tautological social evolutionism with Charles Darwin's biological theories. But the idea that a more civilized, a more organized (even developed?) society is superior to a simpler or more primitive one was a basic part of the fabric of thought in Western society long before Darwin wrote *The Origin of Species* (Malefijt 1974 : 136). The idea of time, of ordered change and progress, is so closely linked to cultural, ethnocentric values that the two are almost impossible to separate, even in anthropological discourse (Fabian 1983). So even though we know that evolutionary change has occurred, we must remain critical of our perceptions and interpretations of that change. It is just too easy to fit our observations to an existing model, to reify our preconceptions, and to conclude that what we have preconceived was inevitable. Our evolutionary ideology is formed of hindsight and is always in danger of becoming self-fulfilling.[1]

No social arena has suffered from the imposition of an evolutionary ideology more than domestic life. The notion of progress seems to suffuse images of domestic life, as do the complementary themes of loss and nostalgia. From Xenophon (1970) and Plato onward, social theorists have pushed families into conformity with their grand theories, ordering them in time. And general attitudes about the past, across the scale from deep nostalgic preservationism to arrogant modernism, have colored most interpretations of domestic life. In discussing how households are involved in cultural change, we must therefore proceed carefully, separating assumptions from observations. The more closely we look at historical and evolutionary models of the household from the earliest time to the present, the clearer the political and ethnocentric assumptions become.

In his introduction to *Household and Family in Past Times*, one of the most influential books on the household in recent times, Peter Laslett criticizes evolutionary theories of household development because they do not fit the facts. He explains the persistence of grand evolutionary theories in the face of contrary evidence as a product of a peculiar nostalgia for an imaginary past (Laslett 1972:4–9, 16–21). I believe, however, that nostalgic blindness to facts about the household has its roots in deeper ideological commitments. Almost every important political or religious movement in the Euroamerican tradition over the last 150 years has had something to say about the household and family. Once progress is defined and a set of values about an ideal society is established, people turn to the family or household as either a symptom of the problem, its potential cure, or both. This blending of the political and academic emerges very early in the study of household and family.

Frédéric Le Play (1806–1882), inventor of modern sociological methodology, who proposed a model of family change and modernization, was never an academic in the strict sense of the word. The son of a small-town customs official, he became an engineer, and then an outspoken writer, reformer, and political activist, ending up as a consultant to Napoleon III, a counselor of state, commander of the Legion of Honor, and the head of a large political following. But to Le Play, the academic and the political were one (1982:283). His interest in the family was intensely political and didactic, flowing from his belief that what happened in the family was a function of what happened to the whole society, and vice versa. By conducting detailed monographic studies of individual families and dissecting their budgets and finances, he wanted to call attention to the pressing problems of society. Each case fit into a historical evolutionary model (Le Play 1982:73–75) that is worth recounting in some detail because it openly states many views that are present but concealed in later work.

Le Play (1982:15) based his ideas of the past partially on his own childhood experience in an isolated part of France.[2] Later, he hearkened to the reign of St. Louis (1226–1270) as the Golden Age of France, after which things went downhill, leading to the revolution when, Le Play (1879:30, cited in Zimmerman & Frampton 1935:75) said, the "three false dogmas—Liberty, Equality and the Right of Revolt"—were forced on the people.

Before the revolution social harmony founded in the family characterized society in Western Europe:

> The elements of social peace were strongly established in private life. Personal interest, harnessed by a sense of duty, led each to respect a master: in the home the children were submissive to the father; in the shop, the workmen obeyed the employer; in the community, the fathers and the employers grouped themselves deferentially around the social authorities. . . . Harmony extended over an entire province through the co-operation of a great hierarchy of families and localities. . . . Today this primary condition of happiness is disappearing little by little in Europe [Zimmerman & Frampton 1935:362].

The mid-nineteenth century was, to Le Play, a time of discord in which "social antagonisms . . . are shaking contemporary European societies to their very foundations" (quoted by Zimmerman & Frampton 1935:362). Drawing a distinction between happy societies and ones dominated by evil, he equated the former condition with tradition and the latter with novelty, meaning rapid social change. "The races which preserve unchanging happiness," he intoned, "remain for the most part in the condition of their ancestors" (quoted by Zimmerman & Frampton 1935:590). "They do not form new 'needs' nor undergo impressions which disturb their mores" (quoted by Zimmerman & Frampton 1935:591). Le Play created an evolutionary scheme that ordered his observed traditional and novel societies in sequence (though not as neatly as Morgan did) (Zimmerman & Frampton 1935:404).

Le Play was very clear about what was going on in modern Western Europe. "A fierce struggle is being waged today . . . between the spirit of tradition and the spirit of novelty." The rise of coal and machines in manufacturing degrades the value of skilled labor, and the entire social order is torn. Wealth becomes the supreme value to the detriment of religion and traditional authority (Zimmerman & Frampton 1935:391–93). The effect of economic change is to turn the working classes from being noble and happy into something repugnant. They lack judgment, are lazy and spendthrift, and are only worsened by philanthropy and assistance that "by exciting insatiable appetites, bring about the degradation of members of the working class" (quoted in Zimmerman & Frampton 1935:530).

Le Play's beliefs led him into reactionary political positions. He opposed representative democracy, universal suffrage, mandatory education, labor unions, and free market economics; and supported church involvement in government, the sanctity of private property, chauvinistic nationalism, and paternal authority in government and domestic life (Silver 1982:3–27). His political program was to slow down the rate of change, preserve existing customs, and have the state intervene to reinstate traditional family patterns (Zimmerman & Frampton 1935:119). Like Denton, Le Play thought that the root of all of the ill effects of progress on society lay in the "destruction of the family," and if the family could be changed back to its traditional state, then the problems would disappear.

Following this dubious logic, Le Play developed an evolutionary typology of the family that is still found in sociology texts. The three types are patriarchal, unstable, and stem families (Zimmerman & Frampton 1935:98; Laslett 1972:17–20). The patriarchal family, found in "simple but strong societies," has a "stable and permanent relationship with its fireside, it is faithful to traditions, and it establishes its married children near the homestead in order to watch over them" (Zimmerman & Frampton 1935:98; Le Play 1982:259). The household is authoritarian, and all that is good in happy societies is realized in a microcosm, even if the standard of living is low.

The unstable family is formed by the breakdown of patriarchal authority. "It has no permanent attachment to its hearth and it is inspired by the lust for social change." There is no generational continuity, and the family is really no more than individuals coming together for a short time. It is found in "complex societies which are suffering," where individuals may have a high consumption of material goods while employed, but "since the individual has no family tradition to hold him in check . . . recurring periods of economic insecurity cause a great deal of physical hardship" (Zimmerman & Frampton 1935:99). The unstable family is a product of industrial development and modernization, in which the various functions of the patriarchal family are stripped away. This in turn forces the government to take on the burdens previously shouldered by the domestic economy.

The stem family is Le Play's bright star on the horizon, a successful adaptation to industrial life. Continuity is ensured by a younger son's remaining in the household after marriage, independence by continuing subsistence production, and income by sending younger members out for industrial work.

> It satisfies both those who are happy in the situation of their birth and those who wish to advance socially or economically. It harmonizes the authority of the father and the liberty of the children. It is formed wherever the family is free and it maintains itself throughout major disruptions of the established order. . . . In brief, European people in becoming more free and more prosperous broke up the patriarchal family, which is too much given to the worship of tradition. They also attempted to repulse the unstable family with its desire for novelty. The stem-family satisfies both tendencies and harmonizes two equally imperative needs—the respect for tradition and the yearning for the new [Zimmerman & Frampton 1935 : 133–34].

This was not simple nostalgia for the past, although that may have been its inspiration. Rather, Le Play based his analysis of the family and its evolution on his belief that civilization was deteriorating, on his study of the geographic distribution of economic systems, of racial propensities, and of statistical data on French families. His cases were ordered temporally into an evolutionary sequence that provided a blueprint for political action (Zimmerman & Frampton 1935 : 565–79). Le Play was an archetype of the reactionary social scientist. His attitude to the family was a mirror for his attitude to progress and the social order. How then, would someone with a very different political viewpoint see the family?

Friedrich Engels (1820–1895) based his *The Origin of the Family, Private Property, and the State* on notes left him by Karl Marx and on the published works of Lewis Henry Morgan. The coauthor of *The Manifesto of the Communist Party* was hardly a reactionary like Le Play, but his views of modern industrial society expressed similar distaste. Modern capitalism was a dehumanizing force, a system that emisserated and enslaved, while destroying the economic and social bonds that had previously tied people together into communities. "By making all things into commodities, it dissolved all inherited and traditional relationships, and, in place of time-honored custom and historic rights, it set up purchase and sale" (Engels 1942 : 70).

Both Marx and Engels tended to idealize the "good old days" of precapitalist society, although they looked further back in time than did Le Play. Before modern civilization, societies were organized communally, and exploitation of one sex by the other, or of one class by another, was unknown. "And what men and women such a society breeds is proven by the admiration inspired in all white people who have come into contact with unspoiled Indians, by the personal dignity, uprightness, strength of character, and courage of these barbarians" (Engels 1942:87). Corruption came not with the French Revolution, but among the ancient Greeks, with the origin of private property and the emergence of a monetary system that encouraged commodity exchange. With civilization comes the state, slavery, the disruption of communities, exploitation of one class by another, and "a permanent opposition between town and country" (Engels 1942:161). Civilization was viewed with the same kind of distaste felt by Le Play. "With this as its basic constitution, civilization achieved things of which gentile society was not even remotely capable. But it achieved them by setting in motion the lowest instincts and passions in man and developing them at the expense of all his other abilities. From its first day to this, sheer greed was the driving spirit of civilization; wealth and again wealth and once more wealth, wealth, not of society, but of the single scurvy individual—here was its once and final aim" (Engels 1942:161).

Engels, like Le Play, equated the condition of society with that of the family, and wove the evolution of the family into the evolution of human social organization. With the benefit of Morgan's wider ethnographic perspective, Engels defined more types of families, including some extinct forms. But he also specified that in social stages of savagery and barbarism the family as a unit is submerged within the larger social groupings of the horde, the tribe, and the gens.

In some barbarian societies there is a transitional patriarchal family in which women and servants are subjugated, for with monogamous marriage inequality enters the family—unlike Le Play, Engels did not look back fondly on the patriarchal Yugoslavian Zadrugas and Hebraic households of the Bible. And when civilization begins the old marriage system breaks down, as do the gens that bind society together, and we end up with the most unequal and exploitative family, that formed by monogamous marriage. Women become property, bound in domestic slavery through a marriage that is no more than a property contract (Engels 1942:71). The decay of the complex communal gens within which families were embedded, "loosening all the old ties of society," was caused by the penetration of monetary relations and private property into the sphere of kinship. At the same time, the state took on many of the functions of the gens and the extended patriarchal family, leaving the family autonomous but also divided into classes on the basis of property (Engels 1942:97). The family became both a victim of the state and a vehicle for its perpetuation; "it exhibits in miniature the same oppositions and contradictions as those in which society has been moving . . . ever since it split into classes at the beginning of civilization" (Engels 1942:60). Engels abhorred the nuclear monogamous family, a creation of the capitalist economy and the state. The family, in the restricted sense of an isolated economic unit, emerges only in civilization and is present only in societies that "are imperfect and split into antagonisms." In this he agreed completely with Le Play.

That Le Play and Engels share a great deal is not a new observation (Nisbet 1966:66–70). They were both nostalgic for the past, distasteful of the present, and programmatic toward the future. Their evolutionary models are based on the premise that political and social evolution is paralleled by evolution of the family. For both, the misery of the present and the lesson of the past justified a sweeping program of social change and political action. Le Play sanctified private property while Marx and Engels despised it. Marx hated organized religion, Le Play was a Catholic activist. Yet, both Le Play and Engels accepted that the traditional institution of the family was obsolete in the modern setting, and sought some accommodation, and in that sense both were reformers.

The past provided a model for an acceptable future, but Le Play looked back a few hundred years to a mythical patriarchal extended family, while Marx and Engels looked into antiquity for an equally mythical communal group based on sharing and equality. While Le Play thought that the problems of society and the state could be solved by reforming the family, Engels and Marx thought that the problems of the family could be solved by destroying and then reforming the state and by eliminating private property. Le Play and Engels largely agreed on the historical direction the family had taken; in the past families were more integrated into the community, were more cohesive, and more involved in production. Progress had stripped the family of functions, creating misery, exploitation, and social strife.

Since Le Play's and Engels's time an incredible amount has been written about the family as it "modernizes," as it is involved in cultural evolution. But beneath the mountain of verbiage little has really changed. While the crude and sweeping models of social evolution proposed by Le Play and Engels (and by Bachofen and Morgan) have been soundly rejected, their models of family evolution live on. If we scratch the surface of even the most sophisticated of recent models of family and household change, Le Play or Engels pop out.

THE HOUSEHOLD IN MODERNIZATION THEORY

Instead of savagery, barbarism, and civilization, we now have under-developed, developing, and modern societies. Hiding the evolutionary assumption behind such euphemisms as "less-developed countries" does not make them go away. Even dependency theory, with its explicit denial that the peripheral society will always evolve into the core or metropolitan society, ends up reclothing the same tired model in a new outfit (see, e.g., Cardoso & Faletto 1979:8). The jargon used in dependency theory to speak of the peripheral economy and society—functionally incomplete, poorly integrated, distorted, fragmented, marginalized, dominated, weak, disarticulated (Caporaso & Zare 1981; Janvry 1981:33)—is reminiscent of Le Play's and Engels's descriptions of the working class of nineteenth-century Europe. Combined with the temporal framework provided by the terms *precapitalist, functionally dualistic,* and *modern* (or *fully capitalist*), they express the same traditional/modern dichotomy they are intended to contradict. Critics of dependency theory who substitute modes of production for socio-economic stage follow the same path when they order modes of production along an evolutionary line from primitive community through semifeudal to capitalist (Janvry 1981:110).

Modernization theory and dependency theory also discuss family and household change. The nostalgia is gone (or is well hidden behind scientific language), and the value judgments are carefully couched, but the family is again seen as the cause, symptom, and product of social change. Once the antagonistic arguments and pointed critiques are stripped away, the most conservative modernization theorist and the most radical dependency theorist have very much the same thing to say about the family. Although their arguments and political points are varied, and their villains and victims different, their assumptions and their historical analyses are very similar.

The basic building block of modernization theory is the distinction between traditional and modern societies and economies, in turn borrowed from the work of nineteenth-century sociologists. Emerging after World War II, the theory posits an evolutionary continuum from traditional to modern, with the fully modern societies represented only by the North American and European principals in that war (Valenzuela & Valenzuela 1981). Modernization was the linear process through which traditional society was transformed, reaching a take-off point whence it made the leap into modernity, through a "cumulative process upwards" (Myrdal 1957).

Theorists such as Levy, Rostow, and Myrdal ordered the nations of the world along temporal scales of modernity and implied that all societies are becoming more and more alike (Levy 1972). What is left is "residual diversity," which sometimes takes the pernicious form of "persistent pluralism" (Deutsch 1973 : 31). Modern society spreads as if by gravity through diffusion. "The historic spread, over the last several centuries, of aspects or by-products of modernization from its fountainhead in northwestern Europe and, later, the United States to the outermost reaches of the world can be viewed as a multifaceted process of cultural diffusion" (Deutsch 1973 : 33). The process, however, is uneven, proceeding at different rates (often blamed on cultural or even psychological barriers, as in McClelland's [1961] "need for achievement" hypothesis). For this reason there is a long period between pure tradition and complete modernity when the two exist side by side in a "dual economy" (see Boeke 1942; Furnivall 1948; Lewis 1955; Singer 1964). The traditional society survives in a truncated or circumscribed form, often as an enclave, alongside the growing modern sector. Thus any complex process or intricate situation of change is dissected into its traditional and its modern components, and everything is referred back to its archetype. Neoclassical economists tend to see the traditional sector as holding back the development of the modern, while Marxists claim that the modern develops at the expense of the traditional, but both share the same categories.

The model of the dual economy has been refuted almost from its inception (see, e.g., Gusfield 1967). Ranis (1977 : 260) thinks we can get around the problems of the dual society model by rephrasing, serving up another half-cooked mess:

> By now . . . sufficient data have accumulated to permit us to look at developing societies in a historical context and to try to isolate meaningful subphases of development. There is no reason to permit the unfortunate "stages of growth" controversy linked to the name of W. W. Rostow to inhibit us in this respect any longer. While no historical inevitability connotation is intended, developing societies do seem to move in certain transitional states between the long epoch of open agrarianism and another long epoch of modern growth. One of the more common transitional states is one of dualism.

He suggests that within the dualistic phase there is a "domestic-market-oriented or primary-import-substitution subphase," followed by either an "outer-oriented" or "export-substitution" subphase or the prolongation of domestic market-orientation through a "secondary-import-substitution subphase."

Like Le Play, the modernization theorists were interested in politics as well as economics, and their politics shared something of his tone. Chirot (1981) places modernization theory squarely in the intellectual armory of the U.S. Department of State during the cold war period. Modernization was rationalization and efficiency, a movement that would bring prosperity and happiness to the peoples of the underdeveloped world, pulling them away from the temptation to follow communism and revolution as solutions to their problems.

Modernization has a place in social science that was prepared by Redfield's influential folk-urban continuum and his laments over the passing of the "little tradition" (Redfield 1941, 1956). In anthropology Geertz (1963: 120) offers a good summary of the conventional wisdom on social modernization: "The [economic or market capitalist] mentality has had its customary sociocultural accompaniments; increasing flexibility of land tenure; growth of individualism and slackening of extended family ties; greater class differentiation and conflict, intensified opposition between young and old, modern and conservative; weakening of traditional authority and wavering of traditional social standards; and even the growth of 'Protestant Ethic' religious ideologies." The family, especially, suffers during modernization. "During a society's transition from domestic to factory industry the division of labor increases and the economic activities previously lodged in the family move to the firm" (Smelser 1963: 35). Specialized institutions that emerge during modernization take functions from the family, leaving a fragmented, nuclearized husk involved only in sharing wages, housekeeping, and child rearing (Parsons 1959).

Parsons used functionalist arguments to explain this change. The nuclearized family is adapted to modern industrial society, so the traditional extended family is no longer a viable institution, and it disappears. Schultz (1977: 251) listed a series of good reasons why the nuclear family is the logical (efficient) institution for the modern economy: "as production activities are modernized, (1) the market is extended which enhances the comparative advantage of nuclear relative to the extended family; (2) as the incomes of families rise over time, the shift towards the nuclear family is a pure income effect; (3) there is less need for intrafamily insurance as markets develop; and (4) there is less demand for many children, as the price of the time of modern mothers increases." The fact that nuclear families predominate is assumed to prove these functional assertions. Goode (1963: 12–17) only reverses the functional arrow when he proposes that modernization and industrialization come about because isolated nuclear, "pre-adapted" families exist. However many layers of scientific-looking garments this proposition is clothed in, it is the same thin, weak old argument inside, and the frail creature continues to stand with no more than shreds of evidence to support it.

Dependency theory includes a diverse and voluminous literature that is now replete with internal divisions and discord. Rather than delve into these complexities, here I will point out the similarities among prominent dependency theorists in how they approach such social groups as the household. Along the way I will show how their views are similar to those of modernization theorists.

Baran (1957) set modernization theory on its head. Rather than comprising modern economies in earlier stages of development, the underdeveloped, traditional world is prevented from developing by the modernized nations. This "blocked development" results from the systematic pillage of the underdeveloped world during the colonial era and continuing forms of economic exploitation. The developed world drains and distorts the dependent, peripheral economy (see Furtado 1970; Cardoso & Faletto 1979: ch. 2).

Frank (1967, 1969) published a most devastating critique of the evolutionary assumptions of modernization theory, focusing especially on the concept of the dual economy. He (Frank 1967:148) showed, for example, that many regions that now appear traditional and isolated are actually being underdeveloped, having once been very prosperous. And he (Frank 1967:22) attacked the temporal metaphors used to suggest that underdeveloped areas are something out of the past, while the developed area is modern: "for 'feudal' and 'capitalist' are not just convenient words; they are names for concepts whose implications, often unconsciously, affect the user's perception of reality well beyond the immediate context in which the words are used." Marxists as well as modernists were judged guilty of using such evolutionary metaphors. Frank (1967:255) identified the three traditional Marxist positions as "a) feudalism pre-dates capitalism, b) feudalism co-exists with capitalism, and c) feudalism is penetrated or invaded by capitalism. These theses are not mutually exclusive; they complement each other; and several writers subscribe to two or more of them." All three positions rest on European history, interpreted as inevitable evolution and imposed on the Third World. Frank's critique of the idea of development, of the evolutionary ordering of societies into a linear tableau, is a historically based analysis that lifts the traditional society out of the temporal vacuum from which evolutionary theory posits that it can escape only by becoming more recognizably modern.

Substituting the words *peripheral* for traditional, *core* or *metropolitan* for modern, and *semiperiphery* for the dual economy is a hallmark of dependency theory. The new terms are meant to deny the inevitability of evolution from one stage to another and to combat the tendency to think in linear terms. Instead of evolutionary order, they are to indicate relative spatial and economic positions (Cardoso & Faletto 1979:8–21). But do they accomplish that end? Unfortunately, what often happens is that the new terms are adopted but the old meanings linger on. The concepts of progress, tradition, and modern are so deeply ingrained that no change of vocabulary can conceal them for long. The underlying categories still exist, even if we deny the possibility of one's changing into another.

Wallerstein's "modern world system" recasts world history as the growth of a world capitalist system that gradually integrates all the world's societies in various ways. In Europe the traditional is always depicted as "a creation of the present, never of the past" (Wallerstein 1976:71). But when his field of view leaves Western Europe the periphery and the semiperiphery do not get equal treatment. Whatever the factual errors of his arguments about the development of the periphery (see Chirot 1981:274–79), Wallerstein ends up making dependency cut two ways. To say that the periphery is dependent leads us to accept that the core societies ("hegemonic powers") are culturally dominant (Wallerstein 1976:223; 1980:65), which is to say that cultural power, if not content, diffuses outward from the modern core to the underdeveloped periphery.

Outside Europe the contradictions in Wallerstein's history are clear. He depicts the rise of capitalist production of many kinds in the periphery during the colonial phase (Wallerstein 1980:128–78), an expansion that transformed all peripheral societies, even if they did not become mirror images of the capitalist core. Instead, they developed attributes particular to their role in the capitalist world system: they became traditional. "Rather than being the vestiges of some distant past conveniently articulated with a capitalist mode of production, they have everywhere been reconstituted in quite fundamental and decisive ways" (Smith, Wallerstein & Evers 1984:8). This follows Amin (1976:328) who said that

> traditional society was distorted to the point of being unrecognizable; it lost its independence, and its main function was now to produce for the world market under conditions which, because they impoverished it, deprived the society of any prospect of radical modernization. The traditional society was not therefore in transition to modernity; as a depen-

dent, peripheral society it was complete, and hence a dead end; its progress blocked. It consequently retained certain traditional appearances, which constituted its only means of survival.

The same idea surfaces in the work of Friedlander (1975:71), who sees traditional Indian identity in Latin America as a symptom and instrument of oppression, and more radically in Martínez Pelaez's (1971), who says that Indians did not exist at all until they were created by conquest and capitalism.

But in these assertions the way is opened for a new evolutionary division of the world's societies, this time into those that existed before the coming of capitalism and those that existed afterward. And what terms do we find being applied to the precapitalist system but the *natural economy* (Evers, Clauss & Wong 1984:27), the *primordial element* (Stauth 1984:92), *pristine precapitalism* (Harris 1982:91), and best of all, *the community* (Wallerstein 1984:20–22).

At the same time we now have a stage in between the primordial self-subsistence precapitalist economy (assumed by Wallerstein's research group to be based in lineages [Smith, Wallerstein & Evers 1984: 8]) and industrial capitalism with its fully waged workers. Wallerstein (1984:19) calls this intermediate stage "partialism," a period when workers are paid wages below their cost of reproduction and so have to pursue subsistence production and activities in the informal sector (see also Janvry 1981:33). It really makes little difference whether this stage is a deliberate creation of the exploiting class, a means of resistance by the oppressed, or a survival of earlier times that has been bent and shaped under external pressure.

World systems theory carries us full circle, back to a social evolutionary typology. The major difference is that Wallerstein begins the penetration by the capitalist system at an earlier stage than modernization theorists. To the modernization theorists, the underdeveloped world's peasants are survivors from an earlier time carrying traditional culture that is essentially different from that of the modern West. To the world systems theorist, these same people are just a poor and exploited part of the capitalist system. The real traditional people lived only in the precapitalist era, before people were corrupted and exploited by extractive and colonial regimes. We are not, it seems, really arguing about the content of the categories, just their boundaries.

The process of development presented by world systems theory also sounds familiar. The Research Working Group on Households, Labor Force Formation, and the World-Economy of the Fernand Braudel Center says the development of the world system led to social specialization. "Where units charged with decision-making and labor-allocation tasks were once relatively isolated and autonomous, now they have become integrated relational structures whose operations are subject to the pressures of the world-economy" (Friedman 1984:50). While absolute standards of living may rise, labor relations become marginalized, patriarchal domination of women more pronounced, and commodification and monetarization of social relations more complete (Smith, Wallerstein & Evers 1984:9–13). This is categorical and evolutionary change; once capitalism came into the world, all else followed. Substituting the world *capitalist* for modern does not change the content.

We find the same ambivalent emotions about progress, the same nostalgia for the past, that have been felt for centuries by people of all political persuasions. While the economic and historical content of dependency and world systems theory is often insightful and important, these paradigms lead to serious trouble when they look at social structure because of the assumptions built into their terminology and their rigidity in analyzing capitalism. They tend to treat capitalism as a thing sui generis, a personified and malign force. Much time is spent explaining how feudalism and forms of extraction other than wage labor (in other words, social and economic systems other than capitalism as defined by Marx) are really aspects of peripheral capitalism, rather than survivals of earlier times or autonomous systems. This is well and good, but it leaves forms of social structure and economic extraction that are outside the modern capitalist system in limbo and denies that they have anything to tell us about the world today. In other words, anything that came before capitalism (or survives alongside it) is so completely different from capitalism that it has no relevance. But human societies before capitalism were not all the same. Some were highly stratified, many had elaborate systems of extraction, and some even had commodities and wage labor. Surely these societies have some relation to the present. Some built enduring social structures that still condition and shape people's responses to capitalism (which itself is a diverse and temporally variable phenomenon). This is the major point of Wolf's *Europe and the People Without History*. But it is amazing how often sociologists and prehistorians act as if there were nothing before capitalism except a few egalitarian tribes. Compare this to the relish with which Braudel (1982) discusses the diversity of non-capitalist economic systems in Europe.

The problems inherent in the dependency and world systems theories become crippling when the unit of analysis becomes smaller and smaller, descending from the nation or economy to the household and family. Wallerstein's research group became interested in households and the domestic sphere because they wanted to understand how the labor force reproduces itself in the Third World where wages are so low. They were also interested in the relationship between capitalism and gender, especially the exploitation of women as expressed within the household. Their analysis of households and kinship is intended to explain how modern capitalism transforms the precapitalist mode of production. Wallerstein (1984:20) believes that the precapitalist state approximated a community of 50 to 100 people who shared everything. This group was closely tied to the land and firmly bound by kinship. But capitalism causes the commodification of everyday life, and capitalists attack the primordial community to break it down, extract its labor, and steal its land.

> Household structures . . . are increasingly commodified, from the preparation of food, to the cleaning and repair of home appurtenances and clothing, to custodial care, to nursing care, to emotional repair. With the increasing commodification of everyday life has gone a decline in co-residentiality and kinship as determinative of the boundaries. The end point of this secular pressure is not . . . the "individual" or the "nuclear family" but a unit whose cohesiveness is increasingly predicated on the income-pooling function it performs [Wallerstein 1984:21].

First the tie with the land is broken, then the bonds of kinship are destroyed, all serving the interests of capitalism, which wants mobile and cheap labor.

The precapitalist community's functions are progressively stripped away until only the pooling of income from wage labor and the rearing of children to be future workers remain. There is a transitional stage, in which much of the Third World is caught, wherein households have to produce for their own subsistence as well as pool wages (Stauth 1984:98). During this stage precapitalist survivals (the subsistence sector) remain encapsulated within the household (Evers, Clauss & Wong 1984:30–33). The end result is grim: "it is the income-pooling lifetime proletarian household—torn from its once indissoluble link to territory, to kinship, and to coresidentiality—that does the most to strip bare the real conditions of life" (Wallerstein 1984:22); and "the underdevelopment of the household to the family (or, in other words, the reduction of production to reproduction) resulted in . . . a family stripped, abstracted, from its material base" (Schiel 1984:124).

Most of the theory presented here is anachronistic, and very little has an empirical basis. The only radical proposition Wallerstein makes is that the household is actually created by capitalism. Before capitalism there were perhaps units that resembled the household, but they were not households because their main function was not the pooling of income for survival in the context of capitalist wage labor. The definition of household is thus made to serve Wallerstein's evolutionary model.

This is similar to Meillassoux's strategy when he recreates precapitalist society in the shape of kinship and lineage, and precapitalist economy as the circulation of women in marriage exchange. In his evolutionary history the household and family emerge from the lineage only under capitalism (Meillassoux 1981:9–50). He takes Sahlins (1972) to task for positing a domestic mode of production based on the household during precapitalist times, for this implies that households were independent (Meillassoux 1981:6; I do not find that Sahlins ever reached this conclusion). In essence this squabble seems to be over whether precapitalist society was characterized by families or lineages, households or the gens. This is more the kind of debate we expect in late nineteenth-century anthropology than in that of the late twentieth century.

But Wallerstein's model *is* a nineteenth-century view that casts capitalism as the ultimate culprit, the family as the ultimate victim. However, there are real insights and important generalizations in *Households and the World Economy*. Household mobility, the diversity of household economic roles, the stratification of households by wealth and social position, and the degree of self-subsistence provided by households are all important variables. But we really need to look at more evidence before we can say that these variables are all changing in some uniform and directional way during incorporation into a capitalist system. Those chapters in *Households and the World Economy* that deal with empirical historical information on households do not depict linear evolutionary change; Martin (1984), for example, shows just how diverse an environment South African capitalism provided for households, and how varied were their responses.

OTHER CRITIQUES OF EVOLUTIONARY MODELS

The Cambridge Group for the History of Population and Social Structure has provided a center for criticism of evolutionary models of the household and family. Laslett and Wall (1972) developed a standardized methodology for describing the household, using census data, and Laslett (1972) applied it to censuses from England, while others provided information from continental Europe and Japan (Laslett & Wall 1972). Looking only at household size, Laslett finds that there is no clear secular trend before, during, or after the Industrial Revolution, until the twentieth century. Household size in England was close to 4.75 persons from the sixteenth to the twentieth centuries, although the rich always tended to have larger households than the poor. In other words, the model of a precapitalist large family giving way to a capitalist small one is empirically untrue in England, although not necessarily in the rest of the world. And even in Japan, where mean household size decreased through history, the trend is spatially inconsistent and uneven (Hayami & Uchida 1972). Size, however, is only one variable in describing households, and Laslett's analysis has frequently been attacked for ignoring activities and functions, which undoubtedly did change during the Industrial Revolution (Creighton 1980; Medick 1976; Wilk & Netting 1984). But Laslett's findings about size stand as a convincing counter to the assumptions of Le Play and Engels, and force us to reexamine many other assumptions as well.

The real problem with Laslett's analysis lies not with the data, but with what implications he draws from them. In pursuing history, his conclusions become ahistorical, seeming to imply that time and dramatic economic change do not affect household form in any way. Instead, "noumenal norms," unconscious and historically resistant cultural rules, shape the entire fabric of kinship and group formation (Laslett 1984:362–65). This essentially takes households out of the economic realm and explains their variability (or lack thereof) in terms of culture and tradition. It does seem true that in some cultures, especially in Asia (e.g., Thailand [Kunstadter 1984], Taiwan [Wolf 1984], China [Thompson 1984]), household form and structure are remarkably stable across ecological boundaries and through dramatic historical change in economy (Wilk 1988). But it is equally true that in many cases households adapt quickly to changes in the economic and political environment (e.g., Niger [Arnould 1984], Lithuania [Plakans 1984], northern Europe [Medick 1976]). The issue of why households are so adaptable in some situations and are so resistant to change in others is important. It will not be driven away by evolutionary assertions.

In several disciplines recent feminist studies of household and family have produced direct and indirect challenges to evolutionary models of the household. A closer attention to the ideology of the household and family, to the dynamic relationship between social structure, cultural ideology, and praxis, shows up clearly in these critiques (see, e.g., Rapp 1978). One major contribution has been to recast temporal arguments in terms of class: the categories capitalist and precapitalist, developed and underdeveloped have been broken down to show that households vary according to class within complex societies. Every economic system has a diverse set of roles available, and households adopt different strategies to take advantage of them (Laslett 1981:250). Diversity is not the result of overlapping linear stages, but rather of adaptive radiation.

Viewing those in the lower classes as backward is an ideological weapon, a tool used by those on the top to maintain a culturally dominant position. Lofgren (1984; see also Frykman & Lofgren 1987), for example, finds that the emerging middle class of the Victorian era in Scandinavia created an ideology of the modern family in opposition to the practices of the working class, which were cast as primitive or unhealthy. The welfare state's intervention in the family's business was thus justified in the name of science, health, and progress. A similar political use of the family as an ideological weapon can be seen in the modern U.S. controversy over the supposedly broken, pathological, and deformed households of urban blacks (Moynihan 1965).

A more specifically feminist attack on evolutionary models of the household points out that some things do not change whatever the degree of incorporation into capitalism, whatever the type of political organization. Women tend to be responsible for the majority of child care even when they participate fully in a capitalist wage economy or in subsistence production (Laslett 1981:241). Similarly, women tend to be responsible for a disproportionate share of household maintenance tasks, what has been called "household reproduction," regardless of the stage of development or the degree of involvement in the capitalist economy. Several studies show that women's domestic work does not decrease dramatically (if at all) when they enter the waged work force (Berk & Berk 1979; Pleck 1985; Berardo, Shehan & Leslie 1987).

The feminist critique of family and household studies focuses on what goes on within the household, on inequalities in how labor and goods are apportioned (Young, Wolkowitz & McCullagh 1981; Moock 1986). There is also renewed attention to the social and economic networks that tie women together outside the realm of the household (Guyer 1981; Freidman 1984:41; Woodford-Berger 1981). This is an important antidote to the tendency to consider households as primordial and undifferentiated units with a perfect community of interests.

In looking at gender differences within the household, however, some have sought to recreate the Marxist evolutionary scheme, proposing that capitalism invariably increases inequality within the household, leading to the subjugation of women and their exploitation in a patriarchal household (Smith, Wallerstein & Evers 1984:10; J. Smith 1984: 66–67). In this way women's position in capitalist societies is equated with peasants' position in peripheral capitalism, an interesting analogy but a dangerous evolutionary statement. There is another, more conservative position that states the opposite, that capitalism tends to free women from the bondage they experience under precapitalist patriarchy (Caldwell 1981). Recent reviews of the empirical evidence support an antievolutionary position, however, that there is no clear and directional relationship between development and gender relations in society as a whole or within the household (Beneria & Sen 1981, 1982). This is exactly what we would expect of a historical process that itself is complex and differentiated, exerting on the household a whole series of legal, economic, political, and ecological pressures.

It is tempting to attach discussions of gender to existing evolutionary schemes, instead of dealing with complex empirical analysis in an area where few reliable data are available. Casting modern housework as an unreconstructed survival of the precapitalist economy, or positing some past era when women had greater economic power, does not advance our knowledge of why gender relations change and vary. Detailed historical analyses of the effect of capitalism on gender roles have difficulty generalizing about even the very short term (see, e.g., Hareven 1982). Gender identity and role is a complex product of ideology, social class, the organization of work, kinship, and the household economy (among other factors), not a simple result of the nature of the macroeconomy or the stage of its evolution.

HISTORY AND ECOLOGY

It is time to offer some alternatives to evolutionary models of the household. Every scheme I have discussed above, whatever its results or specific hypotheses, assumes that there is some tie of necessity and causality between economic change and social change. This seems fine to me, so far. It is even acceptable to go further and state that broad economic changes are likely to induce change in household organization. But it is a crucial error to extract from this the proposition that each stage of economic change will cause a change in the type of household or family in society. To say that a change in one causes change in the other is not the same as saying that a typological link exists. This may seem like a minor quibble, but I think it lies behind the failure of many models of family and household change.[3]

There are several errors in the idea that a type or level of society or social evolution (or even a mode of production) should correspond with a type or size of household. It really does not matter how we construe our social types, how we order the stages of social development, or how elaborated our household typologies become. The errors stem from the lack of historical, regional, and ecological specificity in the types, stages, and definitions of the household. To put it as simply as possible, households do not adapt to a type of society or a stage of development. They are instead concerned to deal with very local circumstances, with problems and issues of a relatively immediate time span. And households themselves are not things, objects such as butterflies that can be easily sorted into objective types, but are instead fluid and changing groups of individuals, often without clear boundaries between members and nonmembers. They are structures of patterned human action, not items in a catalog.

Historical analysis of households has the potential to penetrate evolutionary myths about the household and family. The messy reality of historical data can keep us from overgeneralizing, and it certainly forces us to focus on the dynamics of change instead of static types. As Macfarlane (1977:8) warns, historians often go too far in this direction, sacrificing scope for detail, burying trends in masses of extraneous events. Historical methodologies for studying the household seem to lead back into typologies (see, e.g., Harter & Bertrand 1977).

The worst problem for a historical approach is simply the poor quality of the available data. The census records, estate listings, and birth or death lists that historians usually work with are cultural documents that are difficult to interpret (Hammel 1984; Plakans 1984). They count events but give very little information on what those events meant. Similarly, they induce historians to count groups, households and communities, without giving any information on the meaning or content of, or interconnections between, those groups. Even when historians add more-textured cultural material from other sources such as proverbs, diaries, and literature (see, e.g., Flandrin 1979; Segalen 1983; Herlihy 1984) we are not sure how to relate this to individual household behavior. Questions of cause and effect that should be addressed most directly with historical data are actually difficult to pose, much less answer.

Historical studies, then, suffer from a general difficulty in specifying the economic, political, and ecological environment of households at any time. How can we understand how households responded, if we do not know in detail what they were responding to? A general description of an agricultural economy under severe population pressure (Adams & Kasakoff 1984) is simply not detailed enough to have any explanatory power. It does not deal with the environment at the level of specificity that the farmers themselves are using to make their decisions.

My brief critique of household history leads to the conclusion that the historical approach is necessary but not sufficient. Escaping the shackles of typological and evolutionary ethnocentricities about the household requires more tools, and the best place to find them is in ecological and economic anthropology. While these fields have themselves suffered from too much typological thinking, more-recent work has focused on process, change, conflict, differentiation, and disequilibrium (Orlove 1977, 1980; Fricke 1986: 15–20). In an effort to break away from static models of equilibrium, some scholars now focus on adaptation at the very local and individual level, and there is new interest in the role of choice, strategy, and decision making in culture change (see, e.g., Vayda & McCay 1975; Barth 1967; Bennett & Kanel 1983; Barlett 1980, 1982; Jochim 1981).

Fricke (1986: 17–27) offers a thorough survey of recent theory in cultural ecology, showing how the concepts of adaptive strategies and processes (from Brush 1977 and Bennett 1969) are leading the field away from teleological functionalism and evolutionism. He argues that the household is the logical level of analysis for human ecological studies. Here the individual patterns of choice and strategic behavior can be placed within larger social structures and economic-ecological contexts. Societies adapt in only the most abstract sense of the word, but households adapt in concrete and observable ways. The point of Fricke's study was that the rational adaptive actions of individuals and households can lead to irrational and destructive consequences at the level of larger systems such as communities and ecosystems. This suggests that households are a crucial link between the micro- and macroscales of human systems (a theme that will be discussed in Chapter 11).

At the same time cultural ecologists increasingly recognize that individual and group choices and strategies are limited and shaped by historical circumstance (see, e.g., Netting 1981; Durham 1979; Fox 1977). Often there are very few options once existing social arrangements, technologies, and local ecological histories are taken into account. The long-term interaction of people and environment often leads to a progressive narrowing of choices that Hackenberg (1974) calls "ecosystemic channeling." This signals an acceptance that the environment itself must be defined more broadly if the concept of adaptation is to have any use in the modern world (Collier 1975). From the perspective of a Thai peasant, for example, taxes and landlords are as much a part of the environment as soils and rain; all are out of his or her control and form a part of the context of each decision and choice during the year.

Is the next step to widen our definition of the environment to include those macroeconomic elements that compose the world system? That same Thai peasant family, whether it knows it or not, is today playing an active part in that system, both as a producer of opium for urban U.S. consumers and as a consumer of goods produced all over the world. What it has to adapt to, and hence the choices its members can make, is now partially the result of national and international economic forces. But if we are to understand this household's response, we need to focus on the specific problems and opportunities it is presented with. We need to focus simultaneously on the architecture of the whole system and on the tiny cracks and surface imperfections in that single brick that happens to be in front of us. Following Fricke, I think that the household is the ideal vehicle for moving this enterprise forward. But first we have to redefine the household and its environment in more-specific economic and ecological terms. In this task I have found the concept of the ecological niche, borrowed from biological ecology, helpful.

In ecology a species' niche is the resource space it occupies in the ecosystem, "an organism's share of the limited energy and nutrients available in an ecological system" (Hardesty 1977 : 109), or more broadly "the resources a species uses, where it finds them, and the strategy by which it harvests them" (Diamond 1978 : 323). Ecological anthropologists have calculated the size of niches only for relatively autonomous subsistence systems of hunter-gatherers and horticulturalists, treating the differences in width as an index of economic diversity or specialization (Hardesty 1977; Ellen 1982). At the same time many anthropologists recognize that humans have a unique capacity to make niches for themselves, carving out ecological spaces by finding new resources and strategies.

If we extend the concept of niche to societies that are not isolated, where the environment within which resources are found includes markets for goods and labor, government programs, and a local power structure, we may lose some rigor and the ability to quantify width, but we gain a valuable concept for understanding how people respond to change. In the process, however, the niche becomes a metaphor instead of a biological term. The biologist's work on the ways nonhuman species compete for and define niches, and on how different species exploit the same environment, cannot be directly applied to households without introducing a host of logical errors and shaky assumptions. Barth (1956) fell into this trap in his discussion of Swat, when he used the biological concepts of competitive exclusion and specialization as explanations (instead of metaphors) for political and economic processes.

Despite this history of misuse of the niche concept in anthropology, I will risk using it here. I like it because it is local and specific, defining an "affective environment," narrowing our attention to those aspects of the environment that make a difference in people's decision making and strategizing. The concept of the niche helps us preserve our knowledge that adaptation is an active and dialectical process whereby people change their environment, even as they change themselves and their social arrangements.

Money, markets, land, and different forms of production have provided a changing environment for the Kekchi, in which they have defined a series of niches. I will make every effort to show how the Kekchi were active participants in this process by looking at the variety of choices they have made. As we go further back into time, however, the issues of choice and strategy are harder to define. The large-scale political and economic transformations of nations leave a stronger trace in written history than do the wilful responses of exploited rural people. Our contexts of choice in this study are the individual farmer and the household group. But what is a household? How can we escape using household typologies (patriarchal extended, isolated nuclear) that incorporate the evolutionary assumptions that we are trying to avoid? We need first to define our unit of analysis.

3 The Household as a Unit of Analysis

Recently, Hammel (1984:30) admitted that the "epistemological status of household is . . . much in doubt." I believe that its role in the world economic system is equally in doubt, and I suggest that the two problems are closely related. As I discussed in Chapter 2, evolutionary models of the household and development fail in part because they do not specify what they mean by household or family. I will therefore attempt to define the elusive household and the ways it changes. The goal is to refine and maintain a working definition of the household that remains cross-culturally and historically useful, without using gross typological categories that obscure important variation.

The household is not a corporate thing with the boundaries and motivations of an individual. While all societies have households, the household is always embedded in wider social and economic networks, to greater or lesser degrees. As Guyer (1981, 1984) and Woodford-Berger (1981) point out, there is always a danger of reifying households unless these networks are taken into account. Individuals have different degrees of household membership, and the autonomy of the unit is always abridged by custom, law, or community. The isolated autonomous household beloved of theorists of the capitalist middle class is an ideal type that has little empirical basis, whatever its ideological appeal (Hareven 1982:2).

HOUSEHOLD AS NOUN, HOUSEHOLD AS VERB

Households can usually be identified "on the ground" in a particular cultural setting, but a universal definition is an elusive target. The difficulty in finding a cross-cultural identifying criterion hints at the nature of the problem and the best solution. While in every society a householdlike group or thing can be found, in each place it performs unique mixes of activities and functions. Even in the same small community, each household can appear different: some may be cohesive, some very diffuse; some will be involved in production, others will not. There are, in fact, no universal functions.

If our purpose is to take a census and produce a list, this is no problem. We want to count things, not activities or economic entities. To define the household as a thing for a census, we generally end up picking a unit that meets Hammel's (1980:251) definition of "the smallest [social] grouping with the maximum corporate function." Or we might just dub the most common social unit in a society the household and leave it at that. This is what I mean by the household as noun. But for comparative purposes and for the study of change, this definition is insufficient.

By treating the household as a bounded unit defined by common residence or participation in vaguely defined domestic activities, it becomes a morphological unit of description. Although its exact functional nature remains culturally particular or vague, the household's morphology can readily be described and classified by reference to the relationships between its members. The thing is either extended, multiple, or nuclear, has an average size and a normal developmental cycle.

It is certainly true that morphological household units can be found, counted, and classified (and such schemes abound; see, e.g., Laslett 1972; Harter & Bertrand 1977). But this can obscure more than it illuminates, for households are not just morphologically differentiated butterflies. The processes by which households adapt and change can no more be understood by classifying and comparing household structures than insect evolutionary process can be discovered in butterfly collections. This is not a new complaint or point (see Lofgren 1974; Medick 1976; Carter & Merrill 1979; Mitterauer & Seider 1979; Sanjek 1982). For example, the household group's boundaries can become difficult to draw with precision when all members do not live under a single roof, or when membership is fluid and constantly changing, or when people can belong to two households. These problems may seem petty, for all classifications are imperfect to some degree. But a morphological approach is based on a misunderstanding of the nature of the household, neglecting what the household does in favor of what it looks like.

Studying households as process or as patterned activity is difficult and messy too, mainly because of the tremendous variability in household activities within and between cultures. There is some consensus, however, on a group of activities that form the core of domesticity cross-culturally. Elsewhere (Wilk & Netting 1984; Wilk & Rathje 1982) they are grouped together as production, transmission (trusteeship and intergenerational transfer of property), distribution (including pooling, sharing, exchange, and consumption), biological and social reproduction, and coresidence (meaning shared activity in constructing, maintaining, and using a dwelling). We recognize that these are crude categories in need of refinement, and they are not exhaustive. Common defense, for example, or ritual and legal representation are also sometimes domestic activities.

A workable definition of the household as an activity group requires that these various domestic functions be mapped onto a social group. We have suggested (following Wrigley 1977) that a graphic method such as Venn diagrams can show how the different activities overlap, as demonstrated by Helms (1976) and Hawkesworth (1981). The household proper is the area of maximum overlap. This exercise shows how activities are divided up within the household, as well as the functional links between households and groups or individuals outside. Activity maps locate the household economy in relation to larger economic institutions, to other households, and to the individual members. They also can be used to show how household activities change over time as part of the life course, or during wider transformations in the economy.

So far I have spoken of morphology and activity as two dimensions of households. It may seem that I have been opposing them to each other, although my real intent is to show that they are complementary. But they are not exhaustive either. For households are also cultural units, for which there are codes, rules, rights, and duties. This cultural dimension of the household has been labeled the "household system" (Netting, Wilk & Arnould 1984) and has been subdivided by Carter (1984) into rules and strategies. Rules are culturally sanctioned guidelines for leadership, for recruitment of personnel, and for devolution— the management of property and the division or fission of the household and its resources. Strategies involve management and patterns of decisions within that framework of rules.

Another aspect of the household system is its symbolic and meaningful elements. While some cultures seem to lack an ideal household type (putting cultural weight instead on the family, lineage, village, or other group), in others the ideal of what a household should look like and what it should do has great importance and persistence. Even if only a tiny proportion of the populace can ever live in an ideal household for reasons of wealth, status, or demographic accident, these ideals can persist as elements of ethnicity or class identity. These resistant cultural models (Laslett's [1984] noumenal norms) can be constant in time and space, a stasis common in both stable agrarian class-based societies (e.g., China, Japan, preindustrial England) and in the modern industrial state. Household types may be the locus of cultural warfare between competing ideals of what a household should be. Le Play and Engels can be seen as players in a middle-class struggle to impose nuclear family household ideology on the working classes (Frykman & Lofgren 1987).

There is a wider sense in which households are culturally integrated. As Rapp (1978), Guyer (1981), Linares (1985), and others point out, cultural concepts of gender, age, class, and status, while not always part of the household system itself, have a direct effect on household operation. And because these cultural roles and concepts are deeply rooted in structures other than the household, they may resist forces that change the household.

THE GRAMMAR OF HOUSEHOLDS

How can these three very different modes of description be brought together in the study of changing households? While it is unpleasantly complex, I believe that a simultaneous study of household morphology, activity, and culture is necessary in order to understand how households adapt. This is because the causes, and the rates, of change can be different in each of the three dimensions. For example, the activities households undertake can change quickly while some morphological changes take years or several domestic cycles to become evident, and the household head's ideal role may not change at all. The three dimensions of household variability seem to be functionally linked in a very loose fashion.

How can we reconcile this incoherence with the assumption that the household is a system, with functional integrity? I do not think we can, for the household is not a closed, coherent system. While some subcultures of U.S. society may idealize and venerate an image of the household as a closed, autonomous entity with internal order and harmony between parts, this image has little to do with ethnographic reality.[1] Rather, because households are not independent but emergent institutions (with properties derived from other systems), they always remain open systems. As in studying ecosystems, we have to draw arbitrary boundaries around our units of study for analytical purposes, and, like ecologists, we have a tendency to treat those boundaries as real ones ever after (Moran 1984; Wilk 1989).

The morphology of households, for example, is partially under the household's control through recruitment strategies, timing of marriage, fertility control, and through fission or ejection of members. But the morphology of the household is also a product of health, demographic and stochastic factors, and a kinship system that may have little relationship to the household. The same can be said for household activities and the household system. Gender roles, age categories and norms, legal prescriptions on inheritance and on property all are vital in their effects on the household but are also constituents of the wider socioeconomic system.

The lack of systemic integrity does not mean that households cannot be studied or compared as units, it requires only that they be treated as open systems, not isolated ones. And we already have a number of studies that do that. Some draw connections between changes in the economy and household morphology (Murdock 1949; Spoehr 1947; Lofgren 1974; Wilk & Netting 1984; Medick 1976), and some show how the existing morphological character of the household constrains its potential activities (Chayanov 1966; Rudie 1970; Painter 1984; Hyden 1986). These arguments are basically functionalist and materialist, and tend to follow a normal model of economic causation in which macroeconomic or ecological changes stimulate or force change in household production strategies or property relations, followed by change in household morphology and in the ideology and rules of household composition and conduct.

There are good arguments for alternative models of change. Linares (1984) presents a good case of an initial change in religious beliefs and gender roles that later led to reorganization of activities and morphology. Guyer (1981) finds cases of the value of labor and goods changing first, followed by the household decision-making system and the distribution of power, and only then by activities and morphology. Imported ideals of household organization and role behavior have well-documented effects on Caribbean households (Brown 1977; Rubenstein 1975).

These models assume that household dimensions can be linked in a causal sequence, when in fact the interrelationships are often more complex. Lack of change in one dimension of the household, for example, may provide an opportunity for other parts to change rapidly.

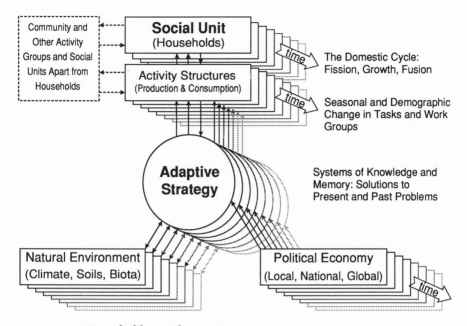

FIGURE 3.1   Households as Adaptive Units

Kunstadter (1984) points to a Thai situation wherein household morphology remained constant despite drastic changes in activity and the household system.

At the very least these studies demonstrate that households are dynamic and changeable, and that presuming stability is a poor way to begin. Contradictions are inherent when dimensions change at different rates, subject to contradictory influence from the socioeconomic environment. Contradictions may propel change for a long time after an initial impetus. Certainly the presumption of some pre- or post-capitalist steady state is unwarranted. The household may be the only place in a social system where these diverse influences and cross-ties come together in a complex knot. Given this complexity it is remarkable that there is any coherence to the household as a system at all; the expectation that order and coherence should be the norm is a source of bias and frustration in household studies (Hammel 1984).

As a means of reducing this complexity to a manageable scale, I will use a simplified model of Kekchi household dynamics, shown in Figure 3.1. The central focus is the adaptive strategy, defined in Chapter 4. Households are depicted as social units that organize production and consumption activities. All elements of the model have continuity with their historical antecedents (shown as time arrows), and they interrelate with each other dynamically, except that the Kekchi adaptive strategy has little effect on the political economy of Belize as a whole. Our exploration of Kekchi life starts at the bottom of Figure 3.1 and moves upward. In Chapters 4 and 5 I focus on the environmental variables, looking at the history of the political economies in which the Kekchi have lived, and at the constraints and possibilities of their natural environment.

4 The Historical and Ethnographic Setting

The form of the modern Kekchi household stems from its production, consumption, and reproduction. Those activities, in turn, are part of a historically based adaptive strategy, shaped and constrained by present and past physical, economic, political, and social environments. The factors that have shaped that adaptive strategy are revealed most clearly in times of change. This formula maintains the traditional focus within ecological anthropology on issues of adaptation, strategy, and the systemic nature of social-environmental interactions. At the same time it avoids the disjuncture between internal and external that characterizes many ecological-anthropological studies that focus on the artificially bounded local community (see E. Smith 1984). As Collier (1975 : 205–12) suggests, the ecosystemic focus of ecological anthropology leads the investigator to wider and wider conceptions of the environment (see also Netting 1965b).

Even if some ecological anthropologists acknowledge that there are outside influences on the local human-environmental relationship, they often disregard them or give them a low priority. Thus Nietchmann (1973) could treat the Miskito as a bounded ecosystem, an entity separate from the political, economic, and historical causes of its own isolation. Highland Latin American Indian communities are treated, in many early ecological studies, as isolates, even as researchers uncomfortably acknowledge the importance of external factors in causing and maintaining that isolation. More-recent studies penetrate the façade of isolation to the economic dependency and exploitation within (see, e.g., Cancian 1972; Wasserstrom 1983; Warren 1978).

All ecologists study artificially bounded units—whole ecosystems are too complex to study in detail. The problem is to remember that the boundaries are artificial. Some ecological anthropologists take refuge in a mythical or assumed past in order to justify leaving the boundaries in place, boundaries needed to build homeostatic models like those of Vayda and Rappaport (1968). Ellen (1982 : 271–72), for example, thinks that "a high degree of system closure . . . was probably a common feature of early human groups. . . . The breakdown of local self-sufficiency marks a key ecological transition." I assert, on the contrary, that all human societies have tended to interact with others throughout history (and in the Americas, before the coming of the Europeans), and that the classical community isolates of ethnography are products of colonial political economy, of historical misinterpretation, or of the anthropologist's cloudy vision. The closed ecosystem is a chimera, the ecologist's equivalent of the timeless traditional culture. Ecological anthropology does quite well without it and can instead open up the debate to issues such as the relative importance of local and political economic factors in shaping a people's culture and social institutions (see, e.g., the chapters in Lehman 1982).

THE KEKCHI IN GUATEMALA: A BRIEF HISTORY

The Kekchi of southern Belize are a small splinter from a much larger population whose homeland is the dissected plateaus and rugged mountains of the Alta Verapaz Department of Guatemala. In 1960 there were over 250,000 Kekchi in Guatemala, and this number is undoubtedly much higher today (Flores 1967; Eachus & Carlson 1966; Osborn 1982 : 10). The 3,600 or so Kekchi in southern Belize, however, have been studied more than those in Guatemala. I know no general ethnography of the Guatemalan Kekchi (though Cabarrus [1974] covers religion and cosmology, and King [1974] discusses ethnicity in Cobán), while for Belize there are works by Thompson (1930a), Howard (1973, 1974, 1975, 1977a, 1977b), Boster (1973), Osborn (1982), Nunes (1977), Schackt (1986), Rambo (1962), McCaffrey (1967), Berte (1983), and Wilk (1981a, 1981b).

Little is known about the Kekchi in pre-Hispanic times. The Alta Verapaz occupies a strategic zone between the lowland forests to the north and the temperate highlands to the south and west, and the Kekchi took advantage of this position to engage in trade and commerce in both directions from at least the Early Classic period (c A.D. 300; see Dillon 1977; Smith 1952), continuing well into colonial times (Villagutierre Soto-Mayor 1983 : 106–7; King 1974 : 25). Archaeology suggests a dense, evenly scattered population that grew slowly but steadily to a maximum just before the conquest (Adams 1972 : 3–8; Bertrand 1982), but we know little about political organization beyond the fact that there was an indigenous nobility. The militaristic Quichean Postclassic polities to the immediate west and south were never able to conquer the Kekchi, suggesting a high degree of political and military organization.

The exact geographic position of the Kekchi at the time of the conquest is not precisely known (see Figure 4.1). Stoll (1884, 1958), Rambo (1964), and Thompson (1938:586) all consider Cahabon, in the highlands, the northeasternmost Kekchi town. Roys (1972), on the other hand, believes that the Kekchi inhabited the lowland town of Chacujal, east of modern Panzós, which was visited by Cortés on his famous march through the lowlands in 1524–1525. Sapper (1985) also places the Kekchi in lowland areas to the east of the highland towns, and Dieseldorff (1909) mentions old land titles in which Kekchi claim ancestral ownership of lowland properties to the north and east. The Kekchi had probably always moved between the highlands and the lowlands, as they do today, colonizing rain forests of Petén and Izabal in Guatemala and moving into southern Belize (Schwartz 1987).

Involved in wars of conquest with the powerful kingdoms of western Guatemala, the Spanish did not make a serious effort to conquer the Kekchi until 1529. By this time Spanish enthusiasm for conquest in the highlands was ebbing; gold had not been found and the conquest of Peru had begun. When the Kekchi and their Pokomchi neighbors put up a spirited resistance, the Spanish paused.

In 1537 the Dominican Friar Bartolomé de Las Casas petitioned the governor of Guatemala for permission to pacify the Kekchi of Tezulutlan (land of war) by peaceful and religious methods, and was granted five years to try. Starting with Remesal's 1619 *Historia* (1966), historians have examined the "great experiment" of Kekchi pacification from a number of perspectives (Ximénez 1930; Saint-Lu 1968). They tend to stress its humanitarian and peaceful nature, in contrast to the violence unleashed on other Maya groups, and thus to deemphasize the dramatic social, economic, demographic, and political transformations of the Dominican period. This lends false authority to the claim that because the Kekchi were never militarily subjugated, their traditional way of life survived untouched through the colonial era (see, e.g., Eachus & Carlson 1966; Dillon 1985:v; Sapper 1985; Sapper 1926). This claim may not be justified.

The Dominicans initially used Indian converts as their agents in pacification, preaching directly only to the Kekchi political elite, but priests physically entered the area by 1539. They assured the Kekchi that existing land rights would be respected and Spanish colonization prohibited, and that the local nobles would retain their status. This in-

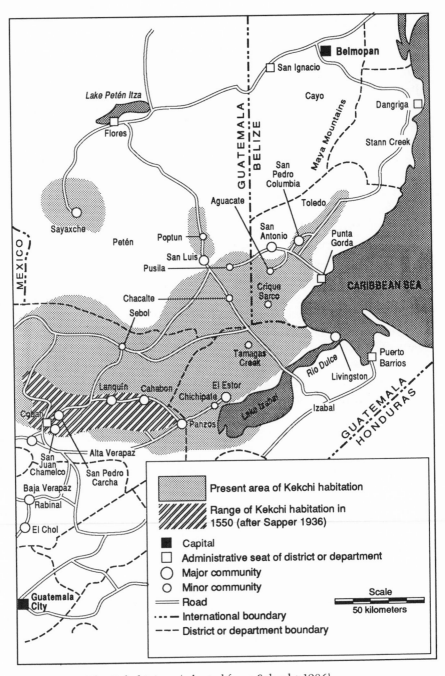

FIGURE 4.1　The Kekchi Area (adapted from Schackt 1986)

centive was yoked to the threat of military conquest, a threat made real by the military authorities' hostility to the Dominican project (King 1974:20). The lesser of two evils, the Dominicans were accepted as the dominant powers in Tezulutlan, and the name of the province was changed to Verapaz (true peace). The Spanish adhered to their side of the bargain, limiting the influx of settlers, nullifying *encomiendas* that had been granted, even removing a military colony, Nueva Sevilla, that had been established on the coast. The ban on immigration was effective in highland northern Verapaz until the nineteenth century. But Spanish settlers slowly drove out the Chol and Pokomchi from the thinly settled, rich farmlands of the Polochic and Motagua valleys of Baja Verapaz.

While the Dominicans were willing to protect part of the Verapaz from external interference, they were not content with political domination and religious conversion of the Kekchi. As early as 1540 they began to change the settlement pattern and social fabric by congregating the Kekchi into towns where they could be counted, taxed, and supervised. This policy became the main focus of conflict between Spanish and Indian in Verapaz for the next 250 years. (The present Guatemalan government's strategic village program is remarkably similar.)

The Spanish found native settlement patterns an impediment. The Kekchi lived in individual households or small hamlets located among their agricultural fields; central places were small and served as markets, religious centers, and residences for the elite. This dispersion suited the moderately intensive agriculture practiced at the time of the conquest (see Viana, Gallego & Cadena 1955; Reina & Hill 1980), but it did not accord with Dominican administrative goals or with their ethnocentric model of a civilized urban society (Farriss 1984:160–61). Over and over in both the highlands and lowlands, the Spanish rounded up the population and brought them to towns, and the Indians would then filter back to the forest. To this day the Kekchi find dispersal an effective counter to the administrative intentions of outsiders (for parallels in Yucatán see Farriss 1984:67–78).

The artificial *reducción* town included people from different areas and political affiliations. The attempt to create a European settlement pattern without a European economy was often disastrous. Sometimes the clerics would try to establish crafts, cloth production, or trading in the new towns, but this was rarely successful. Agricultural production suffered because of the need to establish new farms and change techniques. Sometimes the new community was in a different climatic zone from the old. Households, the major unit of production in pre-

Hispanic times, were disrupted both by forced movement and by the Dominican insistence on breaking up large extended households into nuclear units (Bertrand 1982:67). Reducción expectably worked best in areas where population densities were already high, and where there was already a trading and craft-producing economy.[1]

While the initial reducciones in the core of densely settled central Alta Verapaz were relatively successful, the Dominicans later needed the military to move people into towns. Because they were not as dependent on agricultural production for income as the *encomenderos* in the conquered portions of Guatemala, the Dominicans could more completely concentrate the population. They may therefore have disrupted existing social and economic relations to a greater degree. In areas such as Chiapas, where reducción was less complete, owing to the opposition of encomenderos (Wasserstrom 1983:14–15), the social impact of the conquest may have been less severe.

There was probably a close relationship between agricultural disruption in the reducciones and disease and population decline. In western Verapaz Dominican rule in new reducciones saw annual mortality rates above 10 percent in many of the years between 1561 and 1574 (Bertrand 1982:71). The total population fell by 77 percent between 1560 and 1594 (in Yucatán during a comparable period the estimated decline was between 27% and 42% [Farriss 1984:59]). This decimation in Verapaz came after previous, undocumented epidemics that probably took an even larger toll. The proximate cause of death was, again, disease (including smallpox and measles), but disruption of agriculture may have been at the root of the mortality.

Throughout the late sixteenth and seventeenth centuries, the Dominicans in highland Alta Verapaz made sporadic attempts to extend their political control and reducción policies to the lowlands to the north and east. The Chol, Manche Chol, Acal, and Lacandón there were not as politically organized as the Kekchi had been and lived in smaller, more dispersed villages. They could not be controlled through their chiefs and leaders but had to be rounded up and converted individually. The Kekchi bore the brunt of these campaigns as soldiers on Spanish expeditions and from reprisal raids. Some reprisals were serious enough to threaten the Dominican highland center of Cobán, and in 1648 the Kekchi cacique of Cobán was captured and perhaps eaten by Chol (Stone 1932:248).

The Chol, Itza, and Lacandón were eliminated or deported by the last years of the seventeenth century, and the policy of reducción eventually slowed. A small urban population in Cobán and San Pedro Carcha found some security in a weaving industry and in trading. We know very little of how the Dominicans organized the rest of the rural population. It appears that they set up their own plantations using slave labor (a report from 1769 lists over 700 Kekchi slaves on a single sugar plantation [King 1974:27]). Cochineal and cotton were grown on plantations using either slaves or forced labor. Small factories for weaving and other craft activities were set up and managed by the church. Laborers from Verapaz were sent to work on plantations elsewhere in Guatemala (McBryde 1945:11), suggesting that the Dominicans controlled labor levies. Tribute and taxation were collected as well, in order to support the Dominican regime, and the goods obtained through tribute were traded elsewhere in Guatemala by the church.

Population began to rebound during the colonial period. There were 34,000 Kekchi in 1770, up from a nadir of about 9,000 in 1594 (King 1974:285). Kekchi continued to leave the Dominican highlands for the now empty lowland forests. When the economy later stagnated, many Kekchi also began to migrate seasonally to other parts of Guatemala in search of wage labor or as itinerant peddlers, a practice that continues to the present day.

By its protectionist, paternalistic policies in the Verapaz, the church maintained the Kekchi as an isolated enclave within colonial Guatemala's underdeveloped economy. They stifled native industry and controlled the tiny urban economy; they never created a local managerial class or invested in infrastructure, and this gradually turned the great experiment into a failure. The Dominican establishment was not capable of development—it maintained the Verapaz as if it were an old building that needed only to be swept and painted.

By the early 1800s the church's economic failure in the Verapaz had become increasingly obvious. Dominican misgovernance, corruption, and overtaxation had led many Kekchi to leave the towns and cities for the countryside; gradually the reducción towns melted away. Tax burdens fell more heavily on those who remained, and in 1807 forced labor was instituted as a penalty for those who could not pay.[2] A series of crop failures and a decline in the undercapitalized weaving industry led to more tax deficits, more pressure from the church, and more evasion (Escobar 1841). In the closing years of the colonial regime flight from the Verapaz into the lowland forests increased rapidly (King 1974:27).

Verapaz under the Dominicans was a peculiar kind of colony, but it was a colony nevertheless. It was isolated from the mainstream of the

Guatemalan economy, but it was not an untouched island of tradition, where institutions survived unchanged from preconquest times. Given the dislocations of reducción, population collapse, and church domination of public and private life, it seems unlikely that very much that was pre-Hispanic survived.

It is interesting that in other parts of Guatemala and Chiapas, where colonial domination included an assault on the land base of Indian communities, many of the outward appearances of tradition—regionalism in dress, intensification of community ritual, and closure of community ethnic boundaries—were strengthened far beyond what was seen in the Verapaz. With empty lowlands to the north and east, emigration and flight were always alternatives for the Kekchi, as they were in Yucatán.

When independence came peacefully to Central America in 1821, the church's protection of the Verapaz was already ending, in the face of external pressure and internal resistance. The 18-year struggle for political control of Guatemala that followed was waged between Liberal idealists and the Conservative traditionalists. The Liberals had ties with foreign capital, took the United States as their model of a republic, and had a power base among mestizo small farmers and entrepreneurs. The Conservatives wanted a paternalistic state built on the colonial model, and for the most part their power rested in the landed oligarchy.

Over the next hundred years the Indians suffered more from the reforms of the Liberals (to whom their apparent backwardness was a frustration and an embarrassment) than from the paternalism of the Conservatives (Griffith 1972). Liberal ambitions—obsession with rapid progress, with technology and infrastructure as symbols of modernity—led them to compromise their ideology of equality and social justice when it came to the Indians: someone had to build the new roads, ports, and municipal buildings, and in the process the Indian population might absorb some civilization. Thus it was that under the immediately postcolonial Liberal regime of Morazán the first *mandamiento* law was passed. Leaders of Indian communities had to organize unpaid labor groups for work on public projects, and on the plantations and haciendas that produced export crops. Landlessness and default on small debts, as well as drunkenness and other minor offenses, were defined as vagrancy, punishable by forced labor.

According to the Liberals' theory, the fastest way to transform their underdeveloped country was to import people and capital from developed countries. To encourage such transplanting, huge grants of land were given to sometimes fraudulent foreign colonization companies. In 1834 the Eastern Coast of Central America Commercial and Agricultural Company of London was granted 15 million acres, much of it already occupied by Kekchi. Two villages of Indians were relocated from the highlands to serve as a labor supply, but the European colonists never arrived and the company collapsed (Griffith 1965 : 18, 201–50).

Although foreign colonization policies failed, Guatemala's export economy grew rapidly, based on cochineal and indigo cultivated on expropriated Indian lands with forced or coerced Indian labor (see Woodward 1972 : 50; Cambranes 1985). Ladino settlers began to filter into the Alta Verapaz in the 1830s to produce export crops.

After Carerra, a Conservative, overthrew Morazán in 1839, pressures on Indian land and labor eased for a while. Foreign capital and the growth of plantations were threatening to the landed elite, and a paternalistic rather than overtly exploitative approach to the indigenous population prevailed. The mandamiento was repealed, and many Indian communities were given title to communal lands (*ejidos*) where they were to practice subsistence agriculture. Nevertheless, many communities were coerced to lease their land to ladinos for plantations, and other forms of forced labor continued (Cambranes 1985 : 32–50). Private landownership and cash crop production by Indians had been well established in the eighteenth and early nineteenth centuries. The rise of large-scale capitalist production of export crops in the mid-nineteenth century in Guatemala squeezed Indians out of production because they were competitors, and because mestizos wanted their land and labor. The subsistence orientation of Indian agriculture should properly be dated to this time (see Cardoso & Falleto 1979 : 50–57).

New chemical inventions in Europe during the 1850s drove indigo, logwood, and other dye crops out of the world market, and coffee took their place as Guatemala's export mainstay. The Kekchi took advantage of the market and had the government's help in obtaining seed and technical advice. By 1859 many Indian communities were planting coffee on communal lands (Cambranes 1985 : 64). At the same time foreign and ladino merchants and planters moved into Verapaz, establishing mercantile enterprises, forcing Indians to lease them communal lands, and producing coffee themselves. As ladino population grew, pressures on Indian land and labor increased, and so did resistance. Sometimes Indians would destroy coffee plants on foreign-owned plantations or refuse to report for labor drafts. In 1864 a Kekchi named Melchor Yat spearheaded an uprising against foreign planters and civil authorities. Brutally crushed by the militia, the rebels dispersed to the mountains and the lowland forests (Kelsey & Osborne 1952:268; King 1974:29).

The pressures that led to this rebellion are made clear in a communication from the *corregidor* of Verapaz in 1861: " 'the demands made by the entrepreneurs in the planting season create a lot of problems, because being farmers themselves, the Indians are busy sowing grain and the authorities cannot force them to do someone else's work and leave their own unattended'" (Cambranes 1985:97). Conditions worsened, and

> from 1880 onward, local authorities addressed numerous reports to their superiors in the departmental centers or to the Central Government itself, relating how "the sowing in the communities was never completed for lack of men, because the same people are tied up on different farms," or that the peasants had been taken "en masse" to the fincas, without being allowed to "finish sowing the communal finca with corn for general consumption." Often, it was the women who had to take on tasks once assigned exclusively to men, because the work in the cornfields was left undone [Cambranes 1985:192].

During the 1860s and 1870s a land boom in the alta Verapaz was driven by the German, English, and ladino coffee planters who flooded into the area, some from Belize (Falcón 1970:10–11). The slow erosion of Indian rights became an avalanche in 1871, when a Liberal regime took power under Granados and Barrios. This government openly served the interests of capitalist export producers, many of whom were foreign. The Verapaz went from a lagging area to a leader in the kind of development that the new government favored (McCreery 1983:12–18). Immigrants were again offered incentives, including land and tax exemptions, and repressive labor and land laws were enacted. In 1877 the mandamiento returned, and with it a law that allowed the government to confiscate untitled land, defining most Indian lands in Alta Verapaz as untitled.

What took place in the Alta Verapaz over the next 25 years deserves the name of a "second conquest" (see Farriss 1984; McCreery [1983:12] likens it to a "second serfdom"). The economy became dependent on coffee. By 1900 four German companies controlled almost all trade, including coffee exports and commodity imports. Over 61 percent of all Guatemalan exports went through the hands of Hamburg merchants (King 1974:32–38). In 1890 German companies owned over 300,000 hectares, and a single German firm owned over 50,000 acres of coffee in the Verapaz (Cambranes 1985:143). There were German courts to handle labor disputes, and German social institutions to buffer the planter class from the surrounding Indian ocean. By 1930 the Verapaz was virtually a territorial possession of Germany.

Indians lost most of their land. Precolonial titles were voided on the same day that the export tax on coffee was removed, in 1877. In the land rush that followed many large parcels went straight from the government into the hands of speculators, foreign planters, and even the land surveyors themselves (Cambranes 1985:289–90). Communities that had access to the law and cash bought property as a group.

Communal landholding as a dominant institution in Kekchi life seems to date to the 1870s. In contrast, in prehistoric times, according to evidence given by Sapper (1936), Falcón (1970), and Burkitt (1905), most Kekchi held land individually and in small descent groups. Nobles had estates that were worked by labor levies from communities and resident tributaries, and communities worked some parcels as a group in order to pay tribute and support public projects. In the 1880s and 1890s communal lands were often subdivided into individual plots, and foreigners bought pieces of communal lands. Many Indian parcels were lost to foreigners in default of tiny debts. Most communities never managed to buy land, particularly after 1880 when a form of auction became the dominant practice for granting titles. Indian communities would raise the money for survey and go through protracted legal proceedings to define a land claim but would have to bid against foreign investors. When they lost, the village itself became the property of the planter. Indians were driven out of independent farming and into plantation labor.

Indian labor was put at the disposal of coffee producers by a number of legal and illegal means. Coercion and cheating, bribery and corruption were rampant under the mandamiento laws (Cambranes 1985). *Habilitaciones*—cash advances against future work—were given out by plantation owners, beginning a familiar cycle of endless debt. Added to the burden of misery were plantation stores that charged inflated prices, corporal punishment, the right of pursuit and capture of those fleeing debts, and planter-controlled courts to enforce the law. The cost of catching a runaway laborer was added to his debt.

Most *finqueros* sought a captive labor supply, buying land they did not need in order to obtain the labor of the Indians who lived on it. Only Indians on plantations were exempt from the forced labor gangs, road-building levies, and military conscription that victimized officially free Indians. Each male Indian had to carry two documents that certified his lack of indebtedness and his exemption from military servitude, otherwise he was carried off for road work or conscripted. These laws forced Indian families, even those with land, into the dubious protection of plantations.

The life of plantation *mozos* was like that of a medieval serf. Men had to work two weeks a month on the plantation. During the harvest women and children had to work from sunrise to sundown, until the picking was finished. Women were favored for the exacting task of sorting beans, and children were employed in light work beginning at age seven. Finqueros resisted the law requiring plantation schools well into the 1930s, when only token efforts were made. In this, as in other aspects of life, the finquero had almost unlimited control over his mozos (see Falcón 1970; King 1974).

Finqueros found it onerous to feed their labor force, and this legal requirement was eliminated by the labor law of 1894. After this time most mozos were allowed access to land on or near the plantation for subsistence farming. While they were expected to feed themselves by working two weeks a month (if the finquero did not lend them to the civil authorities during that time), mozos were not permitted to grow or sell an agricultural surplus. Forced to buy supplies from the company store and to borrow from the finquero for emergencies, few mozos could ever pay off their debt from their tiny wages, even with the whole family working. And where could they go if they left the plantation?

Subsistence farmers who owned land or who had shares in communal village lands were fenced in on all sides; the cash economy was dangerous foreign territory. Yet village and town residents needed cash to buy exemption from forced labor and military service, to buy basic supplies, to pay taxes and the costs of cofradías and other community offices. If they grew coffee on their own (usually on contract), they could sell it only to a few buyers who controlled prices. E. P. Dieseldorff, who monopolized the processing and transport of coffee for over 35 years, successfully opposed government plans to build roads into areas where Indians grew coffee, so there would be no competition from other buyers to drive the price up. Most of these areas remain roadless today (Falcón 1970:283).

Most Indians who were not mozos became *meseros* (monthly contract workers) in order to raise the money they needed, or they became *habilitados* working off a specific debt, or *voluntarios* who came to work of their "own free will" (Falcón 1970:322). Where Indian land was scarce people were forced to contract with a finquero merely to get some land to grow food. Where land was more plentiful agents from the *fincas* would circulate before the harvest, pressing large cash advances on workers to bind them for work. A stable labor supply was the chief concern of finqueros, but a free market for labor never emerged. Wage rates remained ridiculously low, well below the cost of reproduction. In 1935 meseros received 18 cents per week. Legal coercion, land pressure, the scarcity of cash, and a lack of alternative work ensured captive and cheap, if unreliable, farm labor.

Many Kekchi opted out of the plantation economy. Some became itinerant traders, spending months at a time carrying goods on their backs around the highlands. The cobanero is still a familiar figure in Guatemala and Belize, plodding routes that probably date from the Early Classic period (Hammond 1978). The weight of their packs and the tiny margin of their profits attest to the few alternatives available at home.

The more common choice was and still is flight. The remoter the area, the harder it was to enforce labor laws and the higher the cost of forced labor. With the reinstatement of the mandamiento in 1877, large numbers of Kekchi fled the densely populated highland region around Cobán for the remote forests north of Lake Izabal and in the Petén. Many highland villages were depopulated and therefore unable to provide their quota of workers. Loss of communal lands also drove many Indians into the unoccupied lowlands in search of subsistence. In 1892 the term that forced labor teams had to work was lengthened from 30 days to 45, and many Indians found the additional burden intolerable. Another wave of emigration began, this time to even more distant areas. But those who fled to Izabal and Petén were no longer safe. The construction of the abortive Northern Railway through Petén beginning in 1884 depended on forced labor from Indian communities in the area, prompting many Kekchi and Mopan to move east into Belize (Cambranes 1985 : 188, 199, 225).

The coffee empire of German capital in the Verapaz did not end until World War II, but the land and labor relations formed during that era have changed little to this date. New nickel and zinc mines in the Verapaz are dominated by foreign capital and continue to dispossess Kekchi communities and exploit their labor (King 1974; Carter 1969). The tragedy of the last 20 years is that land theft, plantation agriculture, and political oppression have now followed the Kekchi into the lowlands.

The 700 Kekchi Indians . . . marched on the Guatemalan village of Panzos last month in a desperate protest against their eviction from traditional farm lands. Some of them carried machetes, the tools of their livelihood in the corn and sugar cane fields. But at the town hall they met soldiers who, after some pushing and shoving, opened fire with Israeli-made Galil assault rifles. "The shooting came from the rooftops, from the windows, from the houses around the square," a young protest leader recalled last week. . . . Several terrified women clutching children jumped into the swift Polochic river and drowned. "We only went peacefully to see the Mayor," said a stunned survivor. "If we had gone to attack, we would not have taken our women and children." . . . The government announced that 38 Kekchis had died in a "peasant uprising instigated by leftist guerrillas, Cuba's Fidel Castro and religious groups." . . . Most of the land now in dispute flanks the "Transversal Strip" where a cross-country road being built from the Caribbean to the Mexican border traverses territory that once only the Indians cared about. In the past two years, say lawyers who assist the Indians, entire thatched-hut communities of Indian peasants have been scattered by developers seeking a share of the oil and nickel deposits and of the booming real-estate market along the road. . . . General Kjell Laugerud, Guatemala's President, is said to own large estates in a "Zone of the Generals" along the strip, while Gen. Romero Lucas, the President-elect, owns more than 78,000 acres. [*Newsweek*, June 19, 1978].

THE KEKCHI IN BELIZE: BACKGROUND TO THE PRESENT

The Spanish never made an effort to control or develop southern Belize after they rounded up the indigenous Chol inhabitants and shipped them off to the highlands in the 1600s. Colonial enterprises initially based on plunder and theft are afterward rooted in the exploitation of labor (Wallerstein 1976:223). The Chol had nothing worth plundering. Because they refused to be congregated into settlements where their labor could be exploited, they were eventually eliminated as a danger to the frontier. With no other sources of slaves or forced labor, the Spanish found it unprofitable to exploit the lowland forests and abandoned them.

While the British government also had no interest in the lowland forests of Central America, independent British entrepreneurs found in them a source of profit. Unlike the Spanish, British merchants and traders had access to all the markets of the world, to capital and slave labor, and their government usually left them alone. British Honduras was only one of several places on the Caribbean shore where British corsairs, buccaneers, traders, and outlaws visited and settled.

The British who settled the coast in the 1640s may have had contact with the Chol and other Maya groups in the south, but there are few records from that time. Early relations between the British and local Maya were not terribly friendly, and the Chol probably learned to avoid the coastal area, frequented by pirates and logwood cutters, at an early date. There is one mention of English corsairs kidnaping Indians from the Temash River area in 1677; we know about this incident only because they caught a Spanish friar as well (Thompson 1972:25). It was a regular practice in British Honduras to keep Indians as slaves as late as the 1820s (Burdon 1934:250, 297; see also Bolland 1977, 1987; Jones 1977 for Maya-British relations). The Mosquito and Waika Indians of the Honduran coast regularly raided the Chol area for male and female slaves who were carried off and sold to the British as far away as Jamaica (Olien 1988). If some few Chol survived by hiding in the forest, as Thompson (1930a) thought, they remained well hidden. A travel account from 1867 mentions "natives" in the forests near the Moho River, which indicates that some remaining Chol may have been living in the district at the time (Swett 1868:33–38), although the term could also have been used for Creoles or mestizos. By the early 1800s, also, a new ethnic group had entered the southern region. Originally deported from St. Vincent to Roatán in 1797, the Black Caribs (now known as Garifuna) arrived in the area of the Moho River and settled along the coast (Gonzalez 1969:21–24, 1986; Taylor 1951; Conzemius 1928). Between 1820 and 1830 the still-extant Garifuna communities of Punta Gorda and Barranco were founded.

British logging began as a small-scale entrepreneurial enterprise, but by the early nineteenth century it was dominated by a few large mahogany companies that drew on London capital. These companies acquired title to vast tracts of land, excluding or buying up smaller concerns, and ran the colony as a company town (Bolland & Shoman 1977: chs. 1, 2). During the eighteenth century logging was confined to central and northern British Honduras, and the south remained in an ambiguous legal status, neither British nor Spanish. The first official claim to a mahogany work in the far south was entered in 1814 (Burdon 1934:166; Gregory 1972:5). By 1827 the legislature of the colony officially claimed the territory, an action supported by the Colonial Office in London, although the southern boundary of the Sarstoon River was not ratified by treaty until 1859 (Bolland & Shoman 1977:46–49).

It took a lot of capital to keep logging crews in such remote areas, and in a short time most of the far south was in the hands of a single concern: Young, Toledo and Company. Founded about 1839, this firm accumulated over a million acres before going bankrupt in 1881. The boom in the southern district did not last long, for the most accessible trees were gone by 1855 (Burdon 1934:373). When markets in Europe were depressed logging firms often found themselves without operating capital and were forced to sell land. But land was rarely sold to the laboring population, the Maya, Caribs, and free colored (Creole). To sell land to these people would encourage smallholder farming, draw labor away from logging, and undercut the lucrative import trade in food. The law made sure that in an empty land of fertile soil, small farmers could not get title to farmland (Bolland & Shoman 1977).

An acceptable alternative was to promote foreign settlement and plantation agriculture, the same strategy used by the Guatemalan Liberals. British Honduras was no more successful. An attempt was made after the U.S. Civil War to settle Confederate refugees in Toledo (Rosenberger 1958; Holdridge 1940). Between 1867 and 1870 the settlers established sugar plantations, mills, and distilleries about 10 kilometers inland from the coast in an area called the Toledo Settlement. Lacking slaves to do the work, the settlement did not provide the living most colonists expected. Some East Indians (mostly Tamils) were imported as workers but soon left to start their own farms in the same area; their descendants remain an important component of the Toledo population. By 1910 most of the ex-Confederates were gone.

The logging firms tried to diversify into plantation agriculture during the second half of the nineteenth century. Young, Toledo and Company had a steam-powered sugar mill and 137 acres in cane in Toledo in 1868, but they could never solve the labor problem, and the industry remained anemic for the next 50 years before dying out entirely. Meanwhile, the sugar industry flourished in the north, not because the land there is more suitable, but because there was a labor supply: Yucatec Maya refugees from the Caste Wars of the 1850s were quickly put to work on cane farms. When low prices drove many mahogany companies out of business toward the end of the nineteenth century, only those with sugar interests in the north survived.

At the end of the third quarter of the nineteenth century Toledo remained the farthest rim of a periphery. After the indigenous population was eliminated nothing remained to exploit except the forests, and the forests did not last long. Colonial and capitalist regimes were stymied when it came to lowland tropical forests. Resources proved difficult to extract, infrastructure was expensive to build and hard to maintain, and the labor force caused endless problems. Workers escaped into forests where they could hide indefinitely and subsist easily, so the cost of coercive labor was high. Technical production problems, market fluctuations and collapses, and competition from synthetics (for indigo, rubber, quinine, and chicle, for example) plagued export crops. Despite all these obstacles, the lowland tropics have a continuing and powerful attraction for investors. Logging and mining do not require large amounts of labor, and they can show a profit if there is adequate starting capital and if prices hold up. When the resource is gone or the price falls, companies simply pull out.

Agricultural capitalism depends on a large seasonal labor supply as well as capital and markets. Southern Belize, like many other "empty lowlands" of Central and South America, has seen hundreds of agricultural schemes come and go over the last century. The principal attraction of the forests is the low price of land, a powerful incentive to farmers from developed countries, where land is the major capital cost. They do not usually understand that the land is worthless without labor and is sometimes worthless even with it. Cattle ranching is the exception, as it uses very few workers. Historically this has been the most successful way for capital to exploit tropical lowland forests, much to their detriment.[3] When schemes go bankrupt, or when they "withdraw from production" in an area, they leave more behind than ecological damage, rotting equipment, and holes in the ground—they leave people.

The borders of British Honduras provided a haven for many different Maya groups during the nineteenth century. Yucatec Maya fled the Caste Wars in the north, and Chan Maya entered the Belize River valley from Guatemala. Toledo was peopled by both the Kekchi and the Mopan; the latter are a lowland Maya group, closely related to the Yucatec, about whom little is known in colonial or precolonial times. Pacified and converted by the Spanish in the late 1600s, they were mostly left alone thereafter, living in widely scattered farming settlements and reducción towns such as San Luís in Guatemala. In 1886 Mopan from the town of San Luís undertook a planned and organized migration across the border into the Toledo District, to escape taxation and forced labor (Thompson 1930a:41; Sapper 1897 : 54; Clegern 1968 : 93). The migration included over 100 initial settlers and many more followers (Gregory 1972 : 14–15). The group first settled near modern Pueblo Viejo and then moved east in 1889 to San Antonio.

This axis, running east-west from San Antonio to Pueblo Viejo through upland hilly country on the southern flanks of the Maya Mountains, is still the center of Mopan population in Belize (see Figure 4.2). San Antonio grew rapidly, from 448 persons in 1891 to 758 in 1901 (BHBB 1901), but then leveled off and grew more slowly to 1,087 in 1980. The number of Mopan in the hill country around San Antonio has continued to grow, as excess population disperses to form small hamlets of three to 10 houses, called *alquilos*.

Some Kekchi probably came with the Mopan settlers. Many Cahabon

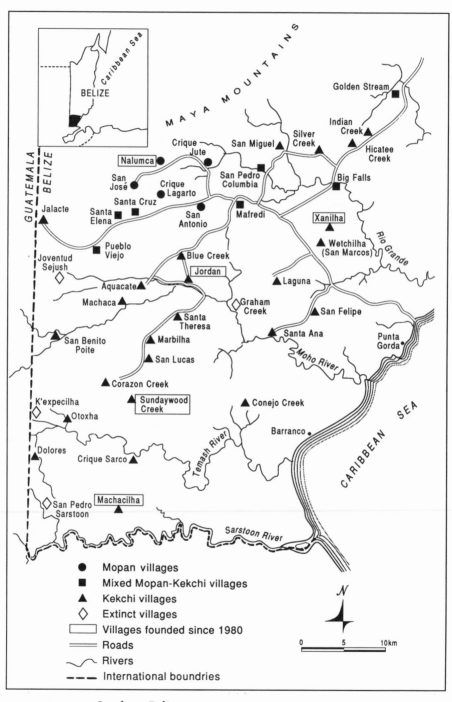

FIGURE 4.2 Southern Belize

Kekchi had already settled around San Luís in 1867 and had begun to intermarry with Mopan there (González 1961:100). Three villages in the hill zone west of San Antonio today have mixed Kekchi-Mopan populations, and this mixing may have begun during the first movements. The Kekchi residents of these villages (Santa Cruz, Santa Elena, Pueblo Viejo) speak a dialect distinct from that of Kekchi speakers elsewhere in the district.

In the early 1940s the colonial government began to encourage corn, rice, and bean production in the Toledo District in order to cut down on the amount of food imported by the colony. This was a safe policy because Toledo lacked significant logging or plantation enterprises at the time, so small-scale farming could not compete for land or labor. Money was invested in building roads, churches, and schools in the larger alquilos. Government buying centers for crops were established. Population once again became more nucleated and concentrated.

The dissected, hilly country where the Mopan settled is a distinct economic and social zone from the Kekchi villages along the Moho, Temash, and Sarstoon drainages. Population density is higher, cash crop production has a long and continuous history, and agriculture is more intensive than in the lowland areas to the south and east. The Mopan, unlike the Kekchi, have a long history as independent small farmers and have never been plantation laborers, and this is reflected in many aspects of their culture and social organization (see Gregory 1972, 1975, 1976).

Although their traditions have therefore been less disrupted by colonialism than have the Kekchi's, the Mopan appear more developed than the Kekchi; they are often seen as more progressive or more modern and are stereotyped as more friendly by many Belizeans. Both cause and consequence is the concentration of infrastructure and development assistance in Mopan villages. Most aid projects, Peace Corps volunteers, and health programs are aimed at Mopan villages. The Mopan have found a political voice and have repeated elected residents of San Antonio to national political office. Differences between Mopan and Kekchi areas have historical roots, but they also stem from the different geographical and economic roles that divide the northern Toledo District from the southern. In the peripheral microcosm of Toledo, the south is a hinterland, a permanent frontier, while the northern and coastal part has been a semiperiphery with closer ties to the market and better infrastructure.

During the colonial period, Spanish colonies were prohibited from trading with anyone but Spain, and British Honduras flourished as an entrepôt for illegal English goods destined for the neighboring colonies. This income tapered off following Central American independence, and some British Honduran merchants invested their capital in land and plantation agriculture. Most of these efforts quickly failed (as similar schemes do today), because they could not find a steady labor supply or a steady market for their produce. One major exception were the plantations of Bernard Cramer on the Sarstoon River in southern Toledo. Cramer succeeded where others failed because he had adequate capital, an outlet to a major port, and a captive labor supply.

Cramer's capital was accumulated as a Belize City trader and land speculator. Land registries from the 1860s in Belize City's Public Records Office are full of his land transactions, first in prime commercial property in the city and nearby Cayes, and then in nearby riverbank locations that had agricultural potential. He lent money to a number of other farmers and merchants and was in partnership for a time with C. W. Dieseldorff, whose family was then moving into the Alta Verapaz and whose nephew would eventually come to dominate the Verapaz coffee trade (BPRO DB2 : 883). Although of German origin, Cramer (like Dieseldorff) moved to London in the 1870s, working thereafter through a local agent, Carlos Melhado. Through him Cramer bought some sugar properties in the north and the booming central coast in 1880 (BPRO DB4 : 67, DB6 : 470, 498). When the mahogany business slumped in the late 1870s, he began to buy up large tracts of mahogany works in the interior at very low prices, or by default of mortgage, accumulating over 510,000 acres. He first bought land in Toledo from the dying Young, Toledo and Company in 1880, acquiring parcels on the Sarstoon, Moho, and Temash rivers (BPRO RT2:F166, 194, 527–32). He continued to buy in Toledo through the 1890s and subdivided several pieces on the Moho, which were sold to prospective plantation owners (BPRO DB12 : 128, PB 1886–1894 : 391, 11, 13–14, 445).[4]

Cramer managed his speculations from the Surrey countryside, while one of his two sons, Herman Joseph, returned to British Honduras to manage the family business. Herman decided to begin a plantation on the Toledo lands and arranged with friends or relatives in the Verapaz to provide Kekchi workers. These Kekchi families were settled at San Pedro Sarstoon, a plantation established between 1881 and 1890 in the southwestern corner of the colony, close to the Guatemalan border. The census of 1891 is the first to mention the settlement, listing 254 occupants, including Cramer's personal servant and a schoolteacher (BHAR 1891 : 40).[5]

The Cramer estates, which grew into the third largest settlement in the Toledo District (the 1911 census lists 328 residents, a school, and a church [Dunk 1921:135]), produced coffee shaded by *castilloa* rubber, and, later, cacao shaded by plantains and bananas (Romney 1959:118). Cramer supplied all the colony's coffee and had a small surplus for export, but his major success was with cacao, exporting a peak of 42,800 pounds in 1906. Informants say that nutmeg, mace, allspice and *achiote* were also grown on the plantation and exported successfully.

Bernard Cramer died in 1903, and his properties were split between two sons. Herman got the properties in the south and continued to live at Punta Gorda and San Pedro Sarstoon until World War I broke out and the plantation closed down for good. We do not know why the enterprise failed. There is no archival evidence that Cramer was shut down as a foreign national at the outbreak of hostilities, as some surmise (Romney 1959:118). He probably had trouble marketing his produce through his German connections, and he may also have had difficulty keeping his Kekchi laborers on the farm. Cramer still had over 95,800 acres when he died in 1947 (BPRO PA24). At some time he had sold his largest Sarstoon estate, over 36,000 acres of forest, to another investor. Although it has since changed hands many times, this Dolores estate, with about 200 resident Kekchi, remains the largest block of private land in Toledo.

While the Cramers brought some Kekchi to the Sarstoon River, others came by themselves, settling the empty region between the river and San Antonio. In 1908 the village of Aguacate had a church (San José Moho), and in the census of 1911 there were 431 persons listed as living on the Moho River. Dolores village, on the northern part of Cramer's Sarstoon estate, had a government school by 1914 (BHBB 1914). A steam-powered sawmill was built on the Temash River in 1910 by two German brothers who were logging in the area, and this may have attracted Kekchi looking for work, establishing the core of the present Temash village of Crique Sarco (Robinson 1985:31; Schackt 1986).

On the Columbia River, in a lowland area east of San Antonio, Kekchi immigrants founded San Pedro Columbia between 1911 and 1914. Between the market centers of San Antonio and Punta Gorda, drawing on the migrants from the Petén and northern Verapaz, San Pedro grew more rapidly than any other Kekchi settlement and remains the largest in the district (784 people in 1980). After Cramer's estate closed, Kekchi families from San Pedro Sarstoon dispersed to found new villages and alquilos. Their settlements (Otoxha, Crique Sarco, Machaca) on major rivers survive to this day, while many other small alquilos have disappeared, leaving only a named creek or crossing. Hamlets formed around temporary logging camps that offered jobs and a market for food.

Toledo administrative history shows long periods of benign neglect punctuated by short periods of activity that mark external interest. The district commissioner in Punta Gorda was mainly concerned with keeping the peace and collecting land use fees from the Indians. Schools and churches were administered by the Catholic diocese, which maintained only tenuous contact with the remoter settlements. The Forestry Department was one of the most powerful arms of the colonial government and showed some interest in the Indians, mainly to protect timber from them. Most of Toledo became Crown Land by the beginning of this century through lapses in leases and tax default. At first farmers were allowed to take out leases on small parcels each year for their fields, but this proved administratively clumsy and inefficient, and evasion was the norm (BAB 1916:MP1472–16, MP1454–16).

In 1924 the colonial government tried to control land, labor, and taxation more efficiently through a form of indirect rule. This system had already been used among the Yucatec Maya immigrants to northern British Honduras (Bolland 1987). Each recognized Indian village, not including alquilos, was granted an Indian Reserve, where they could live and farm under an elected village alcalde who collected a yearly fee of $5 (a significant sum at that time). He was also responsible for settling minor disputes and judging minor crimes within the reserve.[6] These reserves were amended in 1933 to include villages that had been missed in 1924. Already two reserves had been abandoned, and new villages had been established on reserves assigned to others. The reserve system never fit very closely with actual land use patterns but was instead an administrative convenience and fiction.

On these reserves land was used almost without restriction or supervision, but no title could be granted. The system, in fact, made it impossible for Indians to own land in their communities. No communal rights were recognized, and though the Indians had to pay administration costs, they had no part in defining boundaries. The whole system remains under the control of the national authorities, so a stroke of the pen in the capital can eliminate Indians' rights (and this stroke seems increasingly imminent). In cruel irony, those same authorities, from the colonial period to the present, have blamed the Kekchi's footloose migratory ways, their inability to invest in permanent agriculture, on what is claimed as their custom of communal land tenure. They have certainly adapted to the system and may now prefer to keep it, but the reserves are not customary or traditional. They are not really any sort of land tenure, merely community rental from the government, a fact that has been lost in current debate about the future of the Indian Reserves (Romney 1959; Aguilar 1984; Howard 1974; Osborn 1982; Topsey 1987).

Census figures are not available at regular intervals for Toledo (see Table 4.1). The district's total Indian population went from zero in 1886 to about 2,200 in 1921 (of whom about 1,300 were Kekchi), for an average growth of 63 persons per year, mostly immigrants. This rate has never been exceeded. Changes in the rate of immigration since 1921 are attributable mainly to variation in the "pull" of economic opportunities on the Belizean side of the border, and in the "push" felt by the Indians on the Guatemalan side. Government interest in Toledo declined between the late 1930s and the early 1950s, and no accurate census figures were collected. The annual growth rate of 1.97 percent between 1936 and 1966 may be natural population growth, although, given frequent measles and malaria epidemics, a small amount of immigration may be indicated. The real increase in Kekchi population occurred in the 1970s, when mining and cattle ranching expanded into Kekchi territory on the Guatemalan side of the border, and political and economic oppression of Indians increased dramatically.

After the original migration in the 1890s, groups and individual families followed in its path. A case in point is a 1932 petition by six household heads (with 16 dependents) from Chacalte in Guatemala, asking permission to settle at Joventud, near the western frontier (BAB 1932: MP249–32). The settlement of about 40 people from Blue Creek (Izabal District) in the new village of Wetchilha (now called San Marcos) in 1979 is a more recent example.

Most movement of individual households takes the stepwise form found in the Petén by Richard N. Adams (1965). A household settles for several years in each village along a route. At the end of the route small groups split off from the terminal village to begin new hamlets in unoccupied forest. In general, people are unwilling to move to the next village on the route until they have established some sort of kinship or *compadrazgo* connection there. As a consequence, kinship ties link the villages along the routes, and people move in both directions through marriage. What appears to casual observers to be a restless population that aimlessly moves back and forth is actually a slowed stepwise migration, as each household develops a mobility strategy.

For many years the colonial government made little attempt to regulate individual movement across the border by Indians, assuming that the border was somehow invisible for them (which seems unlikely

Table 4.1. *Population of Kekchi Villages, 1921–1980*

Region[a]	Village	1921	1931	1936	1966	1980
S	Dolores	96	113	126	84	193
S	Crique Sarco	89	162	109	133	184
S	Hocotal (Otoxha)	68	27	13	154	182
S	Temashito[b]	56	68	0	0	0
S	K'expecilha	44	20	75	0	0
S	San Pedro Sarstoon[b]	34	20	0	0	0
S	Little Temash[bc]	31	0	0	0	0
S	Conejo Creek	28	0	0	35	42
S	Hicatee[bc]	22	0	0	0	0
S	Joventud (Poite)	0	31	58	37	261
S	San Lucas	0	0	0	77	63
S	Mabilha	0	0	0		57
S	Corazon Creek	0	0	0		32
S	Graham Creek	0	12	1	0	0
N	San Pedro Columbia	261	297	279	545	784
N	San Pedro Alquilos[bc]	54	85	42	0	0
N	Laguna	53	0	0	85	205
N	Condemned Creek (San Felipe)	3	7	22	86	47
N	Big Falls				160	323
N	Indian Creek				0	264
N	San Miguel				266	227
N	Silver Creek				20	175
N	Big Falls Road				54	175
N	Hicatee Creek					110
N	Golden Stream					68
N	San Marcos					66
N	Xanil Ha					18
M	Aguacate	229	120	113	55	149
M	Machaca	173	101	60	0	41
M	Moco River, Santa Ana	31	0	0	40	134
M	Se Jush	22	0	0	0	0
M	Blue Creek	0	51	44	18	145
M	Hinchasones (Santa Theresa)	0	124	137	110	116
M	Jalacte	0	37	0	0	58
M	Jordan	0	0	0	0	56
H	Santa Cruz[d]			34	141	349
H	Pueblo Viejo[d]			54	227	346
H	Santa Elena[d]		239	369	119	177

NOTES: Where population is recorded as zero there were no people present. Where the cell is left blank the village was either not yet established or there are no secure data.

[a] S = Sarstoon and Temash rivers; N = North; M = Moho River; and H = Highland.

[b] Now abandoned.

[c] Location unknown.

[d] Mixed Kekchi and Mopan.

considering their stated desire to hide behind it). Requests by groups of Indians to cross and establish a village were usually handled as a question of where to settle them instead of whether to allow them in or not. Things have changed since Belize's independence in 1981. The influx of political and economic refugees from El Salvador and Guatemala during the late 1970s and early 1980s changed the country's ethnic makeup by making Spanish-speaking ladinos a majority. Many of the refugees, who may number over 25,000, are willing to work for lower wages than Belizeans. The fear and anger prompted by the refugees, or "aliens" as they are called in Belize, led the government to issue new regulations in 1984 requiring all aliens to register and obtain identity cards. It is uncertain how long registered aliens will continue to be permitted to stay in the country, unless they become citizens. Although aimed more at mestizo immigrants in other parts of the country, this regulation affects Kekchi immigrants, who are now classified as aliens even if their children are born in Belize. Few Kekchi ever took out Belizean citizenship, even though they may have lived in the country for most of their lives. All indications are that this has slowed Kekchi immigration and has led to divisions and conflicts between those Kekchi who are citizens and those who are not.

Kekchi population movements in Toledo are not just a product of linear migration from Guatemala. Within Toledo, villages disappear and reappear, and community membership changes from year to year. In Aguacate village in 1978 adults over 20 years old had changed villages on average every 9.7 years of their lives; the most mobile people moved every 5.2 years. Villages, households, and individuals move in response to changing person-to-land ratios, opportunities for wage labor, access to markets for crops, development projects and incentives, kinship alliances, and village politics.

Local population growth has followed road access. The northern zones have seen steady population growth, while numbers in the south have stagnated. The growth in the southern zone since 1980 is attributable to new immigration, while increase in the Moho drainage reflects the construction of roads into that zone in the 1970s, and a consequent flow of people back into the area from north and south.

CYCLES OF ECONOMIC EXPANSION AND CONTRACTION

Toledo still looks like a frontier because each time it has been penetrated the land and its people have been so thoroughly and efficiently exploited that capitalist ventures left nothing behind, except the workers themselves. First it was mahogany; then, under Cramer, cacao, coffee, and rubber. In the 1930s it was bananas and mahogany (again), and today it is pigs, rice, beans, and cacao (again). In each case outsiders have managed to extract what they wanted, at a profit, without investing in the region's development. Up until the 1960s, despite all this activity, Toledo had almost no roads, no markets, no skilled or educated labor, and no self-sustaining economic enterprises; certainly no capital remained behind when profitability declined and the companies left. During each cycle the cash the Kekchi earned was not invested in land or productive resources but was instead spent on consumer goods and necessities, substituting purchased foods for part of their subsistence crop. When they could not find ways to make cash they reverted to subsistence farming, sustaining themselves for the next round of development.

Toledo was therefore not a frontier of capitalism, it was and is a place where peripheral investment enterprises are intermittently conducted. The most striking aspect of those enterprises is that they are usually small and undercapitalized, dependent on limited, fluctuating markets that they do not control. As a result they are unable and unwilling to invest in infrastructure. A cycle of underdevelopment occurs when government fails to invest in roads, schools, communication, marketing services, or other infrastructure because it perceives the region as poor and backward. The lack of infrastructure in turn means that only extractive kinds of capitalist development are profitable or practical there, and in draining the area they further and deepen its status as backward. In the 1860s Toledo was no more backward or marginal than any other part of rural British Honduras. Today, through this cycle, it has become underdeveloped.

In this, Toledo was and is part of the general process of underdevelopment in Belize as a whole (see Ashcraft 1973; Bolland & Shoman 1977; Bolland 1977, 1981). Capitalism practices its own form of shifting cultivation in areas like Toledo. To carry the analogy a bit further, often the area looks like primeval forest, when it is actually a fallowed area within a larger system of exploitation.

Figure 4.3 is a time-line chart that shows each export commodity from the Toledo District. Early logging, sugar, coffee, cocoa, rubber, and banana production have been mentioned previously. The period from 1914 to the early 1930s was one of relative isolation. Nevertheless, the 1931 forestry survey found that Kekchi households kept many hogs (10.8 per household) and a few cattle, suggesting that they were being sold in town, and they grew enough cocoa and coffee to trade with co-

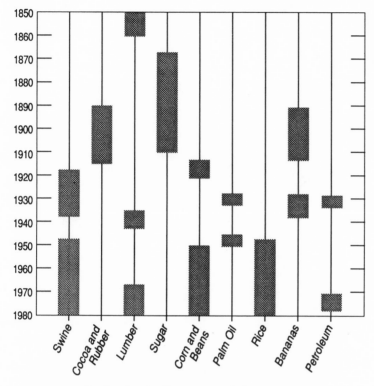

FIGURE 4.3   Production for Export in Toledo, 1850–1980

baneros for other goods (BAB 1936:MP266–33; BAB 1928:MP1279–28).
Even in this time of isolation, the Kekchi produced enough to trade for
manufactured necessities and pay their land use fees.

Although some Mopan and Kekchi were hurt by the loss of wage labor and commodity markets in 1932, at this time schooner captains put
out of business by the end of Prohibition in the United States began to
dock at Punta Gorda to buy bananas instead of rum. Kekchi villages
along the lower Moho and Temash responded quickly, planting on fertile levees and shipping the bananas down the rivers. In 1936 a Kekchi
farmer in Crique Sarco reported making $100 a week from his 40-acre
farm (BAB 1936:MP266–33). The banana boom was short-lived. Farmers had difficulty meeting the strict size and quality standards of the
large companies that dominated the trade, and this drove out the small
independent shipowners who bought in British Honduras. Disease problems hurt production, and in 1938 the trade died out completely
(Romney 1959:127).

As bananas declined, another mahogany boom began. Logging in Toledo goes through cycles based on world prices and extraction costs. Technological improvements lower extraction costs and allow loggers to cut progressively less accessible trees. Gasoline-powered machinery allowed loggers in the late 1930s to cut logging roads deep into the forest. It is hard to guess what kind of impact these logging crews had on the Kekchi. Unlike earlier, labor-intensive logging, mechanized extraction probably offered Indians only short-term jobs clearing bush and locating trees. Depending heavily on canned imported foods, the crews would have been a limited market for Kekchi crops. In the cash-poor economy of Toledo, however, even small purchases would have been important. Logging fell into a decline in the early 1940s after the best lumber was depleted. Since then there have been few technical innovations in logging, and timber extraction in Toledo has been sporadic as prices fluctuate. Foreigners who set up cattle ranches in the 1970s financed their operations with sawmills that cut secondary hardwoods during land-clearing operations, but this lasted only a few years while prices were high. Rosewood was extracted from reserves and Crown Land by private concessionaires in the late 1970s, but no Indian labor was used. In the long run the Kekchi have had little benefit from the logging of their forests.

With the decline of logging in the 1940s the government lost interest in Toledo, and the economy returned to subsistence farming and exporting hogs. In the early 1950s, however, the trade deficit in the colony began to skyrocket, partly because of the increasing cost of imported food. The contradiction of a country with millions of arable acres and an unemployed labor force importing huge amounts of food was not lost on the colonial authorities. Farmers in northern British Honduras were just beginning to shift away from food crops and into sugarcane (Jones 1971), and though some thought that the Creole population of Belize City could be persuaded to become farmers, the government looked south for a solution to the food problem.

From the beginning food purchasing and marketing in Toledo was organized by the government to serve national priorities rather than the needs of small farmers. The government selected the major crops, rice and red kidney beans, because they are staple foods in the urban market. In the early 1950s the government Marketing Board fixed prices for rice, beans, and corn. Between 1951 and 1953 average yearly purchases at the Marketing Board were 795,000 pounds of rice, 35,000 pounds of corn, and 98,000 pounds of beans, entirely from Mopan and northern

Kekchi villages. The southern part of the district produced many of the approximately 2,500 pigs annually shipped north to Belize City, and sold quantities of cacao, coffee, and copal incense to cobaneros (BAB 1953: MP397). Government interest in the area increased, and a Land Use Survey Team was active there between 1952 and 1954 (Romney 1959).

Reports sent back to England by members of this survey team concerning the lack of health care in Toledo's villages led to questions being raised in Parliament. As a result the Colonial Office created the post of Kekchi liaison officer and in 1953 dispatched a young Englishman, Owen-Lewis, to occupy the position (Rambo 1964:14; Nunes 1977). He began a number of successful projects in Crique Sarco, including construction of an airstrip, a regular boat service, and communal cattle pastures, but it was wishful thinking to send a single man, however talented, to develop an entire region.

Owen-Lewis arrived when an economic crisis was beginning in the southern part of the district. Income from selling pigs and cacao was not keeping pace with the rise in the cost of basic commodities. Pigs, like humans, eat corn as a staple diet, and so the amount of corn a farmer could produce with low-technology methods placed an absolute limit on the number of pigs that could be raised, and therefore on the amount of cash earned. Because of difficult trails, rice and other cash crops could not be transported to market. The subsistence economy still required some cash, and cash was becoming increasingly short. Missionaries and schoolteachers, who were seen more frequently in the southern villages at that time, may also have increased people's perceived needs and expectations.

Priests and administrators in Toledo provided a pull factor by encouraging Kekchi from southern and Moho regions to move north where they would be closer to the highway, market, administrators, and priests (Boster 1973:7). By 1951 the ill-conceived movement was under way. All but three households left Santa Theresa to start San Miguel, and the following year most of Aguacate left for San Pedro Columbia. San Lucas, Machaca, and Graham Creek were abandoned, although the larger villages in the district's southern margins resisted relocation. Land for swidden agriculture was already scarce in the crowded northern zone, and new farmers often settled on land claimed by old villages. Less land meant shorter fallow cycles, lower yields, and less produce to sell despite the easy access to market. Many new immigrants also felt burdened by government supervision and interference.

Some migrants decided that roads, hospitals, markets, and other amenities were not worth decreased freedom and access to land for farming and hunting. They returned south, although often not to their original village. Others stayed in the north, seeking new sources of income in small-merchandise stores, wage labor, and new crops, as well as adopting new agricultural techniques. Still others decided to search for land in other directions, moving into areas of Crown Land where no reservations existed, but where leases could be obtained or evaded. Laguna was founded by migrants from San Miguel in 1958, close to the San Antonio–Punta Gorda road. When a highway was built to link Punta Gorda to Belize City in the 1960s, the Kekchi rapidly moved north in a strip settlement along the road wherever they were allowed. Big Falls was established in 1962 by people from Laguna, then came Silver Creek about 1968, Indian Creek in 1972, and Golden Stream in 1974. This is the northernmost area of rain forest near the highway; after this there is pine savannah unsuited for farming. In the late 1970s Mopan and Kekchi from Toledo leapfrogged into the next area of rain forest, about 80 miles to the north in the Stann Creek District, establishing five villages there by 1984.

The 1970s brought new forms of development to Toledo. The government sold several large tracts of forest along the southern highway, close to existing Kekchi villages, to foreign entrepreneurs who cut lumber and used Indian farmers to clear their land for cattle ranching. Cattle were unprofitable (mainly because of high costs and lack of export facilities within the country), and several tried mechanized rice production or orchard crops. What looked in 1978 like an onslaught of foreign capital, competing for land with the Indians and exploiting their labor, had become by 1984 a series of run-down ranches with "for sale" signs in front. Another cycle of development was complete. In 1985 cocoa and citrus began to look like good investments. New capital is turning the ranches into cocoa and citrus farms. One wonders who will pick these crops, especially if most of the Kekchi and Mopan have their own cocoa to pick at the same time. Perhaps Honduran migrant labor will provide the solution, as it has elsewhere in Belize.[7]

In the mid-1970s, following discoveries in Mexico, major oil companies began to explore in Toledo, setting up several camps and eventually digging test wells. As in the previous period of oil prospecting in the late 1920s, nothing was found, and the last camp was abandoned in 1980. Some wage labor was offered to Indians, but when the companies departed they left only herbicide-contaminated clearings in the forest.

In the meantime the national government and the British Ministry of Overseas Development decided to undertake a major rural development project in Toledo, hoping to introduce irrigated rice farming in the abundant seasonal swamps. The Toledo Rural Development Project lasted from 1978 to 1984 and did some valuable research, including a demonstration that irrigated lowland rice is not economically feasible in Toledo. In the end there was little impact on the Kekchi economy, except through wages to day laborers.

A larger impact has been created by the growth of a new cash crop industry in the area—the cultivation of marijuana for export to the United States. Although grown for a long time in Toledo for local trade, marijuana became a big business in about 1980 when middlemen from Dangriga took control of marketing. While producers get very little of the profits from this commodity, it still provides far more cash than any other crop, and in some communities consumer culture is flowering. In San Pedro Columbia one can find two-story concrete houses with electricity and two-car garages standing next to thatched huts with dirt floors. The distribution of income is profoundly uneven, and again the result is little capital accumulation in the district itself.

By far the greatest impact on Toledo District has come through the continuing construction of roads. Unpaved branches of the highway had reached Pueblo Viejo in the late 1960s, San Miguel in 1966 (McCaffrey 1967), and the Moho River at Aguacate by 1972. But the Moho remained a barrier, and the southern district relatively isolated, until 1984 when old roads were improved. A new road, begun with British funding, reached the Temash in 1987 (with help from the U.S. Agency for International Development [USAID]). Roads change the underlying basis of economic decisions by farmers as well as capitalists. By turning the isolated hinterland into an open and accessible area, roads affect people's relationships with the natural environment, their community and family, and with the market and government (Wilk 1984).

CONTINUITY OF PAST AND PRESENT

I would like to emphasize here the long-term continuities in the external pressures on the Kekchi and their responses to them. Throughout the colonial period, in both Guatemala and British Honduras, the Kekchi were faced with a limited range of choices for a very few critical dilemmas. While the last 450 years have included a complex and surprisingly varied sequence of historical events, these events have changed only the outcomes of Kekchi decisions, not the critical dilemmas themselves. Here I am using the word *dilemma* to indicate a crucial choice that has major consequences that cannot be foreseen. The Kekchi know there will be consequences, but not what they will be. That is truly a dilemma.

A trivial example of what I mean by this is the issue of whether to buy clothes from the store or make them at home, which has faced Kekchi households probably from before the conquest to the present. At times the availability of wage work, the relative cost of clothing compared with the value of women's other work, the availability of land for growing cotton, and the need to avoid any indebtedness to finqueros have all changed, and so have the outcomes of Kekchi decisions about clothes. At some times, and in some places, manufactured clothes have prevailed over homemade, and vice versa; but the basic dilemma has persisted even when one outcome has prevailed. The remarkable continuity of Kekchi society in the face of rapid changes in the economic and physical environment depends on a storehouse of knowledge that keeps options open. This knowledge of options may be the best definition of tradition, because it makes it very clear that tradition is an essential adaptation to the extreme spatial and temporal variability of the modern world economy.

Dependence or Flight

The terms *dependence* and *flight* encapsulate a dilemma that has been and remains at the core of Kekchi experience. From the time of the conquest, loss of political independence, land, control of labor, and even the most basic human rights have forced many Kekchi into the position of a dependent peasantry or proletariat. As long as these pressures have been applied the main solutions have been either staying put and resisting (either passively or through the cracks of the system) or picking up and moving to a remote area. History shows a clear relationship between the weight of oppression on the Kekchi and the number who choose flight. Migration to remote areas has never been voluntary except in the sense that some people did it and others did not. In general, most Kekchi would have preferred an independent existence in their temperate and fertile homeland where there are markets, traders, and Indian social and cultural institutions. But this option was not open to most. Isolated farms in an unfamiliar climate, far from medical care, economic opportunity, or relatives, are a last resort for those fleeing something even worse. What is remarkable is that so many remained behind.

Once torn from the highlands, continuing mobility has a lower so-cial and economic cost. Many who fled into the lowlands have con-tinued to move, in search of that ideal combination of access to land, freedom from oppression, and access to markets, roads, schools, and other amenities. Although the Kekchi in Toledo District appear to be forest Indians emerging from a primeval economy into a developed one, they are actually survivors of an exodus, emerging from the waters into what they hope is a promised land.

Subsistence and Trade

The Kekchi have never existed completely outside a market economy of some kind. They want, and have come to need, many products that can be obtained only through trade. Their economy has always hung in a balance between the impractical polarities of pure subsistence and fully waged labor. Subsistence production has always subsidized wage labor, but the degree of exploitation has varied widely, as has the degree of participation in the wage labor force.

The economic and ecological environments in which the Kekchi have lived (neither of which are of their own making) have offered many alter-native ways to obtain cash and to exchange cash for essential goods. The basic dilemma, however, is the contradiction between using labor to produce subsistence crops and selling labor or the products of labor. The ways in which this dilemma has been solved or accommodated have varied widely through time, including petty trade, tenant farming, small-scale cash crop production, complex combinations of waged work and subsistence farming, large-scale cash crop production, community and household redistribution of cash in exchange for subsistence prod-ucts, and so forth. The kinds of strategies adopted are a product of the local ecological situation (e.g., human-to-land ratios, potential for agri-cultural intensification, seasonality of production) and the fluctuating forces of the colonial and then capitalist economies (e.g., prices of com-modities, wage rates, market monopolies). There has been no clear long-term trend, but rather a diversity of strategies in each place over the long term. Flexibility has been the only real constant, as we can see in Kekchi settlement patterns.

Nucleation and Dispersion

The notions of community, village, and town are heavily weighted and problematic in Kekchi society. Those entities have been sources of great suffering, the tools of church and state oppression in present and past. Villages have also been the source of solidarity, socially enacted meaning, political and economic resistance and advancement, and communal action.

In Chapter 8 I argue that the ecologically optimal settlement type is a hamlet of a few families in the center of their shifting fields (cf. Harrison 1976; Farriss 1978). So long as population densities remain low, there will always be tendencies to disperse population into these hamlets. But the balance between a dispersed settlement pattern and one of larger communities has not usually been left up to the Kekchi to determine. Dispersed and isolated hamlets have been unpopular with colonial administrators and missionaries for more than 400 years. Plantation owners have moved Kekchi households and communities around like gaming pieces, to suit their own convenience.

The modern Kekchi of Belize, given ecological, economic, and social incentives, are willing to form large nucleated communities without coercion. Today these incentives include schools, churches, soccer fields, and political leadership that can enforce claims to land. People in Toledo form a variety of settlements in different ecological and economic situations, different solutions to a single basic problem. Rather than being representatives of old and new, traditional and modern, the different community types reflect underlying ecological processes rooted in shifting agriculture and population growth, as well as different relationships to the marketplace and variation in access to basic governmental services. Individual households solve the locational dilemma within this complex regional context, with little regard for what seems traditional.

It is ironic that in attacking the artificial timelessness of conventional presentations of traditional Kekchi life, I have found other timeless patterns. For 400 years or longer the Kekchi have faced the same dilemmas, with a limited number of solutions. In retrospect, the colonial and capitalist systems of exploitation have articulated with the world economy in radically different ways and have used very different methods for exploiting land and labor, but they have also presented a remarkably similar series of constraints and choices to the Kekchi. Perhaps, as Wolf (1982) suggests, some of the similarities between so-called traditional societies in different parts of Latin America and the world are the result of these economic problems and their solutions. Macroeconomic changes are only one side of the story, representing the constraints on Kekchi choice. The potential solutions lie within the realm of their ecological relationships with their habitat and their methods for wresting a living from it.

5 The Physical Setting

Southern Belize is a fascinating place, with a highly variable climate, complex and poorly understood geology, exotic and diverse flora and fauna, and unusual landforms including rivers that disappear into caves. I will here, however, forgo the touristic virtues of the area and concentrate on those details of the physical environment, both exotic and mundane, that provide a context for our understanding of Kekchi life choices. In particular, this means the aspects of the terrain, climate, soils, and flora that are significant constraints in food and crop production. This is a less than straightforward task because scientific understanding of tropical rain forest environments is still evolving. Describing soil types or forest succession leads into fascinating controversies and disputes; in the interest of brevity, I have managed to evade most of them.

LANDFORMS, CLIMATE, SOILS AND VEGETATION

Toledo is naturally divided into two provinces—upland and lowland. The district is essentially the remnant of a flat shelf of hard, white, Jurassic limestone (Campur formation) that has been folded, faulted, eroded, and then partially covered by a complex of mixed, softer Eocene sediments called the Toledo beds (Romney 1959) or Sepur formation (Nicolait et al. 1984). Uplift and erosion have produced a complex terrain, essentially a rugged inland area fringed by a low, flat coastal shelf. Both the limestone and the Toledo beds form the upland hills, while in the lowlands the Toledo beds are flat and the limestones form steep, rugged ranges of hills (see Nicolait et al. 1984:60–63).

The coastal plain varies between 14.5 and 52 kilometers in width and is crossed by four major rivers—Rio Grande, Moho, Temash, and Sarstoon—of which the latter three originate in Guatemala. The most striking features of the plain are the groups of steep, jagged limestone hills that stick up like ancient Maya pyramids, visible from a great distance. On the plain the rivers follow meandering courses between low levees, which they overflow in the wet season. Ocean currents sweeping south along the coast drop sandbars at the mouths of the rivers. These bars restrict river flow during the wet season, causing them to back up and flood large areas (Romney 1959:26).

Swampy terrain restricts settlement of the coastal plain to a few higher points, occupied by the Garifuna villages of Punta Negra, Punta Gorda, and Barranco. Kekchi settlements on the plain are located at the edges of the hills, where they have access to better-drained upland soils, or near the small ranges of limestone hills out on the plain. The exceptions are three villages—Crique Sarco, Conejo Creek, and Santa Ana—located on riverbanks where they can take advantage of levee soils.

Inland topography depends on whether the hills are formed from limestone or from the Toledo beds. The limestone has been folded, faulted, and tipped so the strata lie close to vertical, forming precipitous slopes covered with large jagged boulders. Where limestone is extensive a "cockpit" terrain typical of karst drainage, with many small rounded valleys, caves, and underground streams, is formed. Upland terrain formed by the Toledo beds is gentler and more rounded. The Toledo beds are a complex of thin layers of calcareous sandstone, shale, mudstone, limestone, and tuff. Local differences in soil quality and terrain result from variation in the composition of the underlying rocks. These hills are covered with deep, slippery clay, cut by innumerable seasonally flooded streams, creeks, and gullies. The permanent upland streams flow swiftly at a high gradient. While the lowland rivers build levees and flood large areas, the highland watercourses, especially in the limestone areas, run over irregular courses of rapids, boulders, and waterfalls, and produce no levees. This difference has a major effect on local agriculture.

Climate recording in Toledo has been poor, considering that the climate varies widely over very short distances. The area is classified as wet tropical in the lowlands and wet subtropical in parts of the uplands (Romney 1959). This means an average annual temperature greater than 24 degrees Celsius (C), with no more than one month when evaporation exceeds precipitation.[1] On the coast daily temperatures range from 10 degrees C to about 55 degrees C, with the coldest temperatures between October and December. During the cold months, when "norther" storms and fronts pass through, the temperature often stays below 19 degrees C all day, and chill winds blow into the night. The rest of the year tends to be hot and humid, slightly less humid during the short dry season.

Rainfall patterns are important for understanding agricultural scheduling in Toledo. The important points for the farmer are the degree of dryness during the dry season—if it is too wet clearing fields will be difficult and fallen vegetation will not burn well; the timing of the onset of the rains—if early it will ruin the burn, if late the fields may need to be replanted; and the adequacy of the November–February rainfall for the dry-season corn crop.

Rainfall is most reliable during the peak of the wet season, from June to December, when most days are punctuated by showers, sometimes very heavy (I recorded over 125 mm of rain in less than two hours in Aguacate village). These rains vary widely in strength and duration over very short distances. In June 1981, for example, San José had 18.7 inches of rain, while San Pedro, less than 10 kilometers away, had only 2.4 inches. Two months later, the August rains reversed the imbalance, and San Pedro had 27.5 inches to San José's 13.1 (IFAD 1985: table 9).

Rain is more variable during the dry season than during the wet (and both are more variable than the total annual precipitation). From January to May the standard deviation of rainfall is close to the mean. More crucial is the time of the onset of heavy rains. May is the most variable month—sometimes very dry and sometimes very wet (in Aguacate in May 1981, 1.6 in fell, while May 1982 had 11.4 in). There are often light "iguana rains" in April, but occasionally the heavy rains begin right afterward, while other times they hold off almost two months until the end of June, or even the beginning of July. Many aspects of the Kekchi agricultural system are adaptations to this uncertainty.

Toledo's annual rainfall is variable from place to place, but everywhere it is very high—between 3,000 and 3,800 millimeters. Frequent rain conditions and constrains many aspects of life. Floods make travel and communication difficult or impossible, work stops, and the roads and trails are difficult to maintain. Crops cannot be dried, foods spoil, and firewood must be collected and dried long before it is used. Houses rot quickly and must be built from carefully selected materials; the bare ground around houses erodes and makes village sites a network of gullies.

The poor drainage of many lowland soils greatly limits expansion of swidden agriculture. Otherwise rich soils are covered with standing water most of the year, and even relatively dry areas may flood for short periods at crucial times during the growing season. Sloping soils erode and rainfall quickly leaches nutrients out of them. The unpredictable rise and fall of watercourses makes irrigation impractical (Cayetano, Hickman & Brown 1986:69–73).

Added to these normal climatic problems are periodic hurricanes between May and October, with those late in the season (around harvest time) the most destructive. They seem to be less frequent in Toledo than farther north in Belize; the last major hurricane hit Toledo in 1945 when almost every large tree between the Sarstoon and Temash was downed, killing crops and causing serious hunger (Romney 1959:19).

The Kekchi have a practical, but limited, soil science. They are concerned mainly with telling good agricultural soils from bad and with recognizing a few special problems. Perhaps they would have a more elaborate soil taxonomy if they were not relative newcomers to the area. Yet the potentials and problems of Toledo soils are crucial in shaping agricultural production, migration, and settlement patterns.

Toledo soils, like most in the tropics, have a precarious nutrient balance because of the ease with which rain washes away vital minerals and nutrients.[2] The majority of nutrients are locked up in the vegetation mantle that covers the soil (Lambert, Arnason & Gale 1980; Golley et al. 1975). Therefore, lush tropical vegetation does not necessarily reflect a rich and fertile soil. But tropical soils are not uniformly nutrient-poor or lateritic, as some have claimed (see, e.g., Meggers 1971; Sanders 1962). In fact, the fragile and almost sterile laterites (now called plinthite) that figure so prominently in the literature are quite rare (Sánchez & Buol 1975).

The type of soil-forming parent material directly and importantly influences the texture and nutrient status of the soils, as do topography and drainage (Kellman 1969). The soils of Toledo, for example, are silica-rich, unlike the soils of tropical Brazil that are rich in iron and alumina but silica-poor. Like the soils of adjacent lowland Guatemala, they are relatively fertile, often the equals of temperate soils (Popenoe 1960; Moran 1982:250–51). The richest soils are dark clays derived from the decomposition of limestone. Unfortunately, the steepness of much of the limestone topography means that these fertile soils are often very thin and broken up into small pockets. The fertile limestone soils found on flatter terrain around the bases of limestone hills often suffer from drainage problems, partially because of their high clay content. The important characteristic of the limestone-derived soils is their sustained fertility under shifting cultivation, even after repeated use with short fallow periods. Despite drainage problems the Kekchi make access to these soils a high priority in locating a village.

The soils derived from the Toledo beds vary widely in fertility and usability, depending on drainage and on local rock types. Calcareous sandstone produces the best soils, while sandstone makes the worst. Only small patches of the Toledo bed soils are too steep to use, although even moderate slopes erode quickly. On hilly areas erosion brings new soil nutrients to the surface by exposing bedrock to weathering. Nevertheless, the fertility of these soils diminishes rapidly under cultivation and recovers very slowly. Lower-lying Toledo bed soils also suffer from low fertility and form an impermeable clay pan in the upper layers of the subsoil after exposure to leaching by clearing and cultivating.

Seasonally dry levees are the only areas of the coastal plain that are both fertile and cultivable by low-technology, low-input methods. The swampy areas have great potential if they can be drained. Where water covers the soil for most of the year acid peats accumulate, making the soil unusable even with drainage.

Soil-quality data (from Romney 1959) has been used to perform a site catchment analysis (Vita-Finzi & Higgs 1970) for each of six Kekchi villages (see Table 5.1). A circle, five kilometers in radius, was drawn around each village as the practical limit of soil exploitation. The area of each soil type, judging drainage properties from topographic maps and general soil fertility from Romney's assessments, was measured within the circles, which were adjusted where necessary to match the limits of actual practice. This gives some idea of the variation in the amount of land available; the first four villages are located in the far southern part of the district, which is lightly populated. Aguacate is on the Moho River, closer to the north, and Indian Creek is on the highway in the northern zone.

General descriptions of the fauna and flora of Toledo District are available elsewhere and need not be detailed here (see Romney 1959; Nicolait et al. 1984; Standley & Record 1936). In the more fertile and better-drained areas, the natural vegetation is highly diverse rain forest, dominated in places by such species as ceiba (*Ceiba pentandra*), the cohune palm (*Orbignya cohune*), and quamwood (*Schizolobium parahybrum*). Wet and swampy areas are dominated by lower forests with many palms and sedges. Where soils are thinner and less fertile the forest is lower, less diverse, sometimes thinning out to the mixed savannah-woodland locally called broken ridge. True pine (*Pinus caribaea*) savannahs are found in northern coastal Toledo and in a few patches inland.

Differences in the forest cover are important because they are clues to how the local environment will respond to cultivation. This in turn constrains Kekchi agricultural techniques and settlement. Researchers of shifting cultivation have tended to see it as essentially independent of local soil, topography, and drainage characteristics. The story goes that nearly all the nutrients in the tropical forest are tied up in the vegetation. Slashing and burning releases a "pulse" of nutrients that is used

Table 5.1. *Catchment Analysis of Soil Resources*

	Founding Date	Population	Soil Types (in Ha)					Total Hectares	Levee per Person (in Ha)	Good and Fair Soils per Person (in Ha)
			Levee	Good	Fair	Poor	Unusable			
San Lucas	c 1960	89[a]	0	3,681	819	1,494	463	6,457	0	50.56
Santa Theresa	1932	101[b]	275	2,550	500	1,256	456	5,037	2.72	30.20
Otoxha	c 1916	166[a]	144	1,606	2,581	1,025	600	5,956	0.87	25.22
Crique Sarco	1914	205[a]	526	1,477	4,791	597	463	7,854	2.57	30.58
Aguacate	c 1900	159[b]	163	1,450	1,531	175	2,025	5,344	1.03	18.75
Indian Creek	c 1972	320[b]	0	256	3,038	331	944	4,569	0	10.29

NOTES: Villages are listed roughly from the remotest to the most accessible. The total area within the catchments varies because in some cases international, reservation, or intervillage boundaries exclude some land within five kilometers of the village center. At the same time, the quantity of good land available to each village is underestimated; farmers do in fact go farther out than five kilometers. Also there are many small but usable patches of good soil in some areas shown on soil maps as poor or unusable. Nevertheless, the method used to derive these figures is the only way to arrive at even an approximation of man-to-land ratios without a large-scale agricultural mapping effort.

[a] Population is that obtained by an August 1978 census by the Health Department nurse in Crique Sarco.

[b] Population figures are from my 1979 census; Indian Creek's population was estimated from informants' statements, while the other two villages were completely counted.

by crops, after which the field is abandoned to fallow, which rebuilds the nutrients in the system (Christiansen 1981; Nye & Greenland 1960; Lambert & Arnason 1980, 1982).

While it is true that rain forests are efficient at trapping and recycling nutrients (Ewel 1976:302; Madge 1965), and burning does release many of those nutrients for use by crops, it does not follow that the soil is a passive part of the process. Some tropical forests respond to clearing, burning, and cropping with a natural succession back to a climax community, although this may take hundreds of years (Richards 1952). Other forests are less resilient because of their original floristic composition, topography, drainage, climate, soils, bedrock types, and even the kinds of dormant seeds present in the soil, and they do not simply spring back to their pristine state. In the worst case the clearing may become an eroded wasteland or an impoverished grassland. It is common to ascribe this result to overuse, through shortened fallow cycles or longer cropping periods, and this may indeed be the proximate cause. But identical farming techniques can produce different results in different environments. Shifting cultivation may contribute to long-term stability in some areas and be a shortcut to ecological catastrophe in others.

The putative virgin forests of Toledo are in fact products of human meddling. Many botanists have noted that forests around Classic Maya cities show traces of human disturbances even after 1,000 years have passed (Lundell 1937; Folan, Fletcher & Kintz 1979). Mature forests in Toledo are dominated by three economically useful trees—sapote, ramón, and the cohune palm—that may have become dominant by being spared during slashing and burning by ancient Maya farmers. Cohune palms in particular are hard to kill during swidden preparation, so several cycles of cutting and burning lead to a cohune-dominated forest (Romney 1959:288). These palms offer edible oil-rich seeds, shade and soil protection during the early growing season, building material for houses, and a nutrient-rich leaf litter, and they seem to have a beneficial effect on soil formation (Furley 1975).

Today only small patches of climax forest remain in Toledo District, and most of those are on extreme slopes or in swamps. Most villages use land that has been fallowed for between five and 40 years. What will be the long-term consequences of this cultivation, and how will those areas respond to shorter fallow periods? Some of the limitations imposed by soil-forming parent materials were discussed above. More of the variation in forest communities, and corresponding successional stages, can be explained by drainage quality and topography. Generally the height and species-richness of the flora correspond to the slope of the terrain. High, evergreen broadleaf forest with high species diversity covers hilly areas, and as the terrain gets flatter there is a change to medium and low transitional forests with many grasses and fewer tree species (except in swamps). Finally, on very flat and poorly drained areas there are a few patches of scrubland or savannah dominated by grasses and sedges with a few pines. This gradient of flora is paralleled by diminishing soil fertility and quality.

The natural gradient of high forest to savannah is a visible demonstration that succession from cleared land back to high forest is not inevitable. It shows that topography, parent rock material, and drainage have a direct effect on the kind of forest succession that will follow clearing. In savannah and low or medium broken forest, the fertility of the soil and the diversity of the plant community is not renewed with the passage of time. To the contrary, when grasses and sedges have become established, periodic natural and man-made dry-season fires tend to degrade the plant community by eliminating all but the grasses and fire-resistant trees. A reverse succession occurs, and increased erosion and exposure make the soil ever more compacted, sterile, and nutrient-poor (see Richards 1955:48; Charter 1941; Lambert & Arnason 1980, 1982).

In steeply sloping hilly areas the nutrient regime of the soil is different, and succession goes in the other direction. Erosion constantly breaks down new parent rock material, bringing new nutrients into the soil to replace those lost to agriculture. Similarly, colluvial and alluvial areas receive a constant supply of new soil nutrients through mechanical and water action, providing the sustained soil fertility needed to support luxuriant climax forest and agriculture.

On gentler slopes a fine balance operates. Leaching removes soil nutrients faster than they can be taken up by the vegetation, so the total nutrient balance depends on the contribution of the parent rock to the soil. Because the forest cover is so efficient at recycling and accumulating nutrients and minerals, a diverse and vigorous climax community can be supported on these slopes, even though parent rocks are deeply buried and make only a small contribution to the nutrient regime. But the fund of nutrients in the soil is very low, and under shifting cultivation these areas are poised on the edge of reverse succession. If fallow cycles get short enough, if the soil is left exposed for too long, or if too many nutrients are removed by demanding crops, the forest may not be able to recolonize, and a lower, transitional, grass-infested association will take over. The agricultural potential of an area thus can be permanently lowered, a process that is familiar from other parts of the lowland tropics where Imperata grass has invaded large areas.

Grass should be seen as a symptom, not a cause, of declining fertility. Even on the best soils grass forms a normal part of the early successional community (Kellman & Adams 1970:324–25). But on soils of sustained fertility the grass is quickly shaded out and killed by dense herbaceous and woody growth. By the time the land is used for agriculture again the grass is extinct. On soils of lower fertility dense leafy growth is established more slowly, and grasses are able to survive much longer in the succession. If the plot is recut for agriculture on the same length cycle as more-fertile soils, there is a better chance that grass seed will still be present. Since grasses are often fire-resistant and well adapted to the moisture and light conditions of newly cleared land, they can provide serious competition for young crops. The presence of grass may therefore indicate declining soil fertility, even though the area is still quite capable of producing a good crop from the burst of nutrients freed by burning. This situation has led to some confusion about the reasons for declining crop yields when fallow cycles are shortened or a field is used for several years in a row (Clarke 1976; Vasey 1979). Some believe that soil damage is responsible, while others blame competition from grasses and weeds (Sánchez 1976; Janzen 1973; Nations & Nigh 1980). In reality, both are symptoms of a net outflow in the soil nutrient cycle.

SWIDDEN AND SETTLEMENT

The complexity of the relationships among soils, vegetation, and agricultural systems has barely been penetrated by Western science. How much of the problem is understood by the Kekchi? I think we should remember that they are farmers, not "primitive ecologists," but they have developed rules of thumb that usually keep them out of trouble. They cultivate for only one year before fallowing and try to use forest that has good fertility reserves. These include areas of steep limestone, flat limestone, and gently sloping fertile Toledo beds. As long as agriculture was the main priority for settlement, and there was plenty of good land, these guidelines worked well. But today in the most densely populated parts of Toledo fallow cycles have been shortened and less-fertile land is in use. By trial and error farmers face these new problems, sometimes successfully, sometimes not. The following two short vignettes illustrate the process.

In about 1968 a group of Kekchi from Temash River villages founded a new community that promised easy access to markets. San Felipe was located less than 10 kilometers from Punta Gorda, on a short spur from the northern highway, close to market, shops, and health facilities, and it grew rapidly to about 18 households in 1975. The settlers were attracted by a small range of limestone hills—about 200 hectares of usable high-quality soils—although the fields were steep and exposed to wind and rain. Around the hills were unfamiliar sandstone and shale soils that supported high forest and seemed fertile. But when the farmers turned to these soils after using up the hill zone, they found drainage and weed problems. Worse, the forest did not regenerate quickly enough—it looked as if it might take 20 or 30 years for the plots to be usable again. By 1979 only six households remained; the rest had moved to other new villages that had different (but still new) types of forest.

More a town than a village, the Mopan community of San Antonio has by far the highest population density in Toledo, on a territory that is surrounded and circumscribed by other villages. Nevertheless, farming is still the mainstay of the economy. The community is fortunate to have some of the best Toledo bed soils, highly fertile and capable of sustained yield under a seven- to ten-year fallow. The problems began when fallow cycles were shortened to five years or less. D. E. Johnson (1986) found an average fallow length of 5.7 years in 1984. Grass invasion was a symptom of soil fertility decline, and this was followed by lower yields of corn, more pest and disease problems, and an increase in gully and sheet erosion. Some farmers picked up and moved elsewhere—Mopan communities sprung up as much as 100 miles to the north in Stann Creek District. Some who stayed became part-time farmers, diversifying into honey production, shopkeeping, and petty trade, or they sought to lease additional land outside the reservation. But others experimented and eventually found ways of adapting their agricultural system so they could again achieve a stable productive regime while minimizing soil damage. They began to grow more of the less demanding crops, such as cassava and beans. Their new techniques included planting legumes as cover crops, using a slash-and-mulch technique instead of burning, planting a second corn crop during the dry season on the same field, reducing field size, and switching some of the more fragile land into permanent tree crops such as cocoa and annatto. The rural development project that was supposed to be helping farmers to improve their agriculture could barely keep track of the changes and innovations (TRDP 1986). The Mopan are relative newcomers to Toledo, and they are still learning; in comparison the technical assistance team came and left in the blink of an eye.

6 Land Tenure and Crops

In the adaptations of Kekchi households, agricultural production is the key link between the regional environment and the domestic economy. Households organize labor, distribute the proceeds, and decide about mixing different forms of production. Most of my fieldwork period was spent gathering quantitative data on labor and productivity, and qualitative data on the ways households make decisions. The Toledo Rural Development Project, working at about the same time, gathered summary statistics on production in 15 district villages. Because I am interested in variation in productive strategies and performance among households, as well as villages, my strategy was to concentrate on getting the most accurate data possible from a smaller sample in a single community. I ended the year with annual labor and production figures for 13 Aguacate households, based on self-recording forms, field visits, and biweekly interviews. I have less-complete data from a general survey of all Aguacate farm households, and this is complemented by a similar survey in Indian Creek and a partial survey of Santa Theresa.[1]

I will focus here on how labor is organized in each productive task, for labor organization provides the crucial link between systems of production and social groups (see Terray 1972; Lehman 1982). My working hypothesis is that agrarian social groups, including the household, are constituted partially as work groups that motivate and apply the proper combination of labor, knowledge, and leadership to each chore in an efficient (if not the most efficient) fashion. Existing social form provides a template for acceptable change; innovations are selected and molded according to what is socially and technically practical (Barlett 1982; Brush 1987; Rudie 1970). So social form limits what is possible or preferred in situations of change. By the same token, techniques, crops, or technology, once deemed acceptable and adopted, may lead to social changes over time, changes that were not anticipated or upon which a consensus was never achieved. The process is not always without conflict—the fact that changes in production always change the status quo of wealth and power, that some win and some lose, is one of Marx's enduring contributions to social science.

Anthropologists often assume that changes in productive systems are imposed through political or economic means—an involuntary process whereby workers are placed at the mercy of capital and the marketplace. Population pressure, concentration of land, changes in labor rates and market prices all can force change on the farmer that transforms the social relations of production (see, e.g., Gudeman 1978). But the Kekchi face little external pressure to change their productive system. Their access to markets is limited, true. They also face increasing shortages of land and have little say in legal land tenure. But despite the pressures of government policy and markets, change is mainly motivated by their own desires for greater cash income, for greater participation in national institutions, better health care, education for their children, and more consumer goods. Compared with peasants and farmers elsewhere, the Kekchi have wide latitude in choosing how they will achieve these goals, and they find a diversity of solutions that conserve existing social forms to a remarkable degree.

The transformation of Kekchi production is an unusually clear demonstration that change involves interaction between social form and productive technique, that new forms of production are fitted to existing social groups, at the same time that social groups adapt to new forms of production. The imperfections in achieving these fits, the inequities and the unexpected consequences, the laggards and the antisocial entrepreneur are what make the process dynamic, just as the limitations of the market and prices, the knowledge of alternatives, and the physical environment provide the boundaries and channels for the entire process. I suspect that even in other cases where the limitations seem more prominent, where land is all owned by an urban elite, or where only one kind of crop can be sold, the interplay of choice, technique, and social form is an equally important part of the trajectory of change.

LAND TENURE

The foundation of Kekchi production is the control of land. The official version of Kekchi land tenure is still the reservation system formulated in 1924. Villages were allowed to use reserve land under the authority of a village alcalde, thus instituting corporate village control of land use and making the alcalde a powerful figure who was often the reluctant agent of the government in collecting fees and enforcing regulations. Today the reservation system has been pragmatically altered; as population has moved away from the original reservations the government has created unofficial extensions or has created new, unofficial reserves. In other areas, away from the original reservations, private land tenure has taken hold, usually pioneered by non-Kekchi who find it easier to complete the legal paperwork for leases.[2]

In some areas Kekchi farmers hold leases on blocks of 40 to 100 acres; they also use public land in undeclared reserves farther from the village. From the 1940s the government has occasionally taken steps to privatize land tenure in reservations, and some individual leases have been granted near or even on reserves. And the government has sold large blocks adjacent to reservations to foreign corporations. In short, the legal system of land tenure is confusing and contradictory, and operates pragmatically through continuing negotiation and the exercise of political power.

Within the reservations most Indian communities have developed orderly systems that recognize various degrees of rights to land, depending on the quality of the land, the use it has been put to, and local population pressure. The villages have set boundaries with each other that recognize each alcalde's area of authority. These boundaries are adjusted as villages grow or shrink, and there are frequent court cases that attempt to punish territorial infractions.

The basic principle of village custom is that the man who first clears land from climax forest, who first propitiates the deities of the hills who are the true owners, has a right to return to use it thereafter. In practice, when population pressure is low and large areas of well-fallowed land are available this right is rarely asserted—a fallow length of 15 years or more strains the human memory. In most of the northern zone and in parts of the south where land is getting hard to find, the right to reuse a plot is more formally recognized. If one finds a piece of secondary forest and wants to clear it, one must first locate the man who used it last and ask permission. This usufructory system remains flexible under forest fallow. Also, people move around a lot, so there is little practical difficulty in finding a plot that is not claimed. But when the longer forest fallow has been replaced by a bush fallow system of less than 10 years, usufruct rights are valued and enforced, and rights to the use of land can be loaned, given, or inherited. The alcalde and his court take a stronger role in land disputes. They can, for example, judge that a man's usufruct rights to a plot have lapsed because he has not reused it within a reasonable period. In areas where population pressure is severe the best land has been divided through these rules into what are essentially privately owned plots. Although the owner can rent or lend his land to a village member, he cannot sell it or let an outsider use it.

The usufruct system works differently for land with various uses. For example, absolute rights of ownership are recognized for groves of wild copal trees, which can be acquired by discovery, inheritance, gift, or sale. More-limited ownership is recognized for house-plots; if they are not reoccupied within a few years after abandonment they can be re-allocated by the alcalde. Orchards of cacao, citrus, or other fruit trees are treated as private property and can be rented or sold. Villages tend to be very sensitive about plans to plant large orchards and seek to restrict them because it removes land from the communal pool regulated by usufruct rules, turning it into private property that can be alienated from the village.

Very steep, rocky, or infertile land is public property, a commons used for hunting and gathering. Conversely, the best agricultural land, the seasonally flooded riverbanks, is owned by the person who first cleared it. Although the land can be lent, inherited, or rented, it cannot be sold. These individual rights to land lapse in a few years if the owner moves to another village.

Direct conflict between the practical Kekchi land tenure system and Belizean law and politics cannot be avoided for much longer. Over many years the government has repeatedly expressed a desire to break up the reservations into 40- or 50-acre private parcels that will be given to legal residents (excluding many Kekchi who have uncertain or unsubstantiated citizenship). The latest scheme is part of a development project financed by the International Fund for Agricultural Development, which plans to establish a thousand 50-acre farms despite repeated pleas for caution in changing this complex social and ecological system (Howard 1977b; Osborn 1982; Wilk 1981b). Judging from past experience in Guatemala, Kekchi anxiety over losing their land is quite reasonable.

CORN PRODUCTION

Corn is the Kekchi staff of life. If the seasonal round of planting and harvesting crops is the skeleton, corn is the heart, treated with a reverence and respect not given any other crop. The production of corn, the measure of wealth and security, is wedded to a cycle of ritual that is intended to ensure harmony between the cultivator and the *Tzuultak'a*, the deities of the hills and forest. Rituals are conducted by the community in watch nights (*yo'lek*) of prayer, song, and food, by the household through offerings of copal incense (*pom*) and prayer at the household altar, and by the individual through sexual abstinence, prayer, offerings of incense, and avoidance of certain foods (Schackt 1986; Cabarrus 1974; Thompson 1930a).

Corn is an overarching metaphor for sustenance and belonging. A young man's initiation into Kekchi society comes partially through his apprenticeship to an older man in the community (sometimes his godfather) who teaches him secrets about corn. To say that a woman cooks corn tortillas for a man is to say they are having sexual relations. The complementariness of male corn production and female corn processing and cooking are both symbol and substance of marriage. Festive exchanges of green corn among related households celebrate, renew, and elevate important ties of cooperation and sharing. Cornfields are cleared, planted, and harvested according to lunar cycles, vestiges of a calendar that has been in the heart of Maya communities for at least 2,500 years. Rituals erect a fence that separates corn from other crops. The identity of corn as the true food, without which eating becomes snacking, does not keep the Kekchi from trying new foods and growing new crops. But new foods and new crops are eaten and grown without ceremony, without sanctity. They may sustain the body, but not the heart.

It is difficult to project what slash-and-burn agriculture was like before the advent of steel tools (Wilk 1985). The ax and machete revolutionized shifting cultivation in the sixteenth century. The Kekchi farmer today uses up one or two machetes and two or three files a year, and an ax every four years or so, costing him about $10 to $15 per year. Other important items, such as planting sticks and net bags, are homemade, but fiberglass and jute sacks are increasingly used to carry crops, and some farmers have acquired sprayers for applying herbicides and pesticides to their cash crops.

One of the important elements of corn production technology is the plants' genetic heritage. The Kekchi have accumulated six named varieties of corn in five colors, belonging to four separate races of maize. Each responds differently to moisture and soil conditions and has different storability, flavor, and cooking characteristics. While most men prefer one variety (usually white or yellow), they plant at least three varieties each year, preserving potentially useful genetic variability. The different colors also have ritual significance.

Wet-Season Corn

Each family depends on long-fallow shifting agriculture during the wet season for the bulk of its annual corn supply. In communities with access to large areas of forestland, the long fallow period and one-year cultivation period make this one of the least intensive shifting systems in the world (Ruthenberg 1971: table 3.1). The wet-season corn cycle begins with site selection in January and proceeds to harvest in November and December in steps typical of swidden systems.

The first activity is selecting and marking a field site. The corners are marked with crosses, and pom is burned to propitiate the Tzuul-tak'a. Choosing a plot is complex, based on natural, geographic, social, and supernatural variables. The choice is rarely made by a single farmer; rather, the location and to a lesser extent the size of the field are matters of discussion among men, especially kin, for six months prior to the actual decision. Often a group of men agree to make their fields close together or adjoining.

Location usually balances distance from home and the fallow status of the forest. The swidden field should be as close to home as possible to minimize time spent in transit and in carrying in the crop. The fields cannot be closer than about 1.5 kilometers from the village because the nearer areas are covered daily by free-ranging village pigs, and crops within this pig radius will be destroyed. The farmer wants the longest-fallowed land that is closest to the village, as long as the area meets acceptable criteria for soil, type of vegetation cover, and terrain. Longer fallow generally means fewer weeds, less predation by animals and insects, and higher yields. The logic of labor and the geometry of distance lead to a situation wherein longer-fallowed land is farther from the village.

Marking the field boundaries sets the size of the clearing, reflecting the farmer's judgment of how much corn his family will need for the coming year. He assesses how much corn he has left from the last crop, how much he may have growing in a dry-season field, and how much his family is using, and then estimates how much he will need, leaving a generous margin of error into which he hopes to fit the corn he will feed his pigs. Farmers also think about labor supply: if they are going to be busy with rice production they make a smaller cornfield; if they will have access to the labor of sons or sons-in-law they will make a larger one.

Family size is a fair predictor of the size of wet-season fields. Field sizes for 20 Aguacate farmers correlated positively with absolute household size ($r = .650$, $p < .01$) and with an index of household corn consumption that counts women as 0.8 consumers and children as 0.5 ($r = .694$, $p < .001$). The absolute sizes of 21 Aguacate fields in 1979 ranged from 0.84 to 4.18 hectares, with a mean size of 2.15. Chibnik (1987:89) has calculated the correlation between the number of consumers and the amount of production in a sample of 12 agrarian societies, finding a range from $r = .29$ to .94. While the Kekchi correlation may therefore seem high, suggesting that they are adjusting production to labor resources and consumption needs (living close to the Chayanov slope discussed by Sahlins [1972 : 87–92]), we should remember that we have accounted for less than half (48%) of the variability in field size.

Clearing fields may begin as early as January (the feast of Esquipulas, January 15, marks the start of the clearing season) in climax forest where the huge trees take longer to fell and dry. An early start conflicts with tending and harvesting dry-season corn, so men who are depending on their dry-season fields will rarely cultivate climax forest. In Aguacate most men farm in high secondary forest (from 15 to 30 years old) and begin their land clearing in mid-February. Older men informally discuss timing of labor groups for clearing after church or during other community meetings during January and February, until a consensus is reached on a starting date. Other scheduling complications are that lower forest (shorter fallow) dries more quickly than higher. Cutting too late means the vegetation will not be dry when it is burned, but if a plot is cut too early the fallen vegetation will start to rot and new plants will begin to grow before the burn.

Clearing strategies vary with the kind of forest cover. All farmers use some combination of a village labor-exchange group, their own labor, and smaller groups composed of other household members, friends, and *compadres* or close kin. In high forest the smaller growth will be cleared with machetes by the farmer, or by smaller labor groups, before the large village group comes in and clears the larger trees. The farmer finishes up by himself or with his sons. Kekchi men prefer to clear fields in groups. This preference is based on arguments of efficiency and safety. They say efficiency is greater because men work harder in a group, and because they can divide the labor efficiently and work in teams. Clearing is the most dangerous agricultural task because of snakes and scorpions in the trees and litter, and falling trees. There is also a more positive motivation—clearing in groups is more fun, there is an opportunity to gossip and joke, and there is a ritual meal at the end of the day.

Clearing is ritually important because it is a time when the boundary between human and supernatural, cultural and natural is violated. The forest is the property of the Tzuultak'a (lit. hill-valley). A farmer who wants to use a piece of forest must ask permission and appease the supernatural owners through a sequence of ritual performances. These include burning a candle in the church, a watch night of feasting and prayer, and offerings of incense and prayers each day before work, at lunch, and at the end of the day (Schackt 1986:87–89; Thompson 1930a:50–51).

Burning the field serves many purposes. It physically clears away debris, kills competing vegetation and some of the seeds lying dormant in the soil, drives out pests and insects, and frees nutrients locked up in the vegetation for use by crops. A good burn covers the whole field with gray ash. Because no effort is made to cut up and spread the fallen vegetation around prior to the burn, however, it goes unevenly.

The time for burning depends on the chosen time for sowing and the phase of the moon, as well as the weather. Ideally the field will be burned about a week before planting, but before the first heavy rains fall. Men will often consult nervously with each other, and as the planting season and the rains approach they get more and more nervous, afraid that the rain will come and spoil their burn. Yet if they burn too early the vegetation will begin to regrow before the corn has had a good head start, and the crop will suffer.

Planting brings a festive atmosphere to Kekchi villages. Many community rituals occur at Easter, and the ceremonial meals that precede and follow planting days mean that everyone in the village eats well. At the same time, planting is always an uncertain time because the onset of the rains cannot be predicted. In some years men have to replant the field when the young corn withers. Because planting is a village matter, it is the community elders who make the final decision about when it will start. During March and April these elders will settle on a schedule, trying to accommodate each man's preference for an earlier or later date, although older and more influential men tend to get first pick.

In Aguacate the second week in April was once the preferred time to begin planting, but in the early 1970s there was a sequence of bad years when the rains did not begin until July and the young corn was stunted for lack of moisture. Farmers perceive that the onset of the rains has continued to be late, and they have changed their planting time to the end of April, continuing until about May 20. This flexibility belies the image of the Maya farmer as bound by tradition to a sacred calendar that determines agricultural activities.

Planting is the most ritually important part of the agricultural cycle. Prohibitions on sexual intercourse and on eating certain foods are in effect for two weeks before and after planting. The night before planting a yo'lek, an all-night vigil, is held, and many of the men who will plant the next day attend, playing a game with corn as counters, eating a light meal, praying, burning incense, and playing or listening to music. Early in the morning the *patrón* (the man whose fields are to be planted) passes the bundles of selected seed corn through pom (copal incense) smoke, and then shells it.

At the field the men usually break up into two or three groups, five to eight people each, that plant in a line, using a hard palm-wood planting stick. Usually one group gets squash and bean seeds mixed in with their corn, so a portion of the field will be interplanted. The lines of men move across the field, thrusting into the ground and moving the stick from side to side to open a conical, slanting hole. Seven seeds are thrown into each hole, which is left open as a dew-trap.

The labor input in planting corn was measured directly in hours, and efficiency could be gauged by counting the quarts of seed planted, or the area seeded per hour. It is worth going into this data a bit further as an example of how social considerations of labor-group formation and labor exchange are closely interwoven with mechanical and ecological aspects of the farming system. The working ideal for the planting group is that the same group of men will meet each day (except Sunday) in another field, and finish planting that field in the same number of hours, so that in the end all of the labor debts are canceled out and everyone's field has been finished. Farmers want to see their whole field planted at once, so the corn will grow and mature at the same rate. The interval between burning and planting will then be uniform for the whole field. Nevertheless, sometimes two men will want to plant the same day, and the work group will split into two, so each man gets an insufficient labor force and must call another work group to come finish the job at a later date. Splitting the group also complicates the accounting of who owes days to whom.

In Aguacate in May 1979 there were 26 men in the labor group, and the size of their fields ranged from 0.8 to more than four hectares. Men were not free to adjust the size of the work group to the size of their fields. Instead a man must work for all of the village members who ask him for a day of labor, and then he must call back the days owed to him on his planting day, whether he needs them or not. Some men end up with many hands crowded in a small field; others try to get the workers to finish a vast area in the same length workday. In practice the group would probably go home early in the former case; in the latter they would stay later but still leave the task unfinished. The patrón and his kin would have to return and finish later, but it is hard to get back to planting one's own field because of the obligation to work in others' fields. But planting requires about two hours a day less than clearing or harvesting (about seven hours), allowing each participant time for other urgent tasks in the late afternoon.

The communal labor group has a clear-cut advantage to the farmer during the planting season: having the bulk of the work done at once, at the optimal time after burning. The costs of this participation are high, however. The farmer no longer has control over the scheduling of planting in relation to the onset of the rainy season, he gives up control over his own labor during much of the planting season, and he gets an inflexible amount of labor for planting his own field, regardless of its size. The timing advantage is a powerful one, but does it alone outweigh all these costs? Milpa farmers in northern Belize get acceptable (though lower) yields by planting their fields slowly without the help of a work group (Lambert & Arnason 1982). Communal labor apparently serves other social and economic ends, which we will explore in Chapter 9.

Strict scheduling of the agricultural calendar relaxes as soon as seed is in the ground. Each farmer is then free to adjust his work schedule to his own farm, household, and kin. Nevertheless, the first month of growth is a period of great anxiety, as the fate of the crop is out of his hands. And just because his farm work is less rigorously scheduled, this does not mean he has leisure time. House construction and repair begin in June and July, pigs are driven to market, firewood is cut and stockpiled, and hunting and fishing put variety in the day's *caldo* (stew).

Farmers lump many tasks together under the label of checking the cornfield. A man may stop in his field while on a hunting trip, pull a few weeds, plant some onions, check the crop for animal or pest damage, cut some firewood, and then visit his previous year's field and collect some corn to bring home. This kind of activity is hard to record, and these tasks are underrepresented in my labor survey, but this complex work organization characterizes the growing season. Other accounting problems occur when whole households take outings to the fields during the growing season and do many small chores—planting, weeding, foraging for wild foods, and carrying food home. The growing season is the only time when women and children make regular visits to the fields.

Immediately after the corn begins to sprout, other crops are interplanted in selected parts of the field. Eighty-eight percent of surveyed farmers interplanted, averaging 6.2 species per farmer from a total list of 28 species. Some of the interplanted crops continue to bear long after the corn is harvested, prolonging the plot's yield into the next growing season.

Sometime in July or August a pole-and-thatch building is erected on a high spot in the field, to be used for processing and storing corn. These unwalled structures are simplified versions of houses, using less-durable construction methods and materials, and, like houses, they are built with communal labor. The corn house may also serve as a secondary residence. If the cornfield is in climax forest, more than two hours from the village, the farmer and other friends or relatives may spend several nights at a time there. Where some fields are three or more hours from the village, a household may move out to the field for weeks at a time. Some older men told me that when they were young their families lived at the cornfield for half the year. The ecological, social, and demographic factors that affect this balance between nucleated and dispersed residence deserve more-complete discussion (see Farriss 1978).

Weeding is not a distinct phase of the agricultural cycle in lowland Kekchi villages, although some of the large northern communities, and most Mopan farmers, now weed their fields regularly. In Aguacate weeding is a casual sideline to doing something else, or a spot control in particularly bad areas or of dangerous varieties of weeds. Farmers figure that weeds cause no great loss once the corn gets a head start and consider resistance futile. Farmers in low secondary forest know that a heavy weed infestation will reduce their yields, but they take only sporadic action to control weeds. This makes sense because most households that use low forest are short of labor already. As we will see below, farmers with limited household labor often choose low forest as a high risk–low effort option, and they do not have the time to weed effectively anyway. In northern villages, farmers cultivate low forest because they have no choice (population pressure having reduced the fallow status of the whole area), not because of household labor shortage, and there weeding has become a more regular and integral part of the agricultural cycle.

Risk is one of the major variables in Kekchi agricultural decision making. The most predictable risk in corn production is the most easily managed: predation by mammals. While insects devastate crops in a few years, perhaps one in ten, mammals do damage to every field, every year. Catching them at work means waking early in the morning and walking in semidarkness through the forest, then stalking the last hundred meters to the field. Some men have to borrow shotguns, and the price of cartridges makes every shot an investment. At best the result will be one or two peccaries (*Dicotyles tajacu* or *labiatus*). At worst several shots may be wasted on a multitude of coatimundis that have already destroyed standing corn. If damage is repeated and heavy, a man will plan a nighttime visit to the field. Traps and snares are rarely used. Crop predation is less of a problem in climax forest. The animals of the high bush—white-lipped peccary and brocket—are the least destructive and the easiest to hunt. The smaller and more numerous animals that do the most damage, including coatimundis and rats, prefer the man-made habitats of secondary forest closer to the village. Thus, fallow status and risk are closely to related to each other in corn production through factors other than soil fertility or weed growth.

Green corn is ready in June and July. Household members and kin often go together for the first harvest, burning incense and praying upon arrival. This is a time of celebration and commensality; people exchange gifts of corn or special corn dishes and invite the whole community to open-house meals. Green corn foods are offered on the household altar. Within a few weeks each household harvests almost 2,000 ears.

The beginning of the dry corn harvest is marked by rituals performed by the female head of the household. She burns incense and offers special foods at the household altar, then feeds a special meal to the harvesters as they return from the fields with sacks of dry corn. The rituals mark the passage of corn from the male domain of the field to the female territory of the home.

Timing of the dry corn harvest is flexible and can be fit to the schedules of other tasks, although with long delays there will be more damage and spoiled corn. The physical limit on the start of the harvest is the ripening of the corn in early to late August. All the local varieties have a particularly tight husk that protects the kernels from moisture for some time after ripening. If the corn is not harvested by December, however, the grain will begin to sprout on the ear.

Harvest labor is organized in a variety of ways. Aguacate people say that before the advent of rice farming, in the time when most corn was grown in climax forest, large community labor groups, like those used in planting, reaped corn. Today most harvesting is done by individual households, and by labor groups of three to 10 men. This change is a result of the conflict between corn and rice harvests: rice is easily damaged by birds and must be harvested immediately when ripe; corn is less fragile, so it is scheduled around the rice harvest. There is also increasing diversity in the mix of corn and rice among farmers, so there is less agreement on when and how a large reaping group would proceed. The task of coordinating the labor exchange is much easier with a picked group of five or eight.

Household and household cluster labor resources also influence the choice of a harvesting strategy. A man with sons or brothers in his household may be able to finish the harvest with little outside help, but a man with no grown children will have to form exchange groups with whomever is available, usually other men in the same position.

Women carry corn when they accompany their husbands to the field, but they very rarely go by themselves to get corn. A single load will last a small household for two or three days (depending on the number of pigs to be fed). Carrying corn is a constant demand on the farmer's time, drawing him away from other work, especially in an independent nuclear family household. In larger households the burden is shared among several workers.

By the time a farmer has stacked his corn neatly in the crib, almost a quarter of the crop has already been consumed. The totals, broken down both by area and by hours of labor, are included in Table 6.1. The variability from farmer to farmer is very high, a fact often lost in the averaged figures presented elsewhere for Maya swidden farming (see, e.g., Carter 1969; Lambert & Arnason 1982; Seager 1983c; Nations & Nigh 1980). Data on fallow status from Table 6.1 is summarized in Table 6.2, showing that the Kekchi are correct in expecting higher yields in longer-fallowed forest. There is also a positive correlation between travel time from village to field and yield per hectare ($r = .63$, $p < .05$) because of the ring effect of longer fallow at greater distance. There is no reason to doubt the Kekchi explanations for the phenomenon: shorter-fallowed fields have more weeds, more predators, and more disease.

Labor figures help explain why everyone is not using the higher-yielding long-fallow fields. In all kinds of fallow more work is rewarded with more corn—man-hours of labor per plot and yield per plot are highly correlated ($r = .79$; $r^2 = .62$). This suggests that labor, not land, is the limiting factor in production, and that yield per hectare could be increased through more labor-intensive methods (as experimentally verified by Urrutia [1967]). But higher forest also requires more labor per hectare than low forest, both because it is more work to clear large trees and because it takes longer to get to more-distant high-forest fields, so actual work time per day diminishes. The obvious question is whether or not the extra labor in working high primary forest is repaid in higher yield per man-hour, and the answer in this small sample is no. Primary and high secondary forest, as shown in Table 6.2, yield less per man-hour than low secondary forest, and there is a negative correlation between travel time to fields and yield per man-hour ($r = -.602$).

Why do some farmers still prefer to use primary forest? One possibility is that farmers just do not notice the difference in yield per hour. Another is that they prefer working in high forest for aesthetic reasons

Table 6.1. Wet-Season Corn Yields in Aguacate, 1979

Field Number	Forest Fallow Status	Size (in Ha)	Total Man-Hours of Labor	Total Yield (in Kg)	Kilograms per Hectare	Man-Hours per Hectare	Kilograms per Man-Hour
1	high primary	1.67	1,874.5	4,709	2,820	1,122.5	2.51
2	high primary	2.09	1,410.7	3,708	1,775	674.6	2.63
3	high primary	1.67	1,397.0	3,020	1,808	836.5	2.16
4	high primary	2.51	1,376.5	2,754	1,097	584.4	2.00
5	secondary	1.67	823.5	2,014	1,205	492.5	2.45
6	secondary	2.09	709.5	2,325	1,112	339.5	3.28
7	secondary	2.09	1,031.5	2,724	1,303	493.5	2.64
8	secondary	2.51	480.5	479	191	191.4	1.00
9	secondary	2.51	1,066.0	3,598	1,433	424.7	3.38
10	secondary	1.67	1,036.8	2,197	1,316	620.8	2.12
11	secondary	2.51	934.8	3,204	1,267	372.4	3.43

Table 6.2. Labor Investment and Yield in Different Fallow Lengths

	Fallow Type		
	Primary and High Secondary Forest	Low Secondary Forest	Levees
Mean man-hours/hectare per year	805	419	431
Mean yield (in kg/ha)	1,875	1,274	839
Mean yield (in kg/man-hr)	2.33	2.61	1.83
Average variability in yield[a] (in kg/ha)	61.10	86.70	88.00
Coefficient of variation of yield[b] (in kg/man-hr)	12.60	33.40	42.60

[a] Average variability is defined by Hanks (1972:166) as

$$\frac{(\text{maximum crop} - \text{minimum crop} \times 100)}{\text{minimum crop}}$$

[b] The coefficient of variation is the standard deviation divided by the mean times 100.

(Seager 1983a : 11). More testable is the possibility that there is less risk in primary forest, as shown by variabilities in Table 6.2. Like subsistence farmers in other parts of the world (see, e.g., Coombs 1980; McCloskey 1975; Cancian 1979), the Kekchi pay close attention to risk. They realize that while low secondary forest has the potential for high returns (3.38 kg/man-hr), it also has the potential for very low yields (as low as one kg/man-hr), while primary forest, despite the greater amount of work, lessens the possibility of disaster. As it happens, some households choose to take the higher risk, while others choose the low risk – lower yield strategy (the reasons, detailed below, have to do with household organization and labor supply).

Dry-Season Corn

Moisture is a limitation for corn only during the brief dry season in Toledo; the need to dry and burn the forest imposes seasonality on corn production. While corn can grow at almost any time of year, most farmers plant two annual crops: the wet-season crop described above and a dry-season *sak'ecwaj*[3] in low-lying moist areas and on riverbanks (Wilk 1985). Before turning to our discussion of sak'ecwaj, I should mention that in some years there is a third corn crop, called a *junxil c'al*, or early field. A farmer who finds his corn stocks very low can start an early field in late December or early January. The same methods are used as in the wet season. The farmer plants as soon as he can get a decent burn, usually by the end of February. This is all a risky business, and in some years he may have to plant without burning or recut the field and use it as a normal wet-season field. This early crop is very rare in northern villages except in years when other corn crops fail. This is partially because of land shortage, but also because better access to a cash economy allows farmers to substitute store-bought foods for corn. Many farmers are busy with their bean crop at this time of year as well.

Most people who have studied lowland Maya productive systems have noted the dry-season second corn crop, but most have given it a minor and subsidiary role (Carter 1969; Reina 1967; Reina & Hill 1980; Nations & Nigh 1980). Indeed, yields are lower in this system than in the wet-season milpa. But the Kekchi consider the sak'ecwaj an important and integral part of their yearly agricultural cycle, no second cousin to the wet-season field, but a younger brother. Dry-season double-cropping of seasonally flooded riverine areas is now given more role in the evolution of agroecosystems in the tropics (Culbert, Magers & Spencer 1978; Coe & Diehl 1980; Roosevelt 1980; Denevan 1982;

Siemens 1983; Wilk 1985; Pohl 1985). And researchers interested in the development and intensification of existing agricultural systems see dry-season cultivation of seasonal wetlands as having great potential for intensification and increased productivity (Orozco-Segovia & Gliessman 1979; TRDP 1986; Gómez-Pompa et al. 1982; but also see Chapin 1988).

The Kekchi dry-season system uses different cropping methods from wet-season long-fallow cultivation and is based on distinct land tenure arrangements and labor organization. The ideal location for a sak'ecwaj field is on a seasonally flooded river levee, one that retains some moisture during the dry season but that also slopes enough to drain. Most lowland Kekchi villages are located near suitable land, but the northern communities in highland areas (especially Mopan areas) do not have riverbanks. At one time farmers from highland villages would travel many miles to lowland areas to make a dry-season field, where they would camp for weeks at a time. Most of these areas were subsequently settled by Kekchi, who appropriated the riverbank for their own use. Upland villages have responded by adapting the riverbank system to lower, wetter areas in their upland wet-season fields. The methods, timing, and yields for this double-cropping system are similar to those of riverbank cultivation.

Cultivation in the sak'ecwaj can best be described as slash and mulch. The farmer clears an area from riverine gallery forest by cutting and burning, and seeks to establish a successional community of vines and soft herbaceous growth called *sajal* in Kekchi or *vega* in Spanish. In most cases the desired dominant plant is itself called sajal (or vega bush; *Melathera nivea*), but recently many farmers have experimented with planting kudzu or velvet bean (*Stitzolobium* spp.) in its place. Beginning in November, men clear this tangled mat of bushes and vines with machetes, cutting the plants close to the ground and then chopping them up into a thick mat of green mulch. Corn and other crops are dibbled into the soil beneath. Much of the corn planted is a short-season variety (VS550) introduced by missionaries some years ago that has poor storability or resistance to insects but yields green corn in seven weeks. Clearing and planting extends through December, and may continue up to the feast of Esquipulas (January 15).

Weeding is a more regular practice in the sak'ecwaj because the weeds begin to grow back almost immediately after they are cut. If a lot of rain falls during the dry season, weeding becomes essential and may have to be done twice. The permanence of the fields encourages a resident population of insect, bird, and mammal pests that require constant attention. Besides the horses and village pigs that often stray into the fields, rats and tapirs do the most damage.

Green corn harvest begins in January, and dry corn is broken as early as the first week in February. The latest plantings yield green corn in mid-April and dry corn in May, so staggered plantings allow a household a steady supply of green and dry corn for four or five months. Because of the concentration of pests on the riverbanks, it is impractical to leave the dry corn on the stalk for very long. Windstorms, a danger throughout the growing season, can do great damage to standing dry corn. As soon as there is time, therefore, the corn is carried home, where it is hung on the rafters and stacked in a special corncrib built in the living area. This corn becomes a tactical reserve for the family, cushioning the variation in wet-season corn yield and allowing some flexibility in scheduling trips to haul in wet-season corn. Some households sell a portion of the sak'ecwaj corn if they see that the next wet-season crop will meet household needs.

Sak'ecwaj fields are highly valued because of their sustained fertility. The sajal vegetation keeps out grass competition, and the green mulching protects the soil from compaction, retards water erosion, and maintains soil fertility. Some of the natural vegetation and all the introduced legumes return nitrogen to the soil; riverbank soils are naturally the most fertile in the district even without this special treatment. In Aguacate there is no perceived shortage of levee suitable for sak'ecwaj. Fields are used for a mean of 5.2 years and rested for an average of 2.8 years.

The timing and planting of sak'ecwaj is delicate and requires a balance between the weather, the ecology of the sajal vegetation, and the labor the farmer has available. The weather is important because the corn must have moisture during the first weeks of growth. Given the uncertainty about when the dry season will start, the sooner sak'ecwaj is planted the better. But the rest of the agricultural cycle conflicts. In lowland villages the rice and wet-season corn must be harvested before sak'ecwaj clearing can begin. The larger the wet-season corn crop, the longer the harvest lasts and the less time is available to work on dry-season corn. In the uplands this is also the time of maximum work in the bean fields. The sajal allows the farmer little leeway in scheduling his work. The vegetation grows back so quickly that the corn must be planted within a week of clearing, or it will be smothered by vines and bushes. Farmers respond by clearing and planting on a short cycle, working one small plot and then another, until enough has been done or the dry season begins.

Labor recruiting for the sak'ecwaj is a tricky matter because of these time constraints. Men who finish harvesting their rice or wet-season field early are eager to get started on the sak'ecwaj, but few neighbors are willing to break off their own harvest to help. The seven-day limit on the chopping-planting cycle requires careful coordination of a group of less than seven so each man can clear and plant in sequence. These complications place a premium on small well-coordinated groups of close kin or neighbors. Often a man will work by himself or with other household members for a few days and then call a small group to finish and another small group to plant. Weeding and harvesting are also done with household labor or with small groups.

Because of time limitations (and in some places lack of land or demand), the average area of sak'ecwaj cultivated per household is small. Of 22 Aguacate farmers in 1979, five had no sak'ecwaj fields at all, nine had one field, seven had two, and one planted three fields. The average area planted was 0.995 hectares. In a bad year for wet-season corn the following dry season will see farmers growing about two hectares. Villages in the southern zone tend to have smaller sak'ecwaj fields because they have larger wet-season fields (they divert no wet-season labor to rice production) and more-reliable yields (they have better access to high forest).

Labor per hectare for dry-season corn is not as high or as variable as for wet-season corn; total labor ranged from 107 hours per hectare to 381. Some farmers virtually ignored their crop after it was planted, while others weeded carefully and guarded the field diligently. A lot depended on the other tasks that occupied the farmer and on the amount of labor available. Households that had more than one male worker devoted more labor per hectare to the sak'ecwaj than households with a single adult male could. Farmers who had other resources to fall back on—relatives, or a shop, or a part-time job outside the village—gave little attention to their fields.

Kekchi informants stated that yields in the sak'ecwaj tend to be lower and more variable than in the wet-season swidden where fallow is longer than 10 years, and the figures prove them right (see column under Levees in Table 6.2). The highest yield per hectare is more than nine times the lowest (coefficient of variation is 59%; coefficient for yield/man-hr is 43%). Part of the difference in productivity per hour of labor is due to the labor saved by transporting corn with a horse instead of on human backs. Households that used horses had a mean of 2.06 kilograms per man-hour, as opposed to 1.64 kilograms in households that depended on human labor. There is also a clear increase in pro-

duction (kg/ha) and in productivity (kg/man-hr) with increased application of labor. In other words, the more work the farmer puts into the
sak'ecwaj, the more return he will have. Man-hours per hectare and
yield in kilograms per hectare are highly correlated ($r = .962$ for 10
fields farmed without a horse). This implies that the sak'ecwaj system
could be producing much more corn than at present, although the production function in intensification cannot be specified with this data.

Agricultural intensification, perhaps best defined as the addition of
greater labor, technology, and capital to a given unit of land, has been a
subject of great interest to anthropologists in recent years (see, e.g.,
Geertz 1963; Cohen 1977; Sanders, Parsons & Santley 1979; Turner &
Dolittle 1978; Turner 1985). While this is not the place for an extended
discussion of this literature and the issues it raises, the example of
Kekchi corn production points out that risk rather than absolute yield
may be the crucial factor in the choice of agricultural technique. From
Boserup's (1965) original arguments about intensification, there has
been a tendency to focus on the yield per unit of land and labor in different agricultural systems, and the common conclusion is that because yields per unit of labor decline with intensification, people adopt
intensive techniques under some kind of pressure.

In the Kekchi system, however, variable risk is a major factor in decisions about agricultural techniques (so also is the variable availability
and cost of labor, a topic to be taken up later). Risk operates at several
levels of the system. Seager (1983c:18) estimates that in every 10 years
of wet-season corn production, four will be good (like the year that I
measured yields), two will be excellent (up to 50% higher yield), two
will be low (40% less), and two will be very poor (about 35% of a good
year). Evolutionary theorists can use average yields, but farmers do not
have that luxury, especially where crop storage is inefficient and costly.
Instead, farmers must combine techniques that have different intensity
and yield to ensure an adequate supply of food each year. They do this
by growing corn less efficiently in early-season or dry-season fields and
by planting alternative foods alongside the corn in all fields. Thus,
even without population or other pressure on land resources people
may adopt some intensive techniques to cope with risk of crop failure.
And they may well respond to population pressure on land, increased
labor shortage, or higher demand for agricultural products by changing the mix of different techniques (and crops) that they use, adopting
measures to cope with increased risk of shortfall, rather than declining yields (farmers may actually perceive declining yields as increased
variability).

To move closer to the perspective of the individual farmer, we should recognize that each farm household has a different mix of resources and labor, and each adopts a different strategy in balancing risk and yield. Thus, in Aguacate, young households with less labor tend to choose higher-risk cultivation in shorter-fallow areas because the total labor investment is lower. Households with many dependents and a larger pool of labor tend to pursue a lower-risk, lower-yield strategy, working in high forest. The full complexity of household productive strategies, however, cannot be understood without considering the labor flows between households (a topic that will be taken up in Chapter 8).

In this discussion of intensification I continue an exchange with Turner (1985:201), who was responding to my 1985 writing on Kekchi sak'ecwaj farming. While I certainly agree with his assertion that "increasing need for more output per unit area and time will ultimately lead to a decrease in the fallow cycle of an extensive form of cultivation," this is irrelevant to my argument. Turner continues to think of agricultural techniques as if they were agricultural systems, when in fact any agricultural system consists of a number of techniques, and most farmers—especially subsistence farmers—use a variety of techniques of varying intensity. It may be an elegant abstraction to envision the gradual evolution of extensive to intensive techniques, but the reality is that agricultural evolution may be a lot more like punctuated equilibrium. Even without any increasing demand, people may use short-fallow techniques for a part of their system; intensive and extensive systems often coexist (Boserup 1965: ch. 6; Netting 1977; Grigg 1980). And long fallow may persist, in restricted areas, where there is very high population density.

Corn Production, Settlement, and Intensification: A Simple Model

The dynamics of corn production lead us to a simple model of settlement dynamics. This model ignores such factors as production for the market, food crops other than corn, and the role of political and social factors in the nucleation, dispersal, and fission of settlements, but it is a useful ecological baseline. By modeling Kekchi settlement in the absence of these complicating factors, we can better judge their impact (and add to the literature on the expansion and fission of frontier settlement provided by Logan & Sanders [1976], Harrison [1976], Freeman [1955], and Carneiro [1960]).

Different fallow cycles, labor supply, and yield produce optimal agricultural solutions, depending on the size of a community and its span of occupation. Around new settlements there will be an expanding ring of land in which primary forest has been cleared. Having primary forest close to the village is the optimal situation for Kekchi swidden farming, providing a high yield with low risk. The previous yield figures that show higher yields per hour in secondary forest are deceptive because they do not correct for distance. In Aguacate primary forest is always farther from the village than secondary forest, and the added travel time is a crucial factor. Manipulating primary forest yield by reducing travel time to 15 minutes from a mean of 98 minutes, and adding 50 man-hours per hectare for fencing to keep out pigs (required if the field is only 15 minutes from the village), produces a figure of 2.87 kilograms per hour, about 10 percent more than secondary forest fields. Primary forest therefore yields more than secondary forest when both are at the same distance.

From the recalculated primary forest yields we can estimate the rate at which yield declines as the ring of used forest expands. This is about 0.0065 kilograms per man-hour for each extra minute of one-way travel time—a slope of decreasing return that represents an increasing amount of labor for each kilogram of corn. A community rides down this slope as it remains in the same place for a number of years, and it slips faster if it grows in size.

At some point the declining yield of primary forest production will cross the yield curve of secondary forest (the ring of primary forest is always receding, while the secondary forest is always regenerating). Using the same method of recalculating total yields and labor with different travel time, we find that the yields (in kg/man-hr) from a primary forest field with a 28-minute travel time and a secondary forest field with a 15-minute travel time are the same. If these were exact figures, if the Kekchi were aware of them, and if risk, good hunting, and habit were not factors, we would expect farmers to begin shifting to secondary forest as soon as primary forest is 28 minutes away. In practice the primary forest must be used up to about 45 minutes' travel time before some men begin to switch. And then the transition from one strategy to another is gradual, as people with different household needs and resources choose different strategies. It is not until the primary forest is used up within a two-hour walk from the village that all people give up using it.

At this point, some of the household heads may begin to talk about relocating and starting a new village in primary forestland. What is theoretically important is that pressures that can lead to group fissioning and the founding of new settlements are felt long before any possible carrying capacity is reached (Stauder 1972; Hayden 1975). The constraints on fissioning have more to do with the social problems of motivating enough labor and gaining rights to use new land than with ecological problems of soil exhaustion. The motivations to move have more to do with relative yields in different agricultural regimes than with absolute yields measured against some consumption standard.

To give some numerical skeleton to the body of this argument, we can calculate the amount of time required to use up the forest resources around a hypothetical community. The circle of land within 45 minutes' travel time of a village in rough and muddy terrain is the area of a circle about 1.9 kilometers in radius, or about 1,135 hectares. Based on catchment analysis of six villages, about 67 percent of the land in this circle falls in the range of fair to good soils for swidden farming, and of that area, about half is unusable for reasons of slope and drainage, leaving about 380 hectares. This is the area of primary forest that is cleared before some people begin to switch to using secondary forest, reusing the area already cleared.

Having previously found that the average Aguacate farmer uses 2.15 hectares of forest each year, we can infer that about 176 household-years of primary forest cultivation can be accommodated within the 1.9 kilometer radius. A village of 10 households would exceed this limit in about 18 years, or one of 20 households in half that time. A community of six households could remain within this area in perpetuity, allowing 30 years of regrowth on every swidden plot before it is reused.

Using the same basic figures, we also find that a community of 41 households will use up all of the primary forest within two hours of the village (the present limit) within the 30-year optimum fallow. In other words, 41 households are at equilibrium with a territory with a five-kilometer radius, allowing a generous 30-year fallow. Beyond this size, a village must cope with a declining average fallow length, reaching a critical point when population reaches 80 households, and average fallow falls to 15 years. In practice, historical Kekchi villages rarely reach this size. Only in the northern zone, where cash crop production has become important in the agricultural cycle, are there communities of more than 80 households, or smaller villages on smaller territories. And indeed in this area average fallow lengths have declined to as little as 7.4 years (Johnson 1986:8), and yields and productivity have also fallen. The reason why people stay and cope with this problem rather than moving away must be found in the cash economy.

This simplified model of population size, fallow, and yield defines a framework of costs and benefits that can be compared with actual behavior. In the southern lowland zone of Toledo farmers have a higher-threshold labor cost of production; increased distances to long-fallowed land quickly translate into migration, and community populations remain quite low. In the northern and upland areas farmers are willing to put up with much higher labor costs in corn production, and they stay in their communities long after fallow status has declined to a very low level. (The other costs and benefits, economic and social, that produce this regional variation in agricultural settlement and mobility will be taken up in Chapter 8.)

There is no area where corn is the preferred cash crop. Most farmers produce more than they need as a hedge against risk, and the surplus they sell is a by-product of subsistence farming. Seager (1983c:3–5) estimates that about 8 percent of the corn grown in Toledo is sold to the Marketing Board, with a much smaller amount handled by merchants in Punta Gorda. The total quantity sold has been close to 800,000 pounds per year between 1978 and 1984, even though market prices fluctuated during this time between U.S. $0.07 and $0.11 per pound. Farmers are not very responsive to prices because they do not produce primarily for the market. Although about 85 percent of the corn produced is grown in the wet season, almost half of annual sales are from dry-season production, confirming that farmers first fulfil their subsistence needs, then sell their surplus after judging their annual yield against needs.

OTHER FOOD CROPS

While corn is the staple of the Kekchi diet, meals are not complete without a complement. Often this is a meat or vegetable (or both) stew (caldo), colored with achiote (*xayau*) and flavored with garlic, cilantro, or a combination of these. When other foods are lacking, chiles fried with salt are the basic relish. At other times corn dishes are eaten along with another starchy food that is boiled or roasted—plantains and tubers, for example.

Most Kekchi appreciate diverse sauces and condiments. While few households grow the complete variety of subsidiary crops, an active exchange network moves small quantities of fruits, vegetables, beans, tubers, and plantains from kitchen to kitchen. Many subsidiary crops bear profusely for a short period and cannot be stored. While the okra is bearing, for example, every visitor to the household is given a double handful, and children are sent around the village with gifts of okra for friends, compadres, and relatives. Some households plant the same favorite vegetables in large quantities each year. Knowing that this family will shower the village with a particular food for a few weeks each year, their relatives and neighbors may not plant it.

Each household plants some crops that yield steadily through the year. Perishable foods are freely given as gifts, while dried and storable foods are treated more as commodities. Perishable green beans are given away, but only close kin are given dried beans on request. (The Kekchi make a distinction between gifts given freely and gifts that are asked for.) Otherwise, dried beans are bought and sold for small amounts of cash.

Another category of crops are the subsistence fallbacks. These include most of the root crops and eight varieties of plantains. Usually a complement, they can substitute for corn—first for pigs, then for people—as a corn shortage gets worse. Root crops bear continuously for several months and are therefore left in the ground until needed. The different plantain varieties bear at different times of the year, providing a steady supply of food over an extended period. Households tend to eat root crops and plantains when they are available, saving corn for later.[4] If corn is abundant, most root crops and plantains are fed to pigs.

Finally, there is a group of crops, varying from place to place, that are part of both the household subsistence economy and the wider cash economy. This group includes rice, red kidney beans, cocoa, coffee, and plantains in some places. Farmers can sell small amounts of minor crops in the Punta Gorda market, but demand is very low.

A list of minor food crops, condiments, medicinals, and other domestic plants (excluding ornamentals) is given in Table 6.3, which includes the places these crops are planted. Most of the crops grown in the wet-season cornfield are segregated into small plots in especially fertile soils, usually close to the corn house. Squash is interplanted in the same holes with the wet-season corn. Tree crops and perennials are rarely planted in the shifting wet-season cornfield. A few men established small citrus groves in fields especially close to the village during the 1950s and 1960s when the government gave out citrus seedlings in the hope of establishing oranges as a cash crop. The sak'ecwaj is a favored location for tree crops and such longer-bearing annuals as pineapples, sugarcane, and achiote.

People also plant various foods, medicinal plants, spices, and ornamentals around the house. Each plant must be protected from pigs, chickens, ducks, and horses with a small fence or enclosure, and often the battle is lost. Condiments and spices are often planted in buckets or pots out of the reach of animals, as in the log gardens of rural Panama (Covich & Nickerson 1966) and Yucatán (Redfield & Villa Rojas 1934). The house-plot is the woman's responsibility and property. Sometimes men can be recruited to help in planting or fencing, but women do most of the work. This tends to be a casual affair, pursued in odd moments in the afternoon or evening, not because these crops are unimportant, but because in general they lack pronounced seasonality and can be planted and harvested through most of the year. A few crops provide a small cash income to women. Cotton and agave are used for weaving and twining bags and hammocks, which are sometimes sold. Some women boil achiote seeds into a red paste that is sold in town or to cobaneros. Achiote production began to expand in 1985 when the Marketing Board and a private company began to buy the seed for export, but by 1989 the market had collapsed and prices were too low to justify transport costs.

The minor crops planted in the wet-season field or the sak'ecwaj are usually more seasonal. They are planted with household labor in the two months after the corn is planted. Households often make this an outing, taking lunch and spending the day at the field. Women's participation varies quite a bit—some enjoy the chance to get out of the village, while others dislike the bush and stay at home. Children frequently go along, when they are free from school, and the family often takes this opportunity to gather wild foods or do some fishing.

Scheduling labor for planting, tending, and harvesting minor crops is generally not an issue. These crops take up "available time"—hours that are not productively used in other tasks (see Annis 1987:35–39). I counted a mean of two hours a month in this work, with labor peaks in June, July, and October. But the actual total is probably much greater when the labor of women and children is included, and when odd minutes and hours are added. Perhaps 14 hours per month is a better estimate during the peak months.

Subsistence fallback foods can be divided into two parts—plantains and root crops. Root crops are not nearly as important in Kekchi subsistence as they are to South American lowland forest farmers, even though they offer high caloric yields both per unit of land and per hour of labor (Roosevelt 1980). The Maya preference for corn as a staple instead of root crops has attracted great deal of discussion. Bronson (1966) argued that root crops were more important in Maya subsistence before the conquest, when population densities were higher. Flannery (1982:xix) and Marcus (1982:252–53) contend that root crops were relatively unimportant, or even unknown, in the Maya area before the

Table 6.3. Complementary Food Crops, Condiments, Tree Crops, and Other Minor Produce

a. Minor Food Crops

Kekchi and Creole Names[a]	Scientific Binomial	Planting Locations[c]	Varieties, Their Characteristics, and Uses
Pixp[b]/tomato	*Lycopersicon esculentum*	C,S,A,H	Cherry tomato on creeping vine, often feral
Okr/okra	*Hibiscus esculentus*	C,H	Naj: long pod, tall plant up to 2.5 meters Coc': short, fat pod, small plant
Ch'ima[b]/chocho, chayote	*Sechium edule*	C,S,H	K'ix: green prickly fruit Mac'a k'ix: pale, smooth-skinned fruit
C'um[b]/pumpkin	*Cucurbita* spp.	C,S,H	C'um: flat, round, buff-colored fruit Yocotun: elongated, thin, multicolored fruit
Ceboyx/onion	*Allium cepa*	C,S,A,H	Caki: red, small bulbs Ch'o: no bulb, grows in clusters
Ic[b]/chile	*Capsicum annuum* *Capsicum frutiscens*	C,A,H	Ninki: large, red fruit, small annual bush Coc': tiny, red-orange fruit, large annual bush Jutz': small long fruit, perennial shrub
Anx/garlic	*Allium sativum*	C,H	Grows poorly and slowly if at all
Uts'aj/sugarcane	*Saccharum officinarum*	C,S,H	Saki: large stem, whitish green Cha': large stem, loose, thin, ash-colored skin Caki: thin cane, red to black
Ch'op[b]/pineapple	*Ananas comosus*	C	K'ix: large fruit, spiny leaves Tranjer: smaller fruit, smooth leaves

b. Condiments and Other Minor Crops

Kekchi and Creole Names[a]	Scientific Binomial	Varieties, Their Characteristics, and Uses
Xayau[b]/achiote	*Bixa orellana*	K'ix: red, prickly pod, spice and dye T'uru: reddish, smooth pod, spice and dye Saki: green, prickly pod, spice and dye
Xanchib/ginger	*Zingiber officinale* *Renealmia* sp.[b]	Coc': small leaves, spice Ch'i: large leaf, spice and food coloring
Orek[bd]/oregano	*Hyptis* sp.	Possibly several species, spice
Samat[bd]/unknown	*Eryngium foetidum*	Both wild and cultivated, spice and greens
Ichaj[bd]/nightshade	*Solanum nigrum*	Pot herb when young, seeds boiled
Tep/basil	*Ocimum basilicum*	Grown in buckets, spice
Wangla/sesame	*Sesamum indicum*	Seeds used to make candy
Culant/cilantro	*Coriandrum sativum*	Common spice and pot herb
Pens[b]/allspice	*Pimenta dioica*	Leaves and fruit used as spice, sometimes sold
Iskij/lemongrass	*Cymbopogon citratus*	Leaves used in drinks and other foods
Sel[b]/gourd	*Lagenaria siceraria*	Grown in containers, young fruit eaten
Mai[b]/tobacco	*Nicotiana rustica*	Rolled into large cigars
Nok'[b]/cotton	*Gossypium hirsutum*	K'ani: brown pod, perennial tree cotton Saki: green pod, perennial tree cotton
Mach palau[d]/loofah	*Luffa cylindrica*	Small fruits eaten, sponge

Table 6.3. (continued)

Kekchi and Creole Names[a]	Scientific Binomial	Varieties, Their Characteristics, and Uses
Chau pim[bd]/indigo	*Indigofera suffructicosa*	Dyestuff
Tu'tu'[bd]/girl's booby	*Solanum mammosum*	Ornamental, possibly medicinal
Iq'e[b]/agave	*Agave* spp.	Leaf fiber for bags and hammocks
Ch'alam[bd]/barbasco	*Lonchocarpus castilloi*	Fish poison

c. Tree Crops

Kekchi and Creole Names[a]	Scientific Binomial	Varieties, Their Characteristics, and Uses
Bokūt or ch'elel[bd]/bokoot	*Inga laurina*	Larger fruit than chōchoc
Asēt/castor	*Ricinus communis*	Saki: white stem, leaves and oil medicinal Caki: reddish stem nodes
Leem/lime	*Citrus aurantifolia*	Thin-skinned, used as seasoning
Lamox/lemon	*Citrus limon*	Lamox: rare, thin-skinned Lemonsee: large, thick-skinned, more common
Cheen/orange	*Citrus aurantum* *Citrus sinensis*	Rēre: bitter, used as seasoning and in juice K'i: sweet, popular fruit
Toroni/grapefruit	*Citrus paradisi*	Rarely planted
Saltul[b]/mamey apple	*Calocarpum sapota*	Large, red flesh, very sweet
Muy[bd]/sapote	*Achras zapota*	White flesh, sometimes called coc' saltul
Rūm[b]/hogplum	*Spondius mombin*	Snack food, increasingly popular
Obel[bd]/bullhoof	*Piper umbellatum*	Leaves boiled and eaten
Papā[bd]/papaya	*Carica papaya*	Papā: large cultigen hybridizes with ch'onte Ch'onte: ...

c. Tree Crops

Kekchi and Creole Names[a]	Scientific Binomial	Planting Locations[c]	Varieties, Their Characteristics, and Uses
O[b]/avocado	*Persea americana*		Caki: red skin, small fruit Raxi: green skin, large fruit
Cape/coffee	*Coffea canephora* *Coffea arabica*		Ch'e: (robusta) large tree, large fruit Coc': shrub, small fruit, most common
Pac[b]/custard apple	*Annona reticulata*		Saki: white flesh, smooth skin
Pox[b]/sweetsop	*Annona squamosa*		Sometimes called caki pac, red flesh, rough skin
Anap[b]/soursop	*Annona muricata*		Not widely grown
Pata'[bd]/guava	*Psidium guajava*		Caki: reddish pulp, favorite of children Saki: whitish pulp
Mank/mango	*Mangifera indica*		Cas: small, stringy, purple skin Ninki: red, large, pulpy
Cōc/coconut	*Cocos nucifera*		Rarely planted, but fruit valued
Jōm[b]/calabash	*Crescentia cujete*		Fruit dried and used as container
Sakilte[b]/physic nut	*Jatropha tubulosa*		A common snack food
Chōchoc[bd]/bribri(?)	*Inga edulis*		Pulp from long pods eaten
Masapan/breadfruit	*Artocarpus attilis*		Famine food mostly

[a] If only one variety is known, it does not have a varietal name.
[b] Native to the New World.
[c] A = rice field; C = wet-season cornfield; H = household garden plot; S = dry-season riverbank field.
[d] Semidomesticated.

sixteenth century. Reina and Hill (1980:75–77) think that in early colonial times corn was the staple in the highlands and roots were more important in the lowlands (cf. Harris 1972).

Whatever the historical or prehistoric balance between seed and root crops, it seems that among modern Mesoamerican Indians, among them the Kekchi, corn is king. Root crops are an important adjunct to the diet and serve to back up corn as a staple during times of shortage or crop failure, but corn is always preferred. For this reason, the complex, multilevel, continuously bearing, forest-mimetic "vegeculture" swidden fields found among farmers in Asia (see, e.g., Conklin 1954) and South America (Ruddle 1974) are not usually found in Mesoamerica. As long as corn is the subsistence staple the quantity and diversity of other crops interplanted in the field remains comparatively low, and the period of cultivation relatively short (Beckerman 1983). When one or two corn harvests are completed the field is abandoned, instead of being managed for many years as is common in Asia.

A conventional explanation for the preponderance of corn over root crops in the subsistence system is that corn has higher protein content. But corn also requires better soil than most root crops, so root crops are grown where the soil is too poor, or where population pressure forces a switch to the less nutritious, but higher-yielding, starchy roots (Roosevelt 1980). This idea is based on the theory that protein is the limiting factor among swidden farmers in Amazonia (see Diener, Moore & Mutaw 1980), assuming that with good soil farmers will grow the higher-protein grain (ignoring the possibility of eating the high-protein leaves of the root crops). This does not explain how subsistence farmers know the amino acid composition of their crops, or why they would be willing to put more work into lower yields of corn when they could grow higher-yielding root crops and spend the time thus saved hunting additional protein. In other words, they do not explain why corn should be the default option.

Beckerman (1983) recently summarized the evidence for widespread monocropping among swidden farmers. He thinks it may be more efficient to monocrop because planting, weeding, and other tasks can be done in a single concentrated work period, instead of being spread out over long periods (see also Hames 1983). But these periods of concentrated work may create undesirable labor bottlenecks in the annual cycle, unless there are other activities that demand the farmer's time during other parts of the year. Nevertheless, Hames and Beckerman are right that highly diverse labor-intensive polycultural systems are more likely where land is short or is very expensive to clear (because of the lack of steel tools).

Another reason why Mesoamerican farmers tend to concentrate on corn is that historically there has been a market for corn, because corn stores well and can be easily transported. State intervention in farming goes back at least as far as the fifteenth century when tribute in corn and other seed grains, rather than in bulky root crops, was demanded by the Aztec state. Spanish encomenderos and priests who entered the same trade and tribute system continued to demand corn. Corn went from one crop among many to being the central crop in the subsistence system because it allowed farmers to move back and forth between the subsistence and tributary or market economies. Corn was therefore not necessarily the farmer's choice, nor could the farmer always suit the crop to the local ecology or soil.

One of the few groups of Mesoamericans to remain outside the system that imposed corn as a cash crop are the Lacandón of lowland Chiapas, Yucatec Maya refugees from Spanish colonial control who escaped the tribute and taxation system from the seventeenth century until the 1940s (Thompson 1977). It is no coincidence that until recently these Lacandón had a more widely diversified and polycultural system than any other Maya group. Fields were used for as many as five years in a row, planted with a mixture of seed crops, vegetables, root crops, and longer-yielding tree crops (Nations & Nigh 1980:14).

Nations and Nigh find another reason for a shift from polyculture and ecologically complex fields to monoculture and more-simplified crop mixtures among the Lacandón: the change from dispersed to nucleated settlement. When families lived dispersed in their fields, they could give the constant attention needed to manage the complex ecology. Now that they live in nucleated villages, far from their fields, they have shifted to a system in which they visit less frequently, weed with machetes, and have to abandon the field after two years because of problems with weeds and pests (Nations & Nigh 1980:14–15). Distance from fields may promote the kind of intensive short-term work effort that Beckerman associates with monocropping instead of polyculture.

The colonial *congregación* policy may therefore have caused the original shift from long-term polyculture to short-term monoculture. But can the marketplace and the shift in settlement patterns explain why the Kekchi remain centered on corn and have not shifted back to polyculture and root crops? Or can the focus on corn be best explained as a product of ideology, of the central place that corn takes in Maya religion and ethnic identity (Annis 1987)? Or is this merely a case of cultural conservatism, as the Kekchi only slowly adapt their highland corn agriculture to a new, lowland climate (Carter 1969)? Or it may be that though the Kekchi are no longer taxed directly in corn, they do pay taxes in cash, and they want cash for many other purposes as well. The fact of the marketplace is that corn can always be sold for cash, while root and vegetable crops are hard to sell at best. Corn preserves a farmer's options to convert what he does not need into cash, while root crops can be easily converted only by feeding them to pigs and then selling the pigs.

Today the Kekchi live in nucleated villages, and this keeps them from giving constant attention to their fields, which in turn precludes planting complex polycultures. When I discussed root crops with Kekchi farmers, I was repeatedly told that while they were easy to grow, could be harvested when you needed them, and were good food for both human and pig, there was no use growing a lot of them because peccaries would destroy them. Only in the northern villages, where hunting pressure has kept the peccary population in check, have root crops become a larger part of the diet. Fallow status and corn yields have also fallen in the north, creating an advantage for root crops, which are not as sensitive to weeds or lower fertility.

In sum, the central place of corn in mythology and religion, and its historical importance in cooking, diet, and ritual, may slow the switch to alternative crops, but it can hardly impede making corn part of a more diverse and complex form of agriculture. There are instead good economic and agronomic reasons for depending on corn. The issue of cultural conservatism seems moot, given the speed at which Kekchi production systems change when market opportunities arise, as they have for bananas, cocoa, pigs, beans, rice, and marijuana in the last 60 years.

In his 1969 study of Kekchi migrants in lowland Guatemala Carter concluded that Kekchi farmers are not able to intensify their production or respond to market incentives. He therefore justified continuing latifundia owned by absent landlords in the lowland forests, since the Kekchi would just use them for unproductive subsistence farming. Carter's insistence that Indian swidden agriculture is set in long-standing traditional ways and resists change is belied by his own data. His discussion of agricultural practices shows active experimentation with new techniques of intensification, rapid adoption of new cash crops, and very fast and astute response to market prices. In an otherwise carefully written monograph, tagging Kekchi agriculture as bound

Table 6.4. Root Crops and Varieties in Toledo

Kekchi Name	Belizean Common Name	Scientific Binomial	Varieties and Their Characteristics
Ox[a]	Cocoyam	*Xanthosoma violaceum*	Sakil: white stem Rax: green stem
Balū	Dasheen	*Colocasia esculenta*	Cakal: reddish stem Sakil: pale green stem
Is[a]	Sweet potato	*Ipomoea batatas*	Several unnamed varieties
Tz'in[a]	Yucca, cassava	*Manihot esculenta*	K'an: sweet, yellow stem Raxal: sweet, yellow leaves Sakil: bitter, tall plant
Piyac'	Yam	*Dioscorea alata*	Sakil: white stem joints Cakal: red stem joints
Yampā	Yampa	*Dioscorea trifida*	Sakil: white flesh Raxal: purple flesh
Yamachīn	Chinese yam	*Dioscorea esculenta*	Sakil: white flesh

[a] Native to the New World.

by tradition is a dangerous lapse because it plays into the hands of the Guatemalan elite, who exclude Indians from access to land on the grounds that they would grow only corn (not responding to the market) and would destroy the land by slashing and burning (not responding to population pressure) (see Schwartz 1987).

Seven Kekchi root crops and their varieties are identified in Table 6.4. All of them are reproduced vegetatively by planting corms, parts of the roots, or sections of vines in shallow holes dug with the machete or digging stick. Root crops are planted in the wet-season cornfield in the month after corn planting. All of these plants take more than six months to begin to bear, with cassava taking the longest. Harvest is casual, a few tubers gathered at a time during visits to the field and later shared with other households. Often the crops are replanted as they are harvested, and this continual cycle ensures that some root crops are bearing most times of year.

Table 6.5. Frequency and Quantity of Root Crops Planted

	Coco-yam	Da-sheen	Sweet Potato	Cassava	Yam	Yampa	Chinese Yam
Percentage of farmers							
Aguacate	16	28	16	52	28	20	4
Crique Sarco	61	11	71	84	71	45	21
Indian Creek	40	20	40	80	50	50	10
Mean number of plants[a]							
Aguacate	17	38	3	28	23	24	2
Indian Creek	166	28	31	70	45	134	15

SOURCES: My survey data and Schackt (n.d.).
[a]No data are available for Crique Sarco.

Table 6.6. Frequency and Quantity of Plantain Varieties Planted

	Que-ney	Saki-tul	Tuliyaj	Caki-tul	Parax	Tz'ul-tul	Ala-ban	Caki-saki-tul	Met'tul
Percentage of farmers									
Aguacate	48	68	20	16	40	44	28	32	4
Crique Sarco	55	71	39	42	31	13	32	11	11
Indian Creek	60	70	50	20	20	50	40	50	30
Mean number of plants[a]									
Aguacate	6	19	5	3	4	7	4	8	2
Indian Creek	5	102	15	5	10	20	26	24	11

SOURCES: My survey data and Schackt (n.d.)
[a]No data are available for Crique Sarco.

The average quantities of root crops planted in three study villages are given in Table 6.5. I have no accurate yield or labor figures: labor spent specifically on root crops in Aguacate averaged less than four hours per month during the peak period in June; the rest of the planting and harvesting was done in small snatches between other jobs and was not recorded.

Kekchi farmers in Toledo grow eight varieties of plantain and one kind of banana. They are valued food crops because they require little care—just weeding two or three times a year—and because they continue to bear fruit long after they are planted, thus extending the useful life of the cornfield. Plantains are interplanted in the wet-season cornfield two months after the corn. Yields vary widely depending on the variety. In Table 6.6 the percentages of farmers in each village who plant each variety, and the number planted, are given. About 90 percent of farmers in both villages grow some variety, although Indian Creek farmers have more plants. The most popular varieties are not the most productive, but those that have superior storability after picking, that bear for long periods of time, or that have preferred taste and texture. In Indian Creek the choice of variety is partially dictated by what sells on the market (*queney* and *sakitul*).

CASH CROPS

As mentioned above, the division between cash crops and food crops is not always sharp. All the crops discussed in this section are regularly sold in larger quantities than the crops discussed above.

Cocoa

Cocoa is the cash crop for which southern Belize was famous in pre-Hispanic times (Hammond 1975: chs. 8–9). Until recently the Kekchi produced cocoa for domestic consumption and sold small quantities to each other and to the cobaneros. Recently the Hummingbird Hershey company has begun to buy cocoa from Belizean farmers at a price pegged to the world market (over U.S. $0.75/lb.).

In 1985, with assistance from a Peace Corps volunteer, farmers in 10 villages began to organize groups to pool money and labor and purchase improved seedlings. These village groups have now formed a central organization, the Toledo Cocoa Growers Association, which intends to coordinate marketing, provide credit, and purchase agrochemicals in bulk, with assistance from a large USAID agricultural marketing project. Most of the farmers in this association want to plant cocoa on leasehold land and see the association as a vehicle for helping them to obtain leases. Farmers in San Antonio who do not want to see the reservations broken into leasehold, and who want to plant cocoa on reservation land, quickly formed their own group, the San Antonio Cocoa Growers Association. Despite political interference and land tenure problems, cocoa could become the dominant cash crop in Toledo over the next decade.

Cocoa is also an essential part of daily Kekchi life. Every ceremonial and ritual occasion is marked by the drinking of *cacau*, a brew made from roasted cocoa beans, black pepper, sugar, and sometimes wild vanilla. Offering the drink is a basic hospitality. Now that there is a ready market outlet cocoa is being extracted from the reciprocal economy, and those who have no trees of their own must either buy the beans or substitute a drink made from artificial flavoring and white sugar.

The cocoa tree has acquired a unique place in the Kekchi property system. The rights to land used for other crops can never be sold or rented, but cacau and a few other tree crops can be sold, lent, or rented. The land itself is not actually sold, but the trees are, which is effectively the same thing unless the trees are destroyed, a tactic that has sometimes been used. Cocoa trees are the only possessions that play an important role in inheritance, since they are the only substantial productive resource owned individually. It is possible for the members of a single household to have separate cocoa groves. This joint usufruct is an incentive for sons to remain in, or close to, their natal household after marriage. After the father's death the sons try to maintain the joint enterprise and ownership, but quarrels are common and division eventually takes place. As the value of cocoa increases, this informal ownership and inheritance system, based on negotiation and public consensus, may break down and be replaced by more-formal rules.

People take the ownership of cocoa trees into account in making decisions about residence. Families that have invested effort in establishing groves, or who have inherited a number of trees, are less likely to pick up and move to another village. By the same token the old established families in a village usually control the greatest number of cocoa trees. Mobile households and new immigrants must buy the beans or a grove of trees, until they can establish their own. And establishing cocoa groves on village land can be a sensitive matter, since it effectively removes land from the pool of common property. Permission must be secured from the alcalde before planting and may be difficult to obtain where land is a circumscribed resource.

Fearing that the government will soon break up the reservations, some farmers want to establish a claim to particular parcels by planting cocoa. Older families and others who favor communal ownership resist. Some villagers go outside the reservation to plant their cocoa, figuring that this will establish their rights when that land is finally parceled out. Planting cocoa has therefore become a political issue, calling into question the basis of the land tenure system. In some villages new cocoa groves have been destroyed by those who do not want to see communal land become private property. They point out that only very small amounts of cocoa were planted in past times, and this had no serious impact on communal land. Those who want to plant, in the meantime, argue that the government is behind the program, that there is a ready market, and that change to private tenure is inevitable. In 1986 several villages, under pressure from the government and growers, agreed to let residents plant up to two acres of cocoa. This dispute made it clear that the concern of most communities was equity of opportunity rather than some abstract principle of communal property. What villagers were afraid of was that some entrepreneur among them would establish a huge cocoa farm, eating away at the resources available to the rest. In Guatemala, in the coffee days, many Kekchi watched village caciques establish themselves at communal expense, growing wealthy and gaining political power through the support of the government. This memory is very much alive.

The two species of cocoa planted by Kekchi farmers are cocoa proper (*Theobroma cocoa*; Kekchi *cacau*) and a relative known as *pataxte* in some parts of Guatemala (*Theobroma bicolor*; Kekchi *baalam*). Three varieties of the former are known, and two varieties of the latter. All are planted in well-drained soils, usually in the sheltered valleys between small hills, within two kilometers of the village center. In Aguacate there are over 10 hectares of cocoa in a single area.

Cacau is planted in cornfields that have been abandoned for three to 10 years. In the past no shade was used, but now farmers have begun to leave some natural vegetation as shade, or they plant shade trees. Clearing and planting tend to take place in June when the farmer finishes planting his corn, or in September when the rains begin to slack off. Weeding is done three or more times a year until the plant reaches waist height, after which the plot is cleaned once a year. The trees bear fruit in five years (three for the new varieties), and the main harvest is in March and April. Increased cocoa production will place further burdens on farm labor at the busiest times of the year, when the corn and rice crops are planted. Women and children do most cocoa processing, washing and drying the beans. In the average household this task now occupies two or three working days, but again there will have to be changes as the size of the task increases. If women continue to do most of the processing, and men handle the marketing, equity issues in dividing the proceeds will be raised.

Total yield from the average mature tree is between two and five kilograms of dried seed per year, which works out to about 300–600 kilograms per hectare. New varieties can produce five times this amount. A minimally tended hectare of traditional cacau, requiring perhaps 80 hours of labor per year, yields between U.S. $150 and $300. This rate of return is far higher than that of any other crop, explaining the present enthusiasm for cocoa. Nevertheless, access to land continues to be a problem for some households, especially those in roadside, nonreservation villages where land tenure is insecure.

Baalam is a massive forest tree, relatively unknown in the literature on tropical agriculture, except in Guatemala where its seeds are considered an inferior substitute for cocoa (McBryde 1945:148). The Kekchi prefer baalam to cocoa for domestic use and carefully tend trees they have planted and those growing in the forest. The advantage of baalam is that it bears fruit in October and November (rather than the busy time of the dry season), and the pods fall from the tree themselves when they are ripe. Each tree annually bears between five and seven kilograms of seeds.

In Aguacate in 1980, 56 percent of households owned an average of 44 cocoa trees, and 40 percent of households had an average of six baalam. About 54 percent of those with cocoa had inherited the trees, 22 percent had bought the mature trees from someone else, and only 24 percent had planted the trees themselves. Less than 12 percent of the households in Aguacate had planted cocoa in the previous five years, while all the cocoa in Indian Creek had been planted during that time.

Beans

The Indians of Toledo plant a total of seven varieties of beans, of five different species. The varieties range from red kidney beans (Kekchi *caki kenk; Phaseolus vulgaris*) grown largely for sale to the Marketing Board to those grown entirely for home consumption, with other varieties falling in between. By weight, beans are the third most important cash crop in Toledo, but they have the second highest cash value. Despite agronomists' conclusion that the red kidney bean is poorly adapted to the lowland climate of Toledo District (Seager 1983b), this is the kind of bean that the urban Belizean demands. To promote self-sufficiency in bean production, the government offers incentives to farmers, including high prices (U.S. $0.22/lb in 1978; $0.28 in 1979, $0.50 in 1981) and interest-free seed loans. Most of the beans that are sold to the Marketing Board come from Mopan villages in the northern upland region. Only about 13,000 pounds of red kidney beans and 15,000 pounds of black come from the southern zone, where most of the bean crop is eaten at home. This pattern reflects climatic and soil differences between the two areas, rather than market access.

In the southern villages beans are planted once a year, in September. After the main wet-season crop is harvested, a patch of the field is cleared with a machete. Leaves are chopped into mulch, and the rest of the debris is piled up on the edge of the patch. Seeds are then dibbled into holes spaced about a foot apart, and the field is weeded at least once. Many of the beans are eaten green. In late December or early January the plants are pulled up individually, hung to dry, and brought home where women winnow the beans and dry them.

The household or household cluster provides all the labor for bean production. A major constraint is the bottleneck that occurs when farmers try to finish the corn and rice harvests, at the same time they are trying to get started on the sak'ecwaj corn. Farmers in Aguacate did not plant any red kidney beans during my stay, so I could not gather data on the amounts of work required, but Seager (1983b:6) estimates 50 days per acre.

Farmers in upland zones plant between one and two acres per household in two separate production cycles. The first crop is planted in the wet-season cornfield in September, when the corn is harvested. When the beans are harvested in December, another area is cleared and planted, and this second crop bears in April, at the height of the dry season. Labor groups of up to 10 people clear and plant the larger second crop. Using two production cycles has several advantages. It reduces the amount of time the dried beans must be stored and increases seed viability. For this reason some agronomists have called the first crop a "seed multiplication" crop, although the practice continues even when good seed is available from the government. This production cycle also spreads out the work so other tasks, such as sak'ecwaj, can be pursued at the same time, and extends the bean season into the dryer part of the year when the threat of fungal disease is lower. It also ensures that green beans, a favorite food, are ready for eating twice yearly.

In most northern upland villages beans equal or surpass rice in total cash earnings. Seager (1983b:11–12) estimates that yields vary between 200 and 1,200 pounds per acre, with a mean of 600; return per hour ranges between 1.19 and 2.57 pounds. In 1980 prices, this is between U.S. $0.33 and $0.77 per hour. In three upland villages, Brown and Salam (1985) found an average of 650 pounds per acres from the first crop and 415 pounds per acre from the second, even lower yields per man-hour, especially if the cost of seed is deducted.

As a cash crop, beans have both advantages and disadvantages. They do not require that land be taken out of corn production, there is a constant and ready market, and they can be eaten instead of sold if food is short. On the other hand, they are risky, with an estimated 30 percent chance of total failure. Harvest and processing are labor-intensive and place a heavy burden on women and children, and maintaining viable seed is a problem. The prospects for a future increase in the production of red kidney beans in Toledo are dim. While other varieties of beans grow much better in Toledo and require less care, as long as there is consumer resistance to other beans, and as long as the only market is a domestic one, Toledo farmers will either grow red kidney beans or no beans at all for market.

Black beans, called *er' i kenk* in Kekchi, are another variety of *Phaseolus vulgaris*. Black beans are grown by the same methods as red kidney beans, although usually only one crop is planted. Household labor is used and the area planted is normally quite small. The plants are better adapted than red kidneys to local conditions and are not as susceptible to disease or pests. At one time Toledo exported black beans to the rest of Belize (Thompson 1930a). At that time, however, marketing was in the hands of private individuals, and the beans were carried to the northern districts of the country where the Maya population prefers black beans. As the Marketing Board took over the bean trade in the 1940s, the system was reshaped to serve the demand of the urban population of Belize City, which prefers red kidney beans. The Marketing Board has stifled trade between districts in the interest of increasing the flow to the city. Today the northern districts import black beans from Mexico.

The Marketing Board does buy small quantities of black beans but at about 65 percent of the price for red kidney beans. About 90 percent of the quantity sold comes from the southern zone villages, where the moisture tolerance of black beans outweighs the price differential. Many of these beans are a surplus from production for domestic consumption. At various times the Marketing Board finds itself buying too many black beans, even at low prices, and just stops buying them, leaving the farmers literally holding the bag.

Three varieties of vine beans are grown almost entirely for domestic consumption, by interplanting in the wet-season cornfield. All of them take a long time to bear and are harvested long after the corn matures. They are favorite foods and are often exchanged between households. In Indian Creek farmers claimed that these beans used to be more important, and that they are being displaced by cash crops, but in fact more of these beans are grown in Indian Creek than in Aguacate or Crique Sarco.

Tch'oox, an unidentified species of *Vigna*, yields long, thin pods with bright red beans. They are eaten entirely as a green vegetable. *Tapacal* is a native climbing lima bean (*Phaseolus lunatus*), with black or brown seed, that takes 10 months to bear. *Ch'o kenk*, or rat beans

(*Vigna umbellata*), yield a tiny seed on a thin climbing vine that grows like a weed over the cornstalks. Seed is broadcast on the ground after the corn is planted, maturing after nine months. They are often planted in the sak'ecwaj during the corn harvest so they can be picked when the field is cleared the following year. Although they are the hardiest variety, they are poor producers of seed and are most often eaten green.

During the early 1970s the Marketing Board announced that it would buy any kinds of beans that farmers wanted to sell; at the time the government was planning to export them to other Caribbean Common Market countries, where they would enter duty-free. The buying center was flooded with large quantities of vine beans, but the overseas market never appeared, and after a few weeks the farmers were turned away. This demonstrates that Kekchi and Mopan farmers are willing to convert any food crop into a cash crop, given a market incentive. It also shows that they respond very quickly to those incentives and will keep trying new crops, even though they have been burned by the Marketing Board many times.

Rice

Rice is Toledo District's greatest contribution to Belizean gross national product and to the Belizean diet in general. In the average year small farmers using shifting cultivation produce between one-third and one-half of the national consumption. If the contribution of a single, large, government-owned mechanized farm in the Belize District is subtracted, Toledo rice is three-fourths of annual production (Seager 1983a:1). The total quantity of paddy (not hulled or polished) purchased by the Marketing Board fluctuates from year to year, with a recent low of 3.4 million pounds in 1977/78 and a high of 6.2 million pounds in 1981/82. Promoting rice production in Toledo is a national priority, aimed at making the nation self-sufficient in its urban staple, a goal that has been achieved in most years since 1974. Because of this, most of the government's development and agricultural extension work in Toledo is aimed at rice farming. At times the government has become directly involved in all stages of rice production, providing loan financing, renting out mechanical equipment, selling seed and chemicals, and continuing research on farming techniques.

Production in most of Toledo has been stimulated (and managed) by government policies. A new mill and storage unit was constructed at Big Falls in 1980. When production lags, prices are raised, as if the farmers were a tap that could be opened and adjusted to suit the needs of the urban consumer. But these price rises do not take into account inflation in the costs of consumer goods or crop inputs, nor are they related to the prices of other crops. Thus the price was raised from U.S. eight cents per pound in 1978 to 12.5 cents in 1982, but the amount produced by Indian swidden farmers remained about the same.

Indians produce about 60 percent of the paddy purchased by the Marketing Board. The rest is grown by East Indian, Creole, and foreign farmers in the lowland areas around the highway, who use bulldozers to clear, tractors to cultivate, mechanical sowers, and combine harvesters (Seager 1983a). Each plot is used for four years, at which point weed growth forces fallow for eight to 10 years (a system that Seager calls a "mechanized milpa"). The only thing that makes this system pay is the low cost of land and subsidized equipment. The government essentially works the field for the farmer; the major source of risk is the political issue of who will get priority in scheduling the equipment, a tricky matter when there are narrow windows of dry weather for planting and harvesting.

In 1980 a number of Kekchi and Mopan farmers in the northern zone villages began mechanized production. They formed cooperatives based on labor-exchange groups, with encouragement from the government, and then petitioned for mechanized services. Some groups were successful and became formal grain growers cooperatives in 1983. In that year Indian farmers grew several hundred acres of mechanized rice (Seager 1983a:5). Thus, within the space of four years, Kekchi farmers adopted an entirely new production system based on cash hire of equipment and cash purchase of crop inputs (including herbicides and insecticides), using swidden work groups as a structural basis for cooperation. This rapid change in farming system is almost entirely a product of a windfall profit in the form of subsidized or free farm services. The majority of Indian-grown rice in Toledo is still produced by hand, through shifting cultivation. Because this was the system used in Aguacate and Indian Creek at the time of my fieldwork, I will focus the rest of this discussion on it.

Because of its low value per pound, rice is a cash crop only in areas with access to roads or cheap river transport. Aguacate and Crique Sarco are the remotest rice-producing areas (though a few farmers in Otoxha and Dolores are experimenting with the crop, using mules for transport). As the road network is extended farther south, transportation cost will decrease rapidly and at least a short-term increase in rice production will occur. Even with good transportation the cash return from producing rice is comparable to that from corn, and well below the yield from cocoa, casting doubt on the long-term future of the crop in Toledo (see TRDP 1986).

Rice was a minor food crop in Aguacate for many years before it became a cash crop. In the early 1940s a villager brought some seed back from Punta Gorda and gave it to his compadres and kin, who planted it in small areas of their wet-season cornfields. As food, rice was never anything but an occasional side dish. The first commercial crop was grown in 1963 by a young man who had come from Crique Sarco to live with his father-in-law for two years' bride service. Rice, from the very beginning, was thus disembedded from an existing system of social obligations and rights over labor. With corn and other crops, a man who is living with his father or father-in-law does not work his own field; he works in his father's field and eats from the common pot. As a new crop, rice was not immediately bound by these obligations; a young man could work with his father in the cornfield and work his own rice field when he had free time, and keep the crop. The path to this new independence was not painless—it was beaten against the resistance of fathers, who lost some control over the labor of their sons—but parents have found some compensation, as we will see. A son-in-law is in a more powerful negotiating position because, if faced with strong opposition, he can go home (though he might have to go without his bride). A son, on the other hand, has nowhere else to go if his father turns him out and would find it hard to marry without his father's support.

In 1963 this first rice farmer carried his harvest on horses rented from his father-in-law the 10 kilometers to the highway, and he netted only U.S. $3.50 per hundred-pound sack. The next year his father-in-law compromised with him, and they both grew rice on the same field, although they marked off their own sections and marketed separately. Several other households followed their example, experimenting with new rice varieties acquired from East Indians. The number of farmers producing rice grew steadily until 1975, an exceptionally dry year when much of the crop died. In that year 25 out of 31 households had planted rice. Some farmers who had cut their corn production and increased the amount of rice found themselves without corn to feed their families. Since then the number of farmers growing rice, and the area planted, has fluctuated. In 1979, while I was living in Aguacate, only 11 households grew rice, producing a total of about 23,000 pounds. In 1982, when prices increased and the market for pigs was poor, rice production rebounded to 79,000 pounds.

As a socially disembedded crop, rice is grown with very little ritual. The Kekchi attitude to rice was expressed by reactions to an East Indian schoolteacher who lived in Aguacate in 1979. Although it was against the will of the villagers (and against government regulations), the teacher decided to clear fields and plant corn and rice to supplement his family's diet. As it happened the corn was choked out by grasses, and the remaining ears were eaten by coatimundis, while the rice gave a fair yield. A villager explained to me that the corn was destroyed by the Tzuultak'a because the teacher did not know the proper rituals. But rice is a *caxlan k'en*, a foreigner's crop, so "anyone can grow rice."

The ownership of rice and the rights to the crop are different from those that apply to corn. The male head of each conjugal family owns the yield from cornfields. Although his sons (or coresident sons-in-law) work full-time in the cornfields, on cocoa, plantains, or any other food crop, he manages the product and makes decisions about apportioning it to pigs, kitchen, and market. But young men who still live with their parents can successfully assert a claim to their own rice and make decisions about the products of their labor. Rice therefore gives a young man a chance to divert some of his labor into a crop that will profit him directly. In a time when desire for cash income is rising, especially among young men, it suits the purpose of many parents to allow their sons to earn their own money. Parents argue that if their sons were not allowed to make some money growing rice, they might leave the household. If the son stays, his parents would have to give him some money anyway, both to spend and to pay the expenses of his eventual marriage.

Parents recognize that allowing a son who lives in the household to have his own farm enterprise changes the economic basis of the household. Previously children were completely dependent until they married and had children, and were expected to donate their labor to the household pool. Now they have an independent source of income and practice generalized reciprocity with household members when it comes to food and subsistence crops, but follow a rule of balanced reciprocity in the rice field. The parent's problem is to keep as much of a son's labor as possible in the generalized pool, while allowing him enough time on his own rice to keep him satisfied.

Fathers often try to co-opt their son's enterprise by joining it. They form a cooperative group with their coresident sons in all steps of rice production, trying to blur the separation between the two fields and create a single enterprise. Their two rice fields might be adjacent, they can build a single rice house, work together, thresh together, and market their produce together. Besides bringing some cash income to the father, this cooperation helps the two men schedule their productive tasks and coordinate their rice production with subsistence farming. One man can spend the day in the cornfield intercropping plantains, while the other finishes up the rice planting in both fields. A father thereby promotes the kind of frequent labor exchange that tends to generalize the relationship, making it difficult to reckon exact balances, maintaining the unity of his household. He also, in subtle but important ways, maintains his authority over his sons. The threat to parental roles and power posed by the young man's rice field is thus blunted and domesticated through recourse to the broader forms of economic reciprocity that characterize relationships between all Kekchi farmers.

Of the five young Aguacate men who lived with their parents and grew rice in 1979, all but one cooperated daily with their fathers, who also grew rice. The exception, a son whose father grew no rice, proves the rule, for the ultimate result was that the son married and moved out, setting up his own independent household.

The overriding criterion in choosing a site for rice production is proximity to a road or major path. When the rice is harvested it has a very high moisture content (15% – 18%) and must be marketed immediately or it will spoil. Labor also has a very high opportunity cost at harvest because of competing demands on the farmer's time. While there is overlap between the terrain and soils used for corn and those used for rice, there are some areas suitable only for rice. Steeper and drier slopes are avoided, and wetter, low-lying areas are preferred. The spot must not have standing water or heavy mud during the dry season, because slashed vegetation must dry enough to burn. Nonetheless, proximity to roads is the overriding factor, and unsuitable terrain is sometimes used anyway. Rice fields are rarely cleared at more than half an hour's walk from the roadside.

Because rice can compete with wild grasses, farmers use shorter-fallowed areas. In 1979 about half of Aguacate farmers used fields that had been fallowed less than 10 years. In northern zone villages, where more rice is produced and population pressure on land is greater, over 60 percent of farmers use land that has been fallowed between five and seven years, and 15 percent use land with less than five years of fallow (TRDP 1986:8).

Techniques for clearing rice fields are the same used in the wet-season cornfield, and the labor schedule both overlaps and is similarly constrained by the short dry season and the necessary intervals between clearing, burning, and planting. In Aguacate priority is always given to corn when these conflicts occur, but the balance is more equal in the northern villages. Where rice clearing begins only after the cornfield is finished, field size is partially determined by the amount of time left, and partially by the amount of labor that can be motivated within the household. These limiting factors are balanced against the farmer's need for cash. In higher bush the clearing must begin in late February or early March, so the trees will have enough time to dry. Lower bush can be left until mid- or late March, allowing only a couple of weeks for drying. So shorter-fallowed land gives the farmer more flexibility in scheduling labor.

Rice fields in Aguacate in 1979 averaged just 0.76 hectare, and the largest fields belonged to unmarried men. Average size elsewhere ranges from about 0.5 hectare in heavily populated upland San Antonio to 1.5 hectares in Indian Creek and other lowland northern villages (TRDP 1986:8; Seager 1983a:6).

Most of the labor to clear rice fields comes from the household or the household cluster. Because fewer men in Aguacate cultivate rice, fewer people want to join labor-exchange groups. Also, each farmer has to fit rice labor into his own schedule and finds it almost impossible to meet the obligations and scheduling imposed when the rotating work group is formed. As long as rice fields are small this is not a problem, and most farmers can fit the required three to 16 man-days of labor (about 13 days per ha) into their schedule after the cornfield is cleared. Sometimes several young men will get together and start clearing rice fields while their fathers are still clearing cornfields. This is a source of friction between sons and their fathers, who want help with the subsistence crop. In northern villages, where more farmers plant more rice, the labor arrangements for clearing and planting rice fields parallel those used in corn clearing and planting. More-regular work groups, some rivaling the corn group in size and formality, form right after the cornfields are cleared.

The Kekchi plant rice in the same basic way they plant corn, beginning immediately after the corn planting is completed. Beginning in mid-May, this labor-intensive task continues until mid-June. Unlike corn, rice is planted after the rains begin. The seed is dibbled into holes that are shallower and more closely spaced than for corn. The total planted reflects the amount of work time the farmer has available and the amount of time he expects to have during harvest. Planting is usually done in small work groups, or by a single farmer, so the rice in the field will mature a little bit at a time rather than all at once. A man will go and plant a quart or two of seed about 2:30 P.M. after planting corn in a large communal work group. Often he takes a young son along after school.

Broadleaf weeds are the major problem in rice farming, but in Aguacate few farmers take any countermeasures. In 1979 two farmers hand-weeded, and three others sprayed a 2,4-D-based herbicide. Those who weeded had about 30 percent higher yield, and similar improvements from weeding and spraying have been reported elsewhere (Seager 1983b:9). Where fallow cycles are shorter, weeds are a greater problem, and up to 80 percent of farmers use herbicides. In Aguacate the need for weeding is less clear-cut. Weeding is done with household labor, often in the late afternoon after other work is finished.

Other problems in rice production are rice blast, stem and stalk borers, and leafcutter ants (*Atta* sp). Mammals eat the young shoots, and both rats and birds are pests in the mature fields. In several fields I visited more than 30 percent of the rice heads had been damaged by birds. With the high cost of shotgun shells, the only measure that works is to harvest the rice as soon as it matures.

In larger fields a small thatched hut is built in late June or early July, as a shelter for storing and threshing the grain. A small labor group may be called for a single day to thatch the roof, but usually the house is built with household or household cluster labor. If two men have fields close by they often share a rice house, or a farmer may get by with a simple lean-to.

Farmers cut and thresh rice by hand in this most time-consuming part of rice production. It takes most of the farmer's time that can be spared from corn between September and November. Some of the larger communities get gasoline-powered threshing machines from the government, which farmers can use for a small fee. Only farmers with fields close to the village take advantage of this labor-saving device, because the extra labor of carrying heavy unthreshed stalks from the field is more time-consuming than hand-threshing when the fields are more than 30 minutes from the machine.

Because the timing of the rice harvest is both urgent and delicate, and because it conflicts with so many other tasks, it is hard to gather a group of any size for threshing. Men with large fields do not want to stop work to pay back days of labor they have borrowed. They do not want to get involved in any kind of labor-exchange group at this time of year because it decreases their flexibility. Sometimes a man can find others with ripening rice and put together a group of four or five. Large

Table 6.7. Man-Hours of Labor for Rice Production in Aguacate

Household	Field Size (in Ha)	Finding and Marking	Clearing	Planting	Building Rice House	Checking
8	0.836	9.0	72.0	136.0	43.0	18.0
31	0.350	4.5	27.0	32.0	—	9.0
9	0.836	4.5	90.0	144.0	80.0	13.5
18	0.836	9.0	117.0	136.0	—	18.0
19 (Fa)[a]	1.250	9.0	144.0	108.0	99.0	9.0
19 (Son)	0.836	—	144.0	120.0	—	18.0
17	0.420	9.0	45.0	80.0	—	9.0
16	0.420	18.0	36.0	32.0	—	18.0
23	0.627	9.0	99.0	88.0	49.5	9.0
11	0.836	4.5	72.0	56.0	49.5	18.0
Mean	0.725	13.1	113.5	129.3	36.5	21.4

[a] In the household numbered 19 both father and son plant rice; both men's labor is recorded here.

households or household clusters have a clear advantage because they can plan their rice harvesting in advance, so the household labor pool can deal with each field as it ripens and still send out a worker to harvest corn or begin clearing sak'ecwaj. Some of the larger rice producers, especially shopkeepers who have ready cash, now hire men to help harvest and thresh. These are the only tasks in Aguacate for which wage labor has become acceptable, although infrequent. In each case that I recorded the hired laborer, usually a young man who still lived in his father's house, had no rice field of his own and had no need for a return day of labor anyway. Wage labor is very attractive to these young men, for whom the other option is unpaid work for their fathers.

The market for labor within the village has grown gradually and unevenly, and has so far been confined to this very small sphere. It is mainly the result of increasing diversity in agricultural production strategies. Farmers no longer need the same kinds of labor at the same times of year, and their system of accounting prevents them from exchanging a day of cornfield clearing in February for a day of rice harvesting in October. Wage labor enters through this crack, and also by attracting the most marginal and exploited workers in the indigenous system—young unmarried men. However, once these young men get married they reenter the labor-exchange economy and give up wage labor. In more-northern communities some men are finding ways to

Weeding	Har-vesting	Threshing	Trans-porting	Marketing	Total for All Tasks	Total per Hectare for All Tasks
—	126.0	110.0	36.0	9.0	576.0	689
—	36.0	9.0	4.5	4.5	126.5	361
18.0	243.0	63.0	36.0	18.0	710.0	849
—	144.0	27.0	4.5	9.0	464.5	556
4.5	144.0	72.0	18.0	18.0	625.5	500
22.5	136.0	54.0	18.0	4.5	517.0	618
—	81.0	13.5	4.5	—	242.0	576
—	31.5	9.0	4.5	4.5	153.5	365
—	130.5	49.5	13.5	4.5	452.5	722
9.0	63.0	18.0	22.5	36.0	348.5	417
6.3	154.6	54.1	21.0	13.7	563.5	

combine wage labor with subsistence production, but in these cases the source of the wages lies outside the village.

The first step in threshing rice is to get sacks; this sounds like a minor task, but it usually entails a full day's trip to Punta Gorda or Big Falls to borrow them from the Marketing Board or buy them from merchants. In 1979 one man made three separate trips to Punta Gorda (costing more than $6 each) in order to secure sufficient sacks. One can imagine his frustration as the birds continued to eat his grain.

In the rice house a table is built from cohune-leaf ribs set sharp edge upward, with gaps in between. Two men often work together, one beating the rice heads on the table while the other sweeps up the grain, winnows it, and puts it in sacks. The sacks are carried to the roadside when time, and possibly a horse, is available.

Selling rice is a tense business for many Kekchi, especially those who are relatively new to the job, unused to dealing with government officials, and uncomfortable about feeling at the mercy of strangers. Often a man will make the long journey to Mafredi or Punta Gorda to charter a truck and then will wait in vain on the appointed day. Or the driver appears and demands a higher fee than originally agreed upon. Sometimes when the rice finally gets to the mill, there are long delays unloading and the driver demands more money. The rice may get drenched by an unexpected shower while waiting at the mill, and the

Table 6.8. Household Labor in Corn and Rice Production, 1979

House-hold	Wet-Season Corn Man-Hours	Dry-Season Corn Man-Hours	Total Corn Man-Hours	Rice Man-Hours	Total Man-Hours for Both Crops
19[a]	1,397.0	945.0	2,342.0	1,142.5	3,484.5
9	0.0[b]	355.0	355.0	710.0	1,065.0
18	1,376.5	423.0	1,799.5	464.5	2,264.5
23	1,037.0	710.0	1,747.0	452.5	2,199.5
11	935.0	445.0	1,380.0	348.5	1,728.5
17	1,066.0	932.0	1,998.0	242.0	2,240.0
15	1,874.5	650.0[c]	2,524.5	0.0	2,524.5
16[d]	709.5	587.0	1,296.5	153.5	1,450.0
13[d]	1,031.5	168.0	1,199.5	0.0	1,199.5
12[d]	823.5	312.0	1,135.5	0.0	1,135.5
7[d]	480.5	304.0	784.5	0.0	784.5

[a] Household 19 comprises a father and son. The man-hours given combine the labor of both men.

[b] The head of this household was sick and unable to work during the wet-season corn clearing. He made a large rice field to compensate and purchased corn with much of the income from the rice.

[c] Includes about 200 man-hours' assistance from a 14-year-old nephew who was visiting from another village.

[d] Households 7, 12, 13, and 16 are headed by young men who each live in a household cluster with his father. Three of these young men own shops. All other households listed here are clearly balancing corn and rice production within a set amount of available labor.

wet rice will be rejected and carried all the way home. The average cost of chartering a truck to the rice mill in 1979 was U.S. $30. This works out to about $1.25 per 100 kilograms (or about 6%-8% of the sale price of the rice).

The last stage of the process, the actual sale, has its own indignities. Most Aguacate farmers get the minimum price for their rice because of high moisture content. They distrust the moisture tester and point out that their grain has less foreign matter, fewer weed seeds, and fewer broken grains than mechanized rice, a fact that the government recognizes but does not reward. Finally, they are paid by check, after outstanding debts to the government are deducted. Few Aguacate men have debts, but in other villages land-lease payments, agrochemical costs, and seed-loan payments take a sizable chunk out of the check. And then the farmer has to pay a truck driver to take him to Punta Gorda to get the check cashed, sometimes by a shopkeeper who deducts money for a fee or outstanding debts. The whole sequence, from

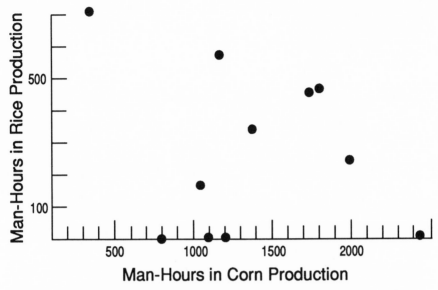

FIGURE 6.1   Cross-plot of Rice Labor and Corn Labor

sacking the rice to getting cash in hand, can take an Aguacate farmer a week and often leaves him feeling frustrated and powerless.

On Table 6.7 I have recorded total rice labor for 10 Aguacate farmers. Planting and harvesting a hectare of rice takes more time than a hectare of corn, but the other operations of clearing, checking, and weeding take about the same number of hours. Fields cut in high secondary forest average 635 man-hours per hectare, while those in low secondary forest take 495. The more land-intensive form of production is therefore less labor-intensive, showing again that labor, not land, limits rice production in Aguacate. Farmers agree, saying that if a man has a lot of labor available he will use high secondary forest for his rice field. Only when labor is short will he use low bush.

The crucial question in how much rice a household can grow is therefore the amount of labor it has available, how this labor can be scheduled, and how rice is balanced with the two corn crops. On Table 6.8 and Figure 6.1 the relationship between corn and rice labor for 11 households is shown. There is clearly a tendency to trade off between corn and rice in a single production cycle—labor spent on corn is deducted from rice labor expenditure and vice versa. The cross-plot shows a relatively straight line along which seven households fall ($r = -.901$ for the seven, $p < .01$), and a cluster of four households that fall well below the line, spending moderate amounts of labor on corn produc-

Table 6.9. *Rice Yields and Cash Value*

	House-hold	Field Size (in Ha)	Total Man-Hours	Total Harvest (in Kg)	Kilograms per Hectare	Kilograms per Man-Hour	Cash Value of Rice (in U.S. $)	Cash Return per Man-Hour (in U.S. $)
High	9	0.836	710.0	1,724.1	2,062.3	2.42	281.03	0.396
	8	0.836	576.0	1,270.1	1,519.3	2.21	207.03	0.359
Secondary	19	1.250	625.5	641.4	513.1	1.03	104.55	0.167
Forest	23	0.627	452.5	453.6	723.4	1.00	73.94	0.163
	11	0.836	348.5	722.1	863.8	2.07	117.70	0.338
Mean			537.0	962.3	1,136.4	1.75	156.85	0.285
Low	18	0.836	464.5	478.1	571.9	1.03	77.93	0.168
	19	0.836	517.0	366.1	437.9	0.71	59.67	0.115
Secondary	31	0.350	126.5	299.4	855.4	2.37	48.80	0.386
Forest	16	0.420	153.5	175.1	416.9	1.14	28.54	0.186
	17	0.420	242.0	136.0	323.8	0.56	22.17	0.092
Mean			300.7	290.9	521.2	1.16	47.42	0.189
Mean of All Fields				626.6	828.8	1.46	102.14	0.237

NOTE: Cash value and return in U.S. dollars is calculated on a base of U.S. 16.3 cents per kilogram.

tion and little or none on rice. All four are headed by young men who live in household clusters with their fathers and have sources of cash income other than rice: three own shops; one is a lay preacher; and one also tends, with his father, a large herd of pigs. Three of the men have only one child, so their households' corn consumption is low.

The other seven households, having no sources of income other than pigs and rice, divide a constant amount of yearly labor between rice and corn. Farmers choose different mixtures based on their corn requirements, their strategy for minimizing risk, their need for cash, and the availability of labor within their household and in the village at large. Below I will show that household composition and structure has important effects on all of the weights and balances in this complex choice. Households at different stages and in different social positions face a changing array of risks and opportunities that structure their agricultural strategies. The effects of household composition on agricultural production are therefore both subtler and more pervasive than the balancing of household labor supply and land use described by Chayanov (1966).

On Table 6.9 we see the yield of 10 rice fields, comparing high secondary forest with low secondary forest. Low forest fields give lower and more variable yields (coefficient of variation [CV] = 62% vs high forest field CV of 39%). Why use low secondary forest at all? Part of the reason is the growing shortage of high forest close to roads. In 15 years of rice farming most of the accessible places have been used, and today the remaining spots are more than half an hour from the road. Younger men and newcomers to the village find that the good spots are already claimed. If a gasoline-powered thresher is available, farmers are also encouraged to use low bush closer to the village in order to minimize the labor of carrying the unthreshed grain in from the field. Another part of the reason is that low forest requires less total labor commitment.

The yields I recorded in Aguacate are below those in northern villages where rice production is more central to the agricultural calendar. In Indian Creek almost every household has a hectare or more of rice, and large labor groups are used in most stages of production. Average yields are about 1,900 kilograms per hectare, more than twice the average in Aguacate (Seager 1983a:11). This may be due to greater use of herbicides and better crop care. Most important, Aguacate farmers did not harvest their rice at the optimum time because they were busy with other things, and they lost a lot to birds and wind. Aguacate farmers in 1979 produced about 2.5 kilograms of corn but only 1.5 kilograms of rice for each hour of labor. Corn can be sold to the Marketing Board

Table 6.10. Variability in Rice and Corn Yields by Fallow Status

	CV Rice Yield (in kg/man-hr)	CV Corn Yield (in kg/man-hr)
Primary Forest	—	12.6
High Secondary Forest	26.4	33.4
Low Secondary Forest	36.2	—

for about 14.5 cents per kilogram, and often merchants in town will pay more. So a man could sell his corn for a return of roughly U.S. $0.36 per work hour, rather than the $0.24 he gets for his rice. So why not just grow more corn and sell the surplus instead of growing rice?

There are a number of economic and cultural reasons why rice is preferred to corn. On Table 6.10 the CVs of yields for corn and rice in different fallow regimes suggest that in shorter-fallowed areas rice yield is less variable than corn yield. As high forest is harder to find, rice becomes a less risky alternative than corn. In other words, rice is a more reliable way to use the short-fallow land close to the village, especially if there is a gasoline-powered thresher available.

Rice can also be grown using land and labor that is not usable for corn. Wetter soils, many of them close to the highway, are used only for rice. And because rice can be planted after the rains begin, men can do productive work at a time when they would otherwise be idle. The marginal cost of their labor at this time is very low, although labor bottlenecks can become serious later in the season when the rice must be harvested.

Culturally, rice is attractive because it is unbound from many of the social obligations and cultural values placed on corn. As Guyer (1984) suggests, the introduction of new crops often allows the renegotiation of social relationships. Rice income belongs to the farmer, whether or not he is living with his father. Corn becomes the province and property of women after it is harvested, while rice stays in the male domain, and the man retains a strong claim on the money he gets for it. Rice may give a lower return to the household, but a much higher return to the individual farmer because he gets to keep more of it. This is an important lesson to agricultural economists, who tend to look at the household as an undifferentiated budget unit in drawing up cost-benefit analyses. The costs and benefits may not be shared evenly among household members (Moock 1986; Guyer 1981).

The Kekchi have historically partitioned their economy into an inward-oriented subsistence system and an outward-oriented system of wage labor and cash crop production. Corn is the mainstay of the diet, while rice is rarely eaten at home. Corn is stored in the field crib, and the surplus and spoilage is fed to pigs, which are both eaten at ceremonial occasions and sold for cash when it is needed. Stored corn and pigs are insurance against hunger, and both can be converted to cash to pay emergency expenses for medicine or to cover the costs of a wedding or a funeral.

To call the subsistence system a precapitalist mode of production is clearly an oversimplification that has little historical accuracy. It is a confusion of a folk taxonomy with an analytical one, for the Kekchi themselves are careful to divide what they consider the sacred realm of corn from modern and profane rice. They perform rituals in all stages of corn production, and they draw close links between the production of corn and those aspects of social organization (communal labor, the alcalde system) that they consider traditional. As Linares (1985) points out, crops have meaning, but these meanings are mutable. For the Kekchi, corn means tradition, subsistence, and stability, and they go out of their way to separate these meanings from the world of wealth, new religions, government intervention, and markets represented by rice. On Figure 6.2 the Kekchi emic classification is contrasted with an etic map of the various crops.

Historically the subsistence system has been quite mutable—recall that the Kekchi have been involved in lowland shifting cultivation for only 100 years, and that 50 years ago they kept cattle as well as pigs. Bananas, once the mainstay of cash crop production, are now a basic

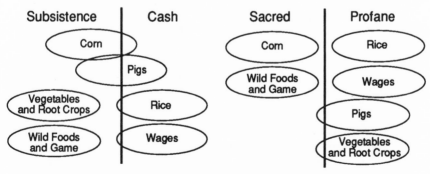

FIGURE 6.2   Analytic and Folk Taxonomies of Kekchi Production

part of the subsistence system. Yet the ideology and meaning of the crops is represented by the Kekchi as timeless. Corn and pigs are crucial today not because they are rooted in the past, and not because they are the subsistence base. They are important because they have been an effective means of moving back and forth between subsistence production and cash crop production without becoming committed to either one. Both corn and pigs can be eaten or sold, they circulate in the domestic economy, in the village gift economy, and the national cash economy. A farmer can never get stuck, overcommitted to one economy or the other, because pigs and corn are mutable. Rice lies outside the corn-pig conversion system. It is hard to store, is not fed to pigs, and does not circulate in the intravillage exchange system. The farmer has no choice of what to do with it. For this reason rice production is uncomplicated; classified as profane it has a place in the Kekchi scheme of things, but it can never take over the center.

THE CRUNCH AND THE RATCHET

The way the Kekchi think about their crops has adaptive significance and has contributed to their long-term independence and survival. Because some crops are sacred they are an effective buffer to the dangerous short-term economic rationality of the market. They reduce the impact of market cycles that drive many non-Indians further and further into proletarianization. In Belize these market cycles take a form I call the "crunch and ratchet."

The crunch is simply a collapse in a lucrative market for cash crops. It happens to farmers all over the world, and it happens frequently in Belize. A perfect example is the drop in sugarcane prices in northern Belize from 1978 to 1986. When prices were high in the 1960s northern Belizean farmers (most of whom were of Yucatec Maya descent) gave up most of their subsistence production and specialized in sugarcane to the exclusion of other crops. When the crunch came they had nothing to fall back on. Dependent on a social, financial, and technical system oriented toward cane, many were driven entirely out of farming when prices fell (ironically a number migrated to Mexico to work as cane cutters). The Kekchi do get caught in crunches; many were hurt when the banana boom ended in the 1930s, and others were financially ruined when the government (with U.S. funding) sprayed herbicide on marijuana fields in 1985 and 1986. But the Kekchi were not driven out of farming by these setbacks. They did not migrate, and they did not starve, because they were not overcommitted to any crop. The sacred nature of corn production and the weight of tradition kept them partially out of this trap.

The ratchet is the second punch in Belizean proletarianization. While the crunch changes systems of production, the ratchet raises standards of consumption. When farmers find a lucrative market for a crop and specialize in producing it, their incomes rise. A lot of that wealth goes into basic goods that raise peoples' standards of living—better housing, schooling, medical care, and wider varieties of foods from the store. When the crunch comes what were once luxuries have now become necessities; standards of living have ratcheted upward and will not go back down. Even if it is physically possible for the farmer to return to subsistence production, the products of his labor now have less value and he cannot satisfy his family's (and his own) needs any more.

The Kekchi are not immune to rising expectations, but they seem less susceptible than other rural Belizeans. I think part of the answer lies again in the sacred nature of corn. Store-bought foods may be tasty, fun, and nourishing, but they are not essential food. Without corn, eating is a snack, not a meal. The values associated with corn production and consumption (and with the consumption of a whole range of other homegrown foods and forest products) are a stable core that provide an alternative to the values of the marketplace. They are an anchor and can become a refuge. A Creole peasant caught in a crunch must return to poverty, but a Kekchi farmer caught in the same market crunch can return to tradition, a viable alternative set of values instead of just the negation of market values.

Seen in this light, tradition becomes a pervasive tool for survival that ensures its own reproduction in the context of peripheral capitalism. I do not mean to make a strictly functionalist assertion here. I do not think that corn is sacred to the Kekchi because it enables them to survive independently. Kekchi culture and values lead the Kekchi farmer to respond to fluctuations in the market differently than the rural Creole or mestizo. Whether it leads to greater exploitation is a more difficult issue. Like poverty, exploitation has both subjective and objective aspects. Whatever the objective measure, most Kekchi feel exploited only in their relations with outsiders and the cash economy, not with each other.

7   Domestic Animals, Hunting and Gathering

It is easy to focus too much attention on farming as the basis of Kekchi subsistence, dismissing game, fish, and wild plants as garnish or foods of minor importance.[1] But domestic animals, particularly pigs, are crucially important in the Kekchi economy, and wild foods are much more important than their frequency in meals would indicate.

DOMESTIC ANIMALS

The ownership of a horse or a mule is one of the few visible dividing lines between rich and poor in southern Belize. Draft animals are relatively expensive (U.S. $200–$300) because demand outstrips supply. They are fed about a kilogram of dried corn each day and are usually tethered to graze in the grassy commons in the village center. Children bring them back to the house at night, where they usually have some kind of shelter in an old pigpen or house. The hardest task is to keep them from straying into someone's corn or rice field. Damage to crops is the most common source of quarrels, witchcraft accusations, and court cases.

A draft animal makes rice and corn production more efficient, easing the labor of carrying grain. One in three Aguacate households owned a draft animal in 1979, although sharing animals within household clusters allowed about 60 percent of farmers steady access. Access to an animal is important in postmarital residence decisions. A single man in an independent household might not use a horse enough during the year to justify the cost; only one independent household in Aguacate owns a horse. Larger household clusters share both the costs and benefits, and achieve economies of scale; all but one of the household clusters in Aguacate have a draft animal.

While draft animals are owned by men, chickens and ducks are owned by women. A woman starts her own flock after marriage from chicks and ducklings given by her mother and mother-in-law. Whatever money a woman earns from selling animals or eggs belongs to her, one of the few ways she can get money that she alone controls. However, she must still get corn to feed fowl from the household granary, so she is not entirely independent. Many eggs and a few chickens end up being eaten at family meals instead of being sold. And the money a woman earns from her flock is often spent on her children rather than herself. Besides this, she must provide fowl for feasts (All Soul's Day, or the Cortés dance, for example), and for meals for smaller labor groups. Most men recognize that women are making a sacrifice and a contribution when they give up two or three birds on these occasions.

Feeding rates for fowl vary, with an average (based on four weeks of records) of about 80 grams of shelled corn per mature animal per day. Most of the time they are fed spoiled and damaged corn that is unfit for humans. The average Aguacate household has 18 chickens and six ducks. Ducks are not as highly valued for food, and they lay fewer eggs, but they are better at foraging for themselves. Geese, turkeys, and guinea fowl have not been successful in most of Toledo because of disease and predation. Parasites and disease are a periodic problem, and every few years cholera kills flocks in some part of the district.

There are no cattle in Kekchi villages today, but, according to censuses taken by the forestry service in the 1930s, cattle were once fairly common. As many as 30 animals were counted in southern zone settlements, and rusting barbed wire fences can still be found in the forest. Several development organizations have suggested that small-scale cattle production could be easily integrated with the existing Kekchi subsistence system (see, e.g., Romney 1959:124–138), and the Kekchi liaison officer established a communal herd at Crique Sarco in the 1950s (Nunes 1977). The village green could be expanded into a pasture, or animals could be grazed in abandoned cornfields, as in central Belize.

Why, then, do the Kekchi not raise cattle today? Part of the answer may be that the market in Toledo has already been filled by East Indians, who live much closer to Punta Gorda. It would be hard for a small producer to undercut these established ranchers. Another possibility is that cows represent too large an investment for the Kekchi. With all the health problems of cattle in the rain forest, and continued work to maintain pasture, the risk may seem too high. A man with twenty pigs can lose two or three and not suffer greatly, but a man with two cows stands to lose half his investment with a single death. Then, too, cows are highly mobile. Unless they are fenced in, they can devastate cornfields and cause discord in the village. In the 1930s there was enough cash around from banana production to allow farmers to buy barbed wire and fence in their animals. Today the price of wire is so high, and money is so tight, that even well-capitalized Texan ranchers have had trouble making a profit raising cattle in Toledo.

Pigs are the crucial bridge between subsistence production and the cash economy for the Kekchi. They live in thatched pigpens close to the house. Each morning they are let out to forage through village and forest, consuming human excrement, wild roots and plants, grass, and small animals (not to mention the odd piece of clothing or book of field notes). They keep down the undergrowth around the village, but they also spread hookworm, pollute water supplies, destroy wildlife, eat crops, and turn the trails into muddy wallows.

Each evening the pigs come back to the pen, where women and children shell corn and feed them. If corn is short the pigs can go three to five days without because they forage, but thereafter they lose weight, stray into cornfields, and may not come home at night. An average ration for a 25-kilogram pig is about 0.8 kilogram of corn per day. They eat mostly spoiled and weevil-infested corn, and smaller amounts of table scraps and peelings, cassava, plantains, and even cohune-palm heart. Many farmers have heard about commercial pig feed supplements, but they are not widely available and few are convinced that they make economic sense (several agronomists agree with them; see, e.g., Seager 1983d).

There have been a number of projects designed to improve swine production in Toledo by improving animal health, introducing better breeds, and encouraging stall feeding with improved feed. None have worked, including one I designed for USAID. Part of the problem is that development workers do not understand the place of pigs in the overall economy, including their storage and sanitation roles (Wilk 1981b). Another problem is that the Kekchi hogs are considered poor quality in the urban market and command a low price. Poor quality means that they are small and fat. This is exactly what the Kekchi prefer—the honored guest at a feast is always given a choice chunk of boiled fat, instead of insulting lean meat. Farmers do not try to raise the enormous pigs beloved of Western livestock science; they would rather have a larger herd of smaller animals (which also reduces the proportional loss of a single animal). Twenty-five kilograms is about the optimum size for slaughter for a feast, providing enough to feed everyone without an unstorable surplus.

Even if the Kekchi were willing to move into producing lean animals, there is still some question about whether it is an economical proposition to raise stall-fed animals in Toledo, given expensive feed supplements, the cost of stalls and medicine, transportation problems, and an uncertain market. Although local hogs do not grow quickly and have low meat yield for carcass weight, they are extremely hardy. They survive despite poor diets and medical neglect. About three-quarters of the Kekchi pigs slaughtered in the Punta Gorda market show major damage from disease or parasites. Swine cholera outbreaks occur every few years and can destroy whole village herds. A rough estimate is a loss of 15 percent annually to disease, predators, and accidents.

Records kept by two men on their swine over a total of three years show that most pigs are sold at 35–40 kilograms, live weight. At an average rate of feeding, pigs get to a salable weight of 24 kilograms in seven months, on 150–160 kilograms of corn. If the farmer sold 150 kilograms of corn directly to the Marketing Board (in 1979) he would realize U.S. $21.75, instead of the $13.35 he would get for his 24-kilogram pig. This may seem to support Romney's (1959:128) assertion that the Kekchi farmer is a "poor mathematician." But as Romney also points out, corn does not walk to market, while pigs do. As distance from the market increases, it makes more economic sense to produce commodities that weigh more per unit of value (Thunen 1966). Another thing that makes the apparent loss of turning corn into pork more rational is that much of the corn being fed to pigs is spoiled and unsalable anyway.

More than just converting corn and refuse into pork, pigs are also storage banks. Storage is a problem with many crops in humid Toledo, where postharvest losses can be up to 50 percent (USAID 1986). Surplus corn steadily declines in value when it is stored as cobs out in the field, while the same corn fed to pigs becomes portable and convertible into cash. Selling corn seems a risky business to the farmer: if he runs out he must pay very high prices to shopkeepers or other farmers to keep his family supplied with staple foods. As long as there is no reliable local market for inexpensive foods, farmers are reluctant to accumulate cash as a hedge against future food shortage. They follow the principle that once something has left the subsistence economy it never comes back. Once corn or rice or pigs are converted into cash, that cash should circulate in the world of goods, not in the village exchange economy. Just as you must give cooked pork and cocoa to your compadres at a baptism, so you must give cash to the truck driver who carries your family to town on market day. Using cash to produce subsistence goods violates these boundaries. Pigs lie on the border of the two economies and allow farmers to stay flexible and keep their options open.

Pigs are male property, although women and children do a great deal of daily care and feeding. Men ostensibly make all the major management decisions, but in practice wives are always consulted before any major action is taken, and women assert some (though variable) authority over the disposition of the pigs and the money from selling them. A man's first sow is a wedding gift from his father, and his godfather is expected to provide an animal or two as well. In practice a young man may not start his own herd for years after marriage, because as long as he resides in his or his wife's natal household, his pigs are raised jointly with his father's or father-in-law's. Years of negotiation between father and son often precede partition of the herd, and this bargaining is an important part of residence decision making.

Most men keep a single breeding sow at a time, because sows eat so much, and they try to sell animals over 45 kilograms for the same reason. More pigs are sold in May and June when stored corn is at a preharvest low (Belize Agriculture Department 1978). My Aguacate pig census was done only once, producing an average figure of 9.4 hogs per household in June 1979. I also took pig-rearing histories for nine household heads, covering the previous 16 months. The average household sold 9.5 hogs each year and ate 2.1. At an average sale weight of 31 kilograms, the sample households earned between U.S. $57 and $304 per year, with a mean of $179, higher than income from rice.

The number of pigs a household keeps is a complex product of local ecological and economic circumstances, and the household's labor supply, developmental cycle, and recent agricultural fortunes. For this reason there are no simple correlations of pig herd size with any single aspect of the household or its economy. There is no relationship between a household's consumer-to-worker (CW) ratio and the number of pigs it owns, except that households with very low and very high CW ratios tend to have few pigs. Because pigs are owned and managed to some extent by household clusters, we should expect membership in a household cluster to affect pig ownership. An independent household (neolocal outside a cluster) owns an average of 6.5 pigs, while a household that is part of a cluster averages 8.4 pigs. I suspect that clustered households have more pigs because there are some economies of scale operating—they can manage a larger number of animals by pooling labor.

The market system for pigs in Toledo is complex and changing. While most of the hogs in the northern and Moho River areas of the district are sold to the Punta Gorda market (and some go to Belize City), some animals raised in the south and west are sold across the border in Guatemala. In 1979 and 1980 the demand for Toledo hogs was high in Belize, prices were good, and about 5,000 pigs per year were sold in Belize. Only a few head, from the southernmost villages, went to Guatemalan buyers. Since that time Belize City buyers have changed their tastes and now buy from other districts where larger, leaner pigs are raised. The number of Toledo's hogs sold in Belize has dropped by more than half, and the number sold in Guatemala has gone up, while total production has declined.

Prices peaked in 1982 at U.S. $0.39 per pound and have declined slowly since then. So during a period of very high inflation the price paid to farmers has declined in real terms. Part of the problem is competition with cheap beef in the urban market, but a more serious factor is the low cost of imported pork products.

Because of European Community subsidies, a 12-ounce can of Danish pork lunch meat sold for U.S. $0.50 in 1983. Given an existing preference for imported goods in urban Belize, how can a Kekchi farmer compete?

PIGS IN THE LOCAL ECONOMY

Like other goods, pigs are exchanged within the village by a different set of rules from those that apply when pigs are sold outside. A man often gives a piglet as a gift to a close relative or compadre if it is wanted or needed, with an expectation of reciprocity in the indefinite future. A more distant relative or friend will usually make a small cash payment for a piglet or young pig, usually a third or a quarter of its market value. But full-grown pigs very rarely change hands between villagers, and if they do it is with the explicit knowledge that a pig of equal weight will be returned within a short time. If a man buys a full-grown pig, he pays close to the market rate. Through these means the village keeps people from exploiting its moral economy, buying pigs at the village discount price and then selling them in the market economy.

There is a general principle at work here, and also a lesson about the relationship between the subsistence economy and the cash economy. If there were no barriers between the two, it would be possible to subvert the subsistence economy for short-term profit. A man could borrow corn from his neighbor at a time of shortage and high price—a moral transaction that requires no interest and allows repayment at an indefinite time—and then sell the corn. He could later repay the corn at his next harvest when corn was plentiful and prices were low. The moral strictures about selling corn, the moral weight attached to corn, make such an action socially impossible and possibly punishable. Tradition and the moral codes it includes are a practical barrier that keeps the cash economy at bay, giving the community a common means of resisting the intrusion of capitalist amorality. Tradition is a common recognition that the rules of the community are different, and those rules ensure a degree of cooperation, forcing individuals to act outside their own short-term economic self-interest. The rules require community members to respond to a different set of economic incentives from those of the marketplace, although they still understand and recognize the rules of the market. Tradition is not ignorance, it is a purposeful strategy that recognizes the logic of capitalist production but encapsulates and seals that logic off in particular parts of life, with mixed success. In the Kekchi case the community labor economy and the household itself are the most protected parts of life, the areas wherein the morality of tradition is most thoroughly enforced, and from which capitalist logic is most completely excluded.

Pigs are killed at all important Kekchi rites of passage, from birth to death. When a new house is raised a pig is slaughtered and the blood is splashed on the corner posts before the head is buried beneath the new hearth. Pork is the sine qua non of hospitality. But there is no evidence that pig consumption is linked to a need for protein in times of stress (cf. Rappaport 1968). Instead the pig is the obvious candidate for ritual importance because it lies on so many important symbolic boundaries, between the subsistence and cash economies, between the world of the domestic and the wild, between the realm of food and that of waste or excrement. I did not study Kekchi cosmology in great detail, so these are really just guesses with some comparative ethnological basis. But there are still some important roles played by pigs in ecological relationships that are a bit like those discussed by Rappaport in *Pigs for the Ancestors.*

As village population increases, pigs become the cause, catalyst, and symbol of intravillage conflict. More than two-thirds of cases judged by the alcalde's court during my stay in Aguacate began with a complaint about a pig's destroying crops (or a person's destroying a pig because it was eating crops). Recent immigrants to a community, or those with tenuous social ties there, are more likely to lose these cases. Conflict provoked by animals probably helps drive these people out, keeping village population below the 80-household equilibrium level. This mechanism works only in the southern zone, where alternative village sites are available and where the regional population density is low in relation to the land base. In the southern zone the costs of moving out of a village are relatively low, and people are more likely to move when conflict erupts.

In the northern zone the option of moving away is not as attractive, and pigs play no part in regulating village size. Where people own land, or where roadside land has become especially valuable, they are less likely to pick up and leave because of fights with neighbors over pigs. In the northern zone few people have surplus corn to feed hogs anyway (a lot more of their effort goes into rice), and they have other sources of cash. Food is more easily purchased with cash, so pigs are not as necessary for storage. Instead of pigs regulating the human population, people end up regulating the pig population. In some villages, such as Indian Creek, people have agreed not to raise pigs at all. In Silver Creek the community decided to limit the number of pigs per household and build a fence around the village to keep them from straying out into fields. Several other communities have set strict limits on the number of pigs that can be kept by each household.

HUNTING AND GATHERING

Compared to the amount of research on hunting and gathering in South America, the record on Central America is very slim, and on Maya-speaking people close to nonexistent (Baer & Merrifield 1971; Pohl 1977). My data lack time depth and are based on small samples, but they show how hunting and gathering fit into larger cycles of production and consumption.

There is one wild nonfood plant that is of tremendous importance to the Kekchi and other Maya peoples. Copal (*pom*, or *uutsuj*; *Protium copal*) is the dried and hardened resin of a forest tree, burned on almost every ritual occasion, to carry prayers to the saints, the Tzuultak'a, and to God (other tree saps including rubber are also used). This practice goes back at least to the Maya Classic period. Today there is a good deal of trade in copal among Kekchi in Belize and with the cobaneros. The cobaneros buy as much copal as they can find, paying more than U.S. $2 per kilogram in 1979. Most of this comes from the southern zone villages where the trees are more common and where there are few other ways to earn cash.

The resin is harvested no more than twice a year from a single tree. Men cut up to 10 small patches of bark from the buttresses and trunk of the tree and scrape the gum from the patches with a wooden spatula three or four times in the next few weeks. About 20 grams are collected from each tree each time. A single trip may produce one kilogram, for a return of $2 for four to six hours of work. The most active collector in Otoxha gathered 25 kilograms a year, limited by the amount his trees would produce rather than by time. Most men get far less than this and may be content with only a kilogram or two for their own use.

Wild foods are an important supplement in the Kekchi diet, but they are essential to subsistence only in rare periods of crop failure and famine. They are an emergency warehouse and otherwise add variety to the diet. If the economy of the south is centered on subsistence agriculture with a second sphere of wild foods, in the north the same subsistence base is supplemented with a sphere of purchased foods. Several Indian Creek men pointed this out to me when complaining about the scarcity of game in the northern rice-producing areas, saying "in Otoxha we had *halau* (gibnut, or paca), *ac* (peccary), and *tiuk* (brocket) with our corn. Here we have sardine, sausage, and beef."

I mostly learned about wild foods when I saw people eating or gathering them, and never reached the end of the list. Because so many wild plants are seasonal or rare, it could take many years to compose a complete inventory, and if the hundreds of medicinal plants are included the job could take a lifetime (see Boster 1973; Roys 1931). I will concentrate on the more important plants and omit those used in basketry, house construction, and making tools, although the majority of Kekchi artifacts, the furnishings of daily life, are made from wild plants, representing a skill and knowledge that deserves study.

The most important snack foods are palm nuts of at least three species that are often eaten during breaks in agricultural work. Cohune nuts (*Orbignya cohune*) are the most important because they are also gathered in large numbers to make cooking oil. The clusters of nuts weigh up to 50 kilograms and when the kernels are cracked and the seed boiled, a clear and tasty oil floats to the surface. At one time it was burned in lamps.

Two other common snack foods are *pok*, the apical shoots of the young wild hogplum tree (*Spondias mombin*), and *tzuc*, the young leaf shoots of a palmlike succulent (*Chamaedora* spp.). Both plants are common in old swidden fields, an environment that also yields large amounts of *Heliconia* leaves (called *mox*) that are used for wrapping and cooking all kinds of foods. Every house keeps a fresh supply of mox on hand to be used as anything from diapers to disposable plates.

The most important wild foods are those used as meat substitutes. *Mococh* is the soft heart of that most versatile palm, the cohune. A single heart, obtained by chopping and splitting the tree, can yield

15 kilograms of food. They are usually cut in the cornfield, for the co-hunes near the village are conserved as a source of leaf for thatching roofs. *Cala'* is the soft base of the young leaf shoots of a palmlike cyclanth that grows in dense stands in abandoned cornfields for two or three years after harvest. While men gather mococh, women often go to fallow fields to gather the tender white shoots of cala', which can be eaten both raw and cooked. A woman can gather about four kilograms in an hour of light work. Also used as a stand-in for meat are a number of species of wild mushrooms, known generically as *ocox*.

Children eat many plants that adults ignore. I saw young children eating green cotton pods, the pulp of cornstalks, green wild guavas and hogplums, and innumerable stems and shoots of trees and shrubs. Men and older children are more selective in picking snack foods to eat while working in the forest.

I should stress the symbiosis between Kekchi agriculture and the gathering of wild foods. Most wild plant foods come from agricultural clearings, and ultimately this is where most domestic plants originated as well. As David Harris (1969) points out, the early stages of forest suc-cession are the natural habitat of many plants that have now been do-mesticated. Clearing a patch of tropical forest, even without planting anything, would be a profitable strategy for hunters and gatherers, since the clearing promotes the growth of many edible plants, as well as attracting animals that can be hunted (Linares 1976).

Wild meat is important in models of tropical forest subsistence de-veloped in South America by ecological anthropologists. Their work tends to concentrate on the most visible and measurable kinds of wild animals—mammals and fish. Influenced by these studies, I counted and weighed samples of fish and game brought in from formal and in-formal hunting trips. But I found I was missing many important foods. People, and particularly children, were always gathering up snails, small fish, crustaceans, amphibians, reptiles, small birds, and eggs that were often cooked and eaten on the spot. Small boys are voracious hunters of small game, using slingshots. Often people find these foods while occupied with something else and do not, unless prompted, re-member eating them.

Kekchi of all ages and both sexes fish. Children catch small fish in creeks and rivers with hook and line. Women sometimes use hook and line, but their favorite technique is to use a bottle as a minnow trap. Men most often use hook and line in the larger rivers, catching cichlids (*tuba*; *Cichlasoma* spp.) that weigh less than 0.5 kilogram, and the larger, bony *machaca* (*Brycon guatemalensis*) that get up to four kilograms. Smaller fish, turtles, crabs, eels, crayfish, and shrimp are taken in smaller creeks and streams with conical fish traps made from cohune-leaf ribs. A man usually gets a few children to help build and tend the trap, which is tied into place in a wooden dam.

The yearly peak in fishing is in June and July, when there is less farm work, but fish poisoning (which I was not able to observe) is a very seasonal method. Many people disapprove of it because it makes whole sections of the river sterile for several months. The leaves of cultivated fish poison (*Chalam*) are beaten into still, low water at the peak of the dry season. A number of families get together to gather the fish that rise to the surface. In some northern villages people use explosives instead of poison.

All twelve men who kept an annual record for me went fishing at least six times a year, not counting short trips to tend traps or short periods of fishing while on the way to do something else. The average was one five-hour fishing trip per month. In 35 fishing trips over six months, the maximum catch was five kilograms, and the minimum was less than 100 grams (though the fisherman came home with a 15-kg turtle instead). Based on several weighed samples, the average yield was 1.7 kilograms of edible fish per 4.5 hour fishing trip, or 0.378 kilogram per man-hour.

The fish population in Aguacate Creek provides a sustained yield of about 900 kilograms of fish per year, from four kilometers of stream, a total area of about a tenth of a square kilometer. This is far higher than the sustainable yield figures given by Gross (1975:528) for the Xingu River in Brazil.

Can fish yields be compared with the average yields of rice or corn for the same hour of work? Should corn yield be converted to a cash equivalent, which can then be totaled against the replacement value of fish (canned sardines)? I do not think so. Work is not uniform drudgery, and to some people sardines taste better than fresh fish. The Kekchi place values on different kinds of work: they would rather do two hours of thatching a roof than an hour of planting rice; they would rather work in a group in high forest than work alone in low bush; and they would much rather go fishing than do most kinds of agricultural work.

Does this mean that fishing should be counted as consumption (leisure) rather than production? No, the fish are eaten, and they provide real protein and calories that are important in the Kekchi diet. Fishing is clearly both production and consumption.

Seventy percent of households in Aguacate owned a gun in 1979, and frequently and at some length people talked about hunting. Nonetheless, game is not central to the Aguacate diet. This may be partially because the price of hunting equipment has recently gone up. Twenty-gauge shotguns rose from U.S. $35 in 1974 to $90 in 1979, and cartridges that cost less than $0.17 each in 1974 were $0.60 in 1979, and scarce at that price. At this cost it does not make sense to shoot small game, unless they are doing serious damage to crops.

Most men hunt in, or on the way to, agricultural fields. They carry guns on most expeditions to the bush and enter their fields as quietly as possible. Other hunting trips are usually taken on weekends. A group of men will sometimes take hunting dogs for an afternoon and early evening. Night hunting uses lights to startle and hold animals in place. Cacao groves and riverbanks are hunted on foot or by boat at night to catch halau. Younger men will take off for two to five days in primary forest far to the west or south of the village. This is much more common in the Mopan highland area where game close to the villages is totally depleted. While men usually hunt in groups of two to five, iguana hunting is a solitary job. Iguanas live in trees on the riverbank and are hunted in October and November when the females carry eggs.

Taste preference is important in hunting priorities. What some prefer, others shun. There is good evidence that preferences for different kinds of food are responsive to economic costs and opportunities, but they also seem to have symbolic values that cannot be reduced to costs and benefits (see the discussion in Ross [1980]). Pohl (1977, n.d.) reports that Yucatec Maya rank meat, setting much higher value on deer than on other wild game. The Kekchi, in comparison, are gourmands rather than gourmets. Most divide animals into edible and inedible and let it go at that. But their inedible category includes animals that other people eat, such as opossum (*uch*; *Didelphis* spp.) and the scaly-tailed iguana (*Ctenosaura similis*). Other inedibles include skunks, rats, anteaters, the weasellike teyra (Kekchi *sacol*; *Eira barbada*), and wildcats. The tapir (*tix*; *Tapirus bairdii*) is the only animal that seems ambiguous, eaten by some Kekchi and avoided by others.

Because pigs are rarely slaughtered, game is the steadiest source of meat in southern zone villages. There is an internal market for game meat within each community. Prices vary from U.S. $0.25 for a quarter of an armadillo to $1 for a quarter of a peccary. Men who live in a household cluster divide their kill with the other cluster members, which usually leaves nothing to sell. This assures those who live in clusters of a steadier supply of meat without having to pay for it; only 12 percent of the men living in household clusters bought game meat

Table 7.1. Hunting Success of Five Aguacate Men, 1979

| | Number of Animals Killed | | | |
	Field Hunting	Night Hunting	Day Hunting	Total
Gibnut	3	4	7	14
Peccary	10	0	0	10
Iguana	2	0	3	5
Brocket	2	1	0	3
Coatimundi	2	0	1	3
Tinamou	1	0	1	2
Armadillo	0	0	1	1
Guan	1	0	0	1
Parrot	1	0	0	1
Total	22	5	13	40

during a one-year period, compared to 82 percent of independent households. The heads of independent households, who are not obligated to give away part of their catch, tend to be more-active hunters than household cluster members. Their incentive to hunt is higher because they can offset some of their cash costs by selling part of the game. This may lead to a pattern like that reported by Pohl (1977, n.d.) in northern Belize, where some young men have become part-time specialists in hunting for cash. This income is socially disembedded in the same way as money from selling rice. Men who live in household clusters do not take this path because for them game remains a part of the economy of reciprocity (even though they must buy a gun and shells in the cash marketplace).

Specific hunting trips averaged 3.6 hours (less than one complete trip) per month in Aguacate. This figure is too low for a variety of reasons, but the average cannot be much more than a single hunting trip a month throughout the year. Some idea of the return from hunting is given in Table 7.1, based on records kept by five men during six to eight months in 1979 (a total of 36 months' record). The success rate seems about half that reported by Pohl (n.d.:7) in northern Belize. The five men caught about 265 kilograms of meat, 69 percent of which required no extra labor because it was killed during trips to agricultural fields. The return from night and day trips was 83 kilograms for about 80 hours of hunting, or about one kilogram per hour, divided by an average of just under two hunters per party for a per hunter yield of 0.49 kilogram per man-hour. This is well above the yield of fishing, and above the hunting yield of typical South American horticulturalists. The Bari, for example, get 0.164 kilogram per man-hour (Beckerman 1979).

But what is the point of comparing these figures? Is an hour of hunting equal to an hour of fishing? Is the social benefit of hunting, including the ability to give meat to people, the same as the social benefit of fishing for which there is usually no surplus to exchange? Hunting is both more and less than a matter of survival to the Kekchi. More because for some men it is a form of recreation and sociability, and less because most do not need the meat in order to survive. Aggregate or average cost-benefit figures for a whole community engaged in hunting or fishing or farming are meaningless; it is the differences between individuals and households that are important. When deciding whether or not to hunt, a Kekchi man does not compare his expectation of return with the average for the village. He thinks about his own costs and his own benefits, his obligations and his commitments to other people, and the needs of his family. Unless we are willing to look at psychology, at why one individual likes to kill mammals and another would rather trap fish, the best way to explain different individual goals is to look at the social and economic matrix of the household.

I do not have the detailed data that would allow me to compare the hunting-fishing-gathering strategies of different households. I did observe that the pace of these activities varies in different kinds of households. Young men in independent households tend to be the most active hunters if they have the cash to buy a gun. They are under the most pressure to make their hunting a paying proposition because their households tend to be cash-poor. They have to justify the cost to their wives by hunting frequently and selling part of their catch. If these young men cannot buy a gun they try to borrow one or train dogs (or both) so they can participate in hunting groups. Women in these independent households do the least fishing and gathering because they usually have infants to take care of on their own.

Older men living in independent households tend to be the most intensive fishermen in the community, using most of the fish traps. Their major goal is not cash but low-cost food with little work. Women in these households also do more fishing and gathering.

The oldest man in a household cluster almost always owns a shotgun, which may have been bought with pooled funds. There is much more sharing of both the costs and benefits of hunting and fishing in household clusters, and this seems to lower the incentive for younger men to hunt. At the same time, access to a steady supply of meat, and access to a shotgun when needed, are incentives to keep young couples attached to the household cluster. Cooperation between women in household clusters tends to free them more often for fishing and gathering expeditions.

There seems to be a steady decline in the importance of hunting, fishing, and gathering in Kekchi villages as they become more involved in cash crop production. Part of this decline is due to overexploitation of the resources. But another part is driven by demand: people replace wild foods with things they buy in stores with cash, and there is a positive allure to a can of corned beef that is not matched by the taste of armadillo. Some Kekchi, especially in the northern zone, are also becoming aware that some wild foods carry a stigma among other Belizeans, that eating such things as river minnows and palm heart brands them as "bushy" in the eyes of schoolteachers, government officials, and foreign preachers. Eventually, of course, hunted and gathered foods become status symbols for the elite gourmet. Once venison has ceased to be the staple food of the rural poor, it can be appropriated as a part of an elite cuisine. Game meat always carries these double connotations of both the top and the bottom of the social scale.

Wild foods are also time-consuming to obtain. In villages where cash crops are important, men are learning to value their labor in a way that may make it seem more economical to purchase goods in shops. As game becomes more difficult to find because of depletion, and success rates go down, the certainty of a can of Spam is liable to be attractive. This opens the way for hunting to become either a specialized economic pursuit, or a recreation.

In the southern villages, in the meantime, hunting and gathering remain a part of the subsistence system, an important supplement to domestic plants and animals, and a means of actualizing social relationships for cooperative hunting and the sharing of produce. But this should not be seen as a part of a traditional subsistence system with any historical continuity. In the homeland of the Alta Verapaz there are no thick tropical forests, no winding rivers dense with overhanging greenery, no jaguars or tapirs or shotguns to hunt them with. Traditional Kekchi hunting is reflected in an old wooden blowgun, kept as a relic and curiosity by an old man in Crique Sarco. Once used for hunting birds in the highlands, it has now become an icon.

8 Economic Change

By this point I have cast doubt on the utility of seeing the Kekchi as moving from some precapitalist mode of production into capitalism or peasantry. Do they fit better into other typologies? Janvry (1981 : 109 – 23) has given us perhaps the most careful analysis of the diverse forms that capitalist and noncapitalist agriculture takes in Latin America. But again we find an evolutionary scheme from the primitive community through semifeudal to capitalist modes of production, and in each mode a series of classes with characteristic farm types. Subsistence farms in corporate communities, which includes Indians, is only a subcategory, a special case of what he calls external subfamily farms within the capitalist mode of production. Nevertheless, Janvry's basic description of the subfamily, semiproletarian family farm fits many rural Belizean households quite well. "These farms cannot insure the needs for maintenance and reproduction of the whole family. And neither can wage levels permit full proletarianization. As a result, peasant households on these farms must rely on both farm production and external sources of income (wage labor, trade, crafts, etc.), a dependence that gives them the status of semiproletarians. These external subsistence peasants constitute the reserve of cheap labor for capitalist enterprises." (Janvry 1981 : 113).

Most Indians in Latin America combine subsistence production with commodity production and wage labor simply because they cannot survive with any measure of security through any single form of production (see Painter 1984). The Kekchi are different because they can get an adequate cash income from simple commodity production, and they are not forced into wage labor or the alternatives through an inability to provide for themselves. The underlying reason for both these differences is land. In Belize the Kekchi have enough land to grow both cash crops and foods for domestic consumption. This makes them a very poor reserve of cheap workers; they have the option of withhold-

ing their labor from the marketplace. It also means that they participate in the capitalist market out of choice. Most peasants in Latin
America, Indian or mestizo, would look enviously upon the Kekchi.

This is not to say that the Kekchi are not exploited. While their
subsistence production does not directly subsidize low wage rates, as
suggested by Meillassoux (1981), most of the cash they earn is spent on
manufactured goods, imported foods, and services provided outside
their communities (cf. Painter 1984:272). Subsistence production
means that very little cash circulates in the village, and little of it stays
there. Subsistence production also subsidizes the price of rice and
beans in the national marketplace. If the Kekchi were full-time specialists in rice production they would have to get a higher price or
heavy subsidies. But compared to exploited peoples elsewhere in Latin
America, the Belizean Kekchi are in a good position. Wage rates for un-
skilled agricultural work are at least five times higher than in Guatemala, and even though the price of rice seems low to the Kekchi, it is
well above the world market price and is therefore a form of subsidy.
The difference in the degree of exploitation is mainly due to the abundance of land, the independence provided by a secure nonmonetarized
subsistence system, and low levels of demand for consumer goods and
services that must be bought with cash.

Social stratification and inequality in wealth is another common
effect of population pressure on land resources combined with commodity production (see Gudeman 1978; Barlett 1982; Netting 1987).
Unequal access to credit and technology and unequal household labor
resources have also been blamed, in different settings, for increased
stratification in rural communities (Stone, Stone & Netting 1984;
Greenhalgh 1985; Netting 1981). The Kekchi area is an especially interesting case in this regard because communal land tenure eliminates
landownership (though not population pressure) as a cause of inequality. Nevertheless there is social differentiation in Kekchi communities.

Because the availability of land is the most important factor underlying the Kekchi's position in relation to the marketplace and the world
economy, predicting the future means looking at population growth:
how will Kekchi production change in response to increased population pressure on the land? My main comparison is therefore between
Kekchi villages that have abundant land and those that have not. In
pursuing this comparison I have included data from my own fieldwork
in Santa Theresa, Aguacate, and Indian Creek, supplemented by material collected by Schackt (1986) in Crique Sarco in 1980 and by Berte
(1983) in San Miguel the same year. San Miguel and Crique Sarco do

more cash crop production than Aguacate, and Santa Theresa does less. Crique Sarco and Santa Theresa have more good land per person than Aguacate, while Indian Creek and San Miguel have less. San Miguel and Indian Creek are in the northern zone along major roads and produce a good deal of rice.

I realize that there are pitfalls and problems with inferring change from synchronic controlled comparisons. To say that Aguacate will look like Indian Creek in another decade is to replicate, in miniature, the fallacies of development theories that compare modern Brazil with nineteenth-century North America. There is a great deal of diversity between villages in Toledo that cannot be reduced to a simple linear developmental model. Each place has unique cultural and histori- cal circumstances. Nevertheless, the comparison of different Kekchi villages is illuminating because it shows some of the systemic rela- tionships among agriculture, population density, markets, and social organization.

The historical data presented in Chapter 5 provide the best key to understanding how these relationships have changed in the past and are likely to change in the future. I would rather have historical records from a single village, so I could gauge changes in individual household organization, agricultural strategies, and demography over time (cf. Ka- shiwazaki 1983; Johnsons 1988). Historical data on economy and social organization, however, are rarely detailed enough for a fine-grained eco- logical and economic analysis. And among nonliterate mobile people such as the Kekchi, we usually have to be content with short-term data that are time-consuming to gather.

I have already mentioned that the Kekchi productive economy is at least partially shaped by demand. Production is so closely tied to con- sumption that we cannot understand one without the other. The major trend in consumption has been the growth in desire for a variety of goods that must be bought with cash (for further details see Wilk 1983, 1988, 1989). The minimum—salt, cloth, machetes, axes, and files—can be bought easily by a southern zone villager with the proceeds from selling pigs, copal, and sometimes beans or corn. But lamps, kerosene, rum, perfume, shotguns, cartridges, watches, white sugar, flour, car- bonated drinks, and a whole spectrum of other goods are harder to ob- tain and more expensive in remote villages, and people rarely have enough cash to buy them. In the southern zone people still substitute labor-intensive domestic products for imports—homemade sugar or honey, cohune oil in lamps, corn beer, woven hammocks. Living in the southern zone means accepting a lower level of consumption, while for many people in the north expectations are rising and new tastes are developing.

Economic anthropology has traditionally focused its attention on how primitive societies constrain consumption through channeling desires into status goods that move in restricted spheres of exchange (see, e.g., Bohannon & Bohannon 1968), through leveling devices such as Foster's (1965) "image of limited good," or through reciprocity that makes accumulation impossible (Sahlins 1972). According to these ideas, when social constraints on consumption break down as a result of acculturation or other economic pressures people are subject to the seduction of the marketplace (Murphy & Steward 1956). Acculturating peoples may be emulating admired foreigners (Stout 1947), or they may be victims of advertising (Ewen 1976; Barnet & Muller 1974) and cultural imperialism (Desieux 1981; Preiswerk 1981).

Materialist cultural ecologists such as Gross and his colleagues, however, argue that desires for imported foods and consumer goods are actually adaptive responses to population pressure, allowing farmers to concentrate on specialized production. And even luxury products are said to have their utilitarian roles: "Relatively few 'luxury' items are purchased by any of the [South American Indian] groups but, where they are, they may be a way of conserving capital because such items as radios, wristwatches and handguns hold their value better than cash, especially in an economy like Brazil's with chronic inflation (Gross et al. 1979:1048–49). Anyone who has watched a wristwatch decay in a tropical rain forest would think twice about buying one as an investment, and there may be more-practical functions for a handgun in the backwoods of the Amazon than fighting inflation. This kind of materialism ignores the political and economic realities of exploitation and manipulation.

What is the adaptive value of selling rice to buy Coca-Cola? Are the South American Indians, and the Kekchi, not being exploited by unequal exchanges in which they sell their labor and produce at low prices in order to buy the goods they want, that they now need, at a high cost? How is this really for their own good and how can it be adaptive? What is needed is a more complete theory of demand and desire, a goal that anthropology is slowly working toward.[1] Douglas and Isherwood (1979) have proposed a more encompassing model of consumption that sees goods as inherently symbolic and social. This breaks down the artificial barrier between the constrained consumption of primitive societies and the consumer culture of the modern West, which Bourdieu (1984) shows to be highly constrained and patterned in its own way (see also Ferguson 1988). Douglas and Isherwood show that the symbolic and the utilitarian are entangled whenever new goods are adopted—the very concept of economic utility is premised on a set of preferences and values that are cultural and therefore partially symbolic. New goods acquire new symbolic values that are used in economic and political competition, and they become tools in contests over reshaping society (Cohen 1981; Wilk 1988).

NEW ROLES, NEW FOODS

In most studies of agricultural change, systems of production are measured against a constant "consumption standard." We figure out how much corn or rice, clothing, tools, and utensils a family needs each year, and look at how much productive work is required to meet those needs (Gudeman [1978] calls what is left over a surplus). But those needs that constitute the standard of living are culturally and socially defined and they change all the time. In the Kekchi case the social definition of needs is in flux, and different standards exist within each community. People are actively negotiating and discussing the values of goods, and there is political and social conflict over changing standards and values. The conflicts have public (community) and private (household and individual) dimensions that are best exemplified by two sorts of goods: food and housing.

Given the dispersed nature of Kekchi agriculture and the lack of task specialization, it was difficult to measure the quantities of many minor crops and wild foodstuffs that were produced. But people in the village were very self-conscious about food in front of me, and I could not measure food on its way to people's mouths. Nor could I follow people around to catch them snacking or eating out in their fields. Instead I paid five men to keep daily records, in small notebooks, of everything they ate for two to four weeks at a time, and checked their records every five days. The data come from the months of September through December, a time when corn and game are abundant, but when plantains, beans, and root crops are scarce. At this time of year there are no large communal work groups, so few pigs are slaughtered and pork is rarely eaten. As a representation of a generalized Kekchi diet it may be poor, ignoring women and children as well as seasonal variation, but for my limited comparative purposes it is adequate.

Most Kekchi eat three meals a day. Women rise between 4:00 and

5 : 00 A.M. to begin grinding corn for tortillas, the main element of the morning meal. Coffee with sugar and small portions of leftover meat or vegetables from the previous evening are also common.

The midday meal is light, and men often carry it to the fields wrapped in a leaf. Tortillas and ground chile fried with salt are the basis, with breakfast leftovers for women, and wild foods from the bush for working men and children. The evening meal, taken betwen 4 : 00 and 6 : 00 P.M. is the major meal of the day though it is not a formal family event. Men sit in the living area of the house, and their wives bring them (and guests) tortillas in a gourd, bowls of caldo, and calabashes of coffee, cocoa, or corn porridge. Women eat separately in the kitchen while children circulate back and forth.

Corn dumplings (*poch*) and tortillas (*cua*) are the essence of any meal. The verb *to eat* (*cua'ac*) is the active form of the word for tortilla, and eating a meal without corn is usually called snacking (*k'uxuc*). In the northern zone this ideal is changing, as wheat tortillas, bread, and rice are being accepted as starchy staples in the same category as corn (if not completely equal). Dumplings and tortillas are usually accompanied by a thin stew (caldo, or *xya'al tib*). The stew usually contains chile and achiote, and may also have onion, garlic (imported), and several common local herbs. Chicken, pork, and fish are boiled fresh, while game is often roasted and smoked first.

The results of my small survey are best shown as the number of days a particular food appeared in any meal (see Table 8.1). Counting a food by meals instead of days is deceptive because people eat small quantities of meat or fish at a succession of meals until the supply is gone. A single small catfish might go into caldo in the evening, and some pieces will be eaten with breakfast, lunch, and dinner the following day. For each meal a family member will say, "I ate fish." Very rare items may, however, be overrepresented by my method of tabulation. I have included on Table 8.1 Berte's (1983 : 169–70) data from San Miguel, which included 42 households for a week each from August to October 1980. Although the season is comparable, her figures are percentages per meal rather than per day, so they may overrepresent the amount of meat, eggs, and fish in the diet.

What comes through most clearly from the table is the degree to which the diet is composed, for most people, of a single starchy staple and a variety of minor supplements. Corn and chile are the commonest foods eaten by all groups. The average Aguacate respondent ate 12.8 tortillas a day, which works out to almost 950 grams. This is more than the 635 grams reported by William Carter (1969 : 137) or the 771 grams given by Cowgill (1962:277), but my sample comprises only working-age men. A separate dietary survey of women found that they ate about 635 grams of corn tortillas a day. These rations provide, from corn alone, about 3,500 kilocalories of food energy per day and 110 grams of protein for men, and 2,300 kilocalories and 70 grams of protein for women (Wu Leung & Flores 1961:14–17). Thus the one staple, in ordinary times, covers basic energy needs.

Beans are not common in the Aguacate or San Miguel surveys. In Aguacate almost all the beans eaten were bought in shops, since the local bean harvest was not yet in. Even at their peak beans do not come close to being a staple food. When we add these purchased beans to all the other items from shops, we find that purchased foods appear on the menu during 69.4 percent of the days reported for all five men. Does this mean that the subsistence economy has already been completely invaded by market goods? Should we expect to see progressive replacement of grown foods with purchased ones?

If we break down the sample of five men into two groups, the issue of dietary change becomes clearer. Two of the five men sampled were shop owners. Both made small wet-season milpas and grew a few vegetables and fruits, but most of their energy went into rice. They also spent three or four days each month buying and transporting goods for their shops, and many afternoons tending their stores instead of working in their fields. They do not depend on their farming for their whole livelihood. Instead they have partially withdrawn from the village labor-exchange economy because their farming is constrained by a lack of time at crucial phases of the productive cycle. (They are the only men in the village who make a regular practice of hiring farm labor).[2]

The shop owners ate most of the purchased foods (79.2%) in the survey, and ate less wild foods and game. They get some food from relatives, but otherwise they substitute canned meat, eggs, chicken, beef, and beans. There are only three shopkeeping households in the village, while there are 27 units headed by full-time farmers. The whole village is not gradually changing from a subsistence diet to one based partially on purchased foods (the model considered by Dewey [1983]). Instead the transition is profoundly unequal. A small minority in the village depends daily on purchased food from within the village and from as far away as Brazil and Taiwan.

We should not expect a smooth gradient from south to north, with the south providing its own subsistence needs and the north mixing in larger proportions of purchased foods. Although northern zone San Miguel farmers have a higher cash incomes, they do not consume a great

Table 8.1. *Food Consumption in Aguacate and San Miguel*

| | Aguacate | | | | | | San Miguel |
| | Three Farmers[a] | | Two Shopkeepers[b] | | All Men[c] | | |
	Number of Days	Percentage	Number of Days	Percentage	Number of Days	Percentage	Percentage
Domestic Products							
Corn tortillas	57	100.0	52	96.5	109	98.2	92.1
Rice	7	5.2	28	51.9	31	27.9	6.4
Plantain	0	0.0	5	9.3	5	4.5	1.9
Root crops	3	5.3	0	0.0	3	2.7	1.9
Corn dumplings	4	7.0	1	1.8	5	4.5	2.8
Corn porridge	5	8.8	0	0.0	5	4.5	0.0[d]
Vegetables	5	8.8	0	0.0	5	4.5	7.8
Fruits	10	17.5	0	0.0	10	9.0	5.5
Chile	29	50.9	33	61.1	62	55.9	90.0[e]
Chicken	6	10.5	13	24.1	19	17.1	13.7
Eggs	8	14.0	11	20.4	19	17.7	7.7
Pork	5	8.8	0	0.0	5	4.5	6.1
Total domestic animal products	19		24		43		
Wild Foods							
Fish	8	14.0	1	1.9	9	8.1	7.6
Gibnut	7	12.3	7	12.9	14	12.6	2.2

Peccary	9	15.8	0	0.0	9	8.1	0.8
Iguana	2	3.5	0	0.0	2	1.8	0.0
River snails	2	3.5	0	0.0	2	1.8	0.0
Cohune nuts	4	7.0	0	0.0	4	3.6	0.0
Armadillo	0	0.0	0	0.0	0	0.0	2.4
Cala'	4	7.0	0	0.0	4	3.6	0.0
Cohune-palm heart	6	10.5	0	0.0	6	5.4	10.5
Total	42		8		50		
Purchased Foods							
Flour tortillas	7	12.3	30	55.5	37	33.3	6.5
Wheat bread	3	8.8	2	3.7	7	6.3	0.8
Red kidney beans	5	5.3	12	22.2	15	13.5	4.7
Beef	0	0.0	2	3.7	2	1.8	1.4
Bottled soft drinks	0	0.0	1	1.8	1	0.9	1.4
Canned lunch meat	0	0.0	5	9.3	5	4.5	2.0
Kool-Aid drink mix	0	0.0	3	5.6	3	2.7	?
Packaged biscuits	1	1.7	2	3.7	3	2.7	0.8
Hard candy	0	0.0	4	7.4	4	3.6	1.4
Total	16		61		77		

SOURCES: My figures are used for Aguacate. Data for San Miguel are from Berte (1983).

NOTES: [a] The three farmers reported a total of 57 days.

[b] The two shopkeepers reported a total of 54 days.

[c] For all men, the number of recorded days is 111.

[d] Porridge is included with corn dumplings.

[e] Berte includes chile used as a spice in caldo. My Aguacate data refer only to fried chiles eaten with tortillas.

deal more purchased food, and they do not eat more rice (Berte 1983 : 167).
The major difference between Aguacate and San Miguel is that San Miguel families more frequently substitute canned meat (especially sardines) for wild meat, and they use fewer wild vegetable foods. Some
families that run out of corn substitute store-bought flour and rice for a
short period during the year.

The same patterns are found in Indian Creek, where a minority of
families eat most of the imported and purchased foods, and the majority
still depend on their own produce. Inequality is the essence of transition
from subsistence production to purchased foods. A few households that
have the necessary human resources and capital have stepped into entrepreneurial roles, changed their farming methods, and commodified
their relations with other households. They no longer reciprocate labor
with labor. They do not benefit directly from the flow of goods out of
the village, since the farmers deal directly with the government or with
wholesalers, but they do profit from selling manufactured and imported goods to their fellow villagers. In the beginning this could be
seen as task specialization, but shortly we see real differences in wealth
and consumption.

INCOME, CONFORMITY, AND INEQUALITY

In 1979, 31 Aguacate households had incomes ranging from U.S. $28 to
$357 with an average of $249.[3] A sample of 10 Indian Creek households
had 1979 incomes from $103 to $967 with a mean of $485 (including
some wage labor).[4] Annual income in remoter villages such as Santa
Theresa is close to $125.

While households may vary in their relative wealth and status within
each community, the uniformity of housing expresses an ideology of
equality. Conformity to community housing standards is a visible expression of willingness to conform to other norms and ethics, including sharing land, participating in communal labor groups, and accepting the alcalde as the legitimate judge of conflicts (see Wilk 1983). In the
northern villages new consumption patterns have emerged. Most cash
is channeled into vehicles, consumer durables (e.g., radios, televisions),
housing, and furnishings. While in the southern villages all houses are
virtually identical in materials and style, in the north there is a diversity of housing.

In Aguacate money left over after buying basic foodstuffs, clothing,
and tools is spent mostly on personal consumer goods, items that belong to an individual rather than the household. About the only com-

mon consumer good that is household rather than individual property is a radio or tape player.[5] In 10 Aguacate households with mean expenditures of $242, $130 went to taxes, tools, white lime, basic foods, kitchen equipment, and clothing; $14 went for expenses related to children's schooling; and the remainder went to a wide variety of consumer goods including cosmetics, luxury foods, toys, alcohol, cigarettes, personal items such as hats and running shoes, and a few major items such as musical instruments, bicycles, shotguns, and radios. No expenditures related to housing were recorded except for $7 spent on a small kitchen table used for making tortillas, and a few dollars on nails for building a household altar.

Indian Creek is not the richest community in the northern zone, but cash income is more than double that of Aguacate. In the northern zone a significant number of villagers have wage income, and a few get remittances from relatives working outside the community. A disproportionate amount of cash goes to men rather than women (cf. Linares 1985; Nash 1983). While in the remoter communities men and women share income from sale of pigs, and women have their own sources of cash, in the northern villages women's economic power has declined relative to men's (Gregory 1987).

Some of this cash is spent on personal consumer goods and on consumables, but most is invested in houses and furnishings. This investment begins by substituting purchased construction materials for gathered ones, within the context of the traditional Kekchi house. The next step is to a non-Kekchi style of house, often a simple two- or three-room wooden house with an iron roof, common among all the ethnic groups of rural Belize and costing about U.S. $900. In 1979 in Indian Creek there were two of these "Creole" houses, one occupied by a Mopan Maya schoolteacher and the other by a Kekchi preacher. In 1985 there were five, and more were under construction. The very wealthiest Kekchi, people with salaried jobs or income from marijuana, hire masons to build concrete-block houses in a style common in the well-to-do northern parts of Belize. Striking contrasts can now be found in the richest villages, where three-story concrete-block houses with two-car garages, balconies, and electricity sit next to old thatch houses still used as pigpens or occupied by poorer relatives.

The rise in income above U.S. $300 per year, then, has led to a change in the kinds of goods purchased. This change is not really a shift from necessities to luxuries. Rather, a large percentage of income has always been expended on luxuries and consumer products, but they have been personal luxuries—liquor, clothes, jewelry, and the like. When income rises above a certain threshold cash is reallocated to household luxuries and consumer goods—items that belong to the household as a corporate group rather than to individual members. This increase in income could be allocated directly to such individual luxuries and consumables as motorcycles, extravagant clothing, jewelry, cosmetics, and foods, but it usually is not.

Besides spending money on houses, northern villagers spend on medical care and educating their children. High school in Belize is costly, and several Indian Creek households spend more than half their income on tuition, board, clothing, and books. Investment in children is similar to spending on houses and furnishings, in that those who earn the money do not spend it on themselves.

Altered housing styles and the reallocation that accompanies greater participation in the cash economy is not a shift from spending on necessities to spending on consumer goods. Housing and education replace personal adornment and personal consumption; investment in household property replaces spending on individual property. The new pattern of investing (including now the lease-purchase of private land in some areas) has important long-term social and economic consequences (to be discussed in Chapter 10); not the least of which is that inequality, concealed and almost invisible in southern communities, has become more obtrusive in the north (Wilk 1984). The same pattern can be found in Kekchi political life.

Political institutions in most Kekchi villages are a truncated form of the civil-religious hierarchies known from elsewhere in Mesoamerica (see Schackt 1986). The civil offices are the alcalde, a second alcalde, and from three to eight ranked village policemen. The alcaldes are paid by the government and are assisted by a relatively permanent village secretary who also gets a small stipend. The religious hierarchy consists of four or five *mayordomos* who are responsible for maintaining the church building and for sponsoring fiestas. The civil offices require a good deal of time, while religious offices can consume money as well. Those who have been alcaldes in the past acquire a special status and form a council that meets to advise the present alcalde and help him judge disputes. These elders also choose candidates for all offices each year, and their choices are ratified in a general village meeting.

In the past the ideal power career was to begin at the lowest-ranking mayordomo or policeman station, and then alternate between the two ladders, serving one office every other year. In a very small village one could rise quickly. Now that Protestant sects have objected to the linkage of the two hierarchies, most villages allow people to climb the policeman-alcalde ladder without entering the mayordomo hierarchy. In northern villages political life is further complicated by the Village Council system established by the government in the 1960s. Although it is supposed to be an elected governing group, in fact the Village Council remains a public service group composed of young men who have little political authority (see McCaffrey 1967).

This political system looks very egalitarian on the surface, but in practice there is inequality. Rising in the hierarchy requires continuous residence in the community, so the longtime settlers dominate and recent immigrants have little voice. The older residents are in the elder council that chooses candidates and voices decisions at public meetings and court cases. The division between old residents and new sometimes solidifies around religious or political party factions (Schackt 1986; Howard 1975, 1977b), but an underlying basis is unequal access to the best land. The old settlers control the rulings of the alcalde court in land disputes. While the system inducts new immigrants into the hierarchy, they have to climb very slowly in status and power over the years. Access to the best resources can also be gained by marriage. A new immigrant family can sometimes marry off children strategically and build a close alliance with the established core of long-term residents.

Most villages are still divided into a powerful core of old-timers, who have a great deal of social investment in the community, and a fringe of "floaters," people who have few ties to the village. It does not take much stress to dislodge the fringe members and send them off to another community. Some stay and are incorporated into the core group, but many move on. Some floaters never settle down, ensuring their continuing marginal status. They acquire reputations as troublemakers or careless farmers and may have problems with witchcraft. The growing importance of cash crop production challenges this system of inequality. Access to the market is not controlled through kinship ties and is not completely monopolized by the core village faction, or by the group of elder men who voice its interests. Many of the new sources of income and power are socially disembedded from the kinship and authority system. But the old power structure can defang this threat by gaining some control over land and the cash economy.

The first two shops in Aguacate were opened by men who belonged to the fringe faction, and both were short-lived. One mysteriously burned down in the night, and the other shop owner left the village after a series of misfortunes he attributed to witchcraft.[6] Only the more established members of the village can withstand the social pressures and problems that occur when cash exchange and business become the daily staff of life. As one man asked me, "What can you do when your father-in-law refuses to pay his bill?" Today all three of the major shops in Aguacate are owned by sons of "big men," two of whom head the longest-established families in the village. The shops began as joint ventures between sons and fathers who contributed the starting capital. Thus the shops followed the familiar mode of cooperation and exchange between father and son in a patrilocal household cluster.

Another, more-general means of controlling new sources of power within the village is through selective emphasis on particular aspects of egalitarian norms. James Gregory (1975) reported this phenomenon in San Antonio and interpreted egalitarian ideology there as a response to an increased potential for inequality, instead of as a traditional vestige. To Gregory, the image of limited good is not a precapitalist vestige, but a foil aimed at checking the accumulation strategies of village capitalists, an "expectation of reciprocity." He implies that people realize that the principles of market exchange are antithetical to those of the village economy. In a number of villages, as in Aguacate, the first entrepreneurs who displayed their newfound wealth too obtrusively were threatened and sometimes punished. In Aguacate none of the shopkeepers has tried to build a tin-roofed house or buy a vehicle yet; their wealth is channeled into less-visible paths, into imported food and personal consumer goods. They have more leisure and their work is not as strenuous.

In conversations with Aguacate shopkeepers I heard a strident advocacy of all things foreign and modern. These men argued against many aspects of the Kekchi way of life and criticized their fellow villagers as backward and unsophisticated. They told me that corn and beans are hard to digest, that white rice is good because it can lighten the skin, just like white sugar and white flour. Canned meats are more nutritious than fresh meat, soft drinks are good food, and powdered milk is the best thing for babies. They advocate English over Kekchi and doctors over Kekchi curers. There is more than a trace of defensiveness and hurt in these statements, the sound of someone claiming to have quit a job when he was really fired. In the tug-of-war between entrepreneurs and big men, each denies the value of the other's symbols of success, the underpinnings of his legitimacy. The contest for power works partially through the definition and redefinition of norms and values, particularly the value of goods.

In reality both kinds of power are interdependent. Despite the fact that all parties agree that this situation is completely new, a recent development, an intrusion of the modern capitalist world into their traditional way of life, there have been capitalist entrepreneurs in Kekchi society since at least the sixteenth century (and probably before that). The whole theme of conflict between the village moral economy and the heartless immorality of the marketplace (use values vs exchange values if you will) is so explicit, so overt, it seems like a rehearsed drama rather than an improvisation. I think this is because it is an old, old story. The power of the male elders, based on their place in the kinship network, on their control of precedent and land, is perpetually opposed to the power of money and foreign goods. The first kind of power is always cast as old, and the second as new; the actors accept this definition of their roles and play out a familiar struggle. But each exists only in opposition to the other. In Kekchi history and across Kekchi geography the balance of power has shifted many times, but neither actor has ever been driven from the stage.

In northern Toledo village entrepreneurs seem less constrained, more powerful, more secure in their alternative way of life. Gregory (1987) speaks of a "young men's revolt" in San Antonio. The young could defy their elders because they are less dependent on the village for food and labor. In Aguacate the group whose power is based on access to cash coexists uneasily with the hierarchy based on access to land and village offices. In some of the remoter southern villages the world of cash value is represented only by the village schoolteacher (an outsider who is paid in wages and must buy his or her food) and a few young men who dream of joining the army, going to high school, or traveling to Belize City to find work.

Whatever the fluctuations of the past, this time the cash economy is here to stay, and the ethos of modernity is gaining strength with no sign of slackening, although the various cultural awareness movements now active in Toledo have taken the voice of tradition into national politics. The direction of future changes will depend largely on the government's approach to the land issue and the direction that the Toledo agricultural economy takes in the next decade. If capital-intensive forms of production come to dominate, entrepreneurs with capital will have a great advantage. This has happened in the Stann Creek valley, where small subsistence farmers lack the capital to invest in citrus and are forced into low-wage jobs in order to get the cash they now need (Kroshus 1987; Moberg 1987).

CHANGES IN PRODUCTION

The Kekchi would agree with Gudeman's (1978:3) statement that "when we talk about subsistence we should cease using the term only to designate standards of living or a form of agriculture . . . and realize that production for consumption is radically different from production for exchange." As I have argued above, this is an emic representational model of the Kekchi economy, not a historically accurate etic depiction. What really separates the subsistence economy from the capitalist economy, as Gudeman (1978:57) also points out, is the behavior of the producers and the cultural system that underlies it. Simply put, people erect barriers around their subsistence economy, aiming to keep it autonomous, and thereby deal with the external economy from a position of strength instead of dependency. This often means maintaining a separate sphere of values (both moral and economic) within the household and village economies. But the prejudices of the anthropologist and the cultural map of a people themselves often combine to create a false image of an encapsulated and timeless subsistence economy that obscures the real interdependence of the parts. We do not further the study of rural people by breaking their economy down into artificial bits (see, e.g., Annis 1987 on "milpa logic"). This only provides ammunition for the development workers and agencies who want to treat the rural economy as a bunch of "production systems" that can be approached one at a time (a rice project, a cattle project, a cocoa project). Ecological anthropology makes its most important contribution to rural development when it stresses interconnections and the folly of studying the whole by isolating individual bits and pieces.

I will try here to stress interconnections and approach the issues of change and population pressure on land resources, moving geographically from the north ("modern") to the south ("traditional"). The idea of a dual economy divided into subsistence and cash sectors goes so deep in our conception of modern Maya life that it is difficult and sometimes tortuous to describe change without lapsing into the old vocabulary of traditional and modern, timeless and innovative.

Indian Creek is a two-kilometer strip of houses along one side of the southern highway. The land on the other side of the road is owned by a foreign firm engaged in large-scale rice, cattle, and cocoa production. Villagers find intermittent employment on the ranch, and they use ranch land for milpa rice. Farm trucks carry villagers into town, and the farm staff buy some goods from village shops. On the other hand, the ranch owns most of the land that the village will need for future expansion, flat land that is easily cultivated by machinery, rather than the hilly land on the village side of the road. The hills have no convenient places for sak' ecwaj, while the ranch has good levee land.

Land is a major constraint and a worry to farmers in Indian Creek. At the time of my fieldwork Indian Creek was only 11 years old, and the original reservoir of primary forestland had not been exhausted, even though the 60 households were far from equilibrium with forest re-growth. In 1980 the villagers were quasi-legal squatters—there was no reservation, but the government recognized that the farmers were there and gave them permission to use Crown Land. Leases were just begin-ning to be available, and several East Indians were the first to apply, gaining leaseholds on land already occupied by Kekchi, which led to some acrimonious disputes. In 1985 the government finally began sys-tematically to survey the land into roadside house-plots and 40-acre parcels arbitrarily placed on the hills. Each household head (males only) and some younger men were given leases on these parcels, which they use for permanent crops while continuing to use forestland to the west for milpas.

Land tenure and geography both constrain farming in Indian Creek. Few pigs are kept, so less corn is needed for domestic use than in Agua-cate. The lack of levee land forces Indian Creek farmers to plant the dry-season crop in low-lying parts of the wet-season field, so yields are lower. Many men prefer to spend October to February working on the ranch instead of farming. The proximity of the new Big Falls rice mill makes rice cheaper to transport and allows Indian Creek farmers easier access to credit, chemicals, and mechanical equipment than in Agua-cate. And the legal ownership of land (plus the growing shortage of high forest) has stimulated planting tree crops.

Indian Creek is a recent settlement, so it is not a very good place to look at the effects of population pressure on agricultural production. In Table 8.2 we see that Indian Creek farmers still have a good deal of primary forest and high secondary forest within a short distance of the village. Nevertheless, farmers use low secondary forest knowing they will have low yields, because they simply do not have the time to clear high bush. Low bush can be cleared more quickly, giving them time to prepare large rice fields.

San Miguel is a better example of the effects of population pressure on the productive cycle because it was settled in the early 1950s and has limited land boxed in by San Pedro Columbia to the south and Silver Creek to the north. Farmers have adapted by producing much less corn and keeping fewer pigs. Compared with Aguacate, they grow a smaller wet-season corn crop and a larger dry-season crop. They put almost as much work into the dry-season crop but get lower returns because they use shorter fallow. Their corn economy tends to be leaner with more periods of true shortage than in Aguacate. But they also have more cash and better access to markets and shops. They work more

Table 8.2. Percentages of Fields of Three Fallow Types in Five Toledo Communities

	Low Secondary	High Secondary	Primary Forest
Aguacate (1978 and 1979 corn)	15.1	60.6	24.2
Indian Creek (1979 corn)	22.2	33.3	44.4
San Miguel (1979 and 1980 corn)	28.5	71.5	0.0
Santa Cruz (1983 corn)	64.0	44.0	0.0
Silver Creek (1983 corn)	95.0	3.0	2.0

SOURCES: Data for Aguacate and Indian Creek are my own. Data for San Miguel are from Berte (1983:184). Data for Santa Cruz and Silver Creek are from TRDP (1984:26–27).

in rice and bean production, spreading out the planting and harvesting of rice for a longer part of the year.

One of the surprising contrasts between Indian Creek and Aguacate is that crop inventories are larger and production is therefore more diverse in the northern area where cash crop production is greater. The average Aguacate farmer grows 18.6 of 69 censused crops and varieties, while in Indian Creek the mean is 23.5 crops (t significant at $p < (.01)$. Schackt found an average of 20.4 varieties per household in Crique Sarco, which is more involved in cash crop production than Aguacate, but less than Indian Creek.

Anthropologists often assume that agricultural systems become less diverse and more specialized as they become more market-oriented (see, e.g., Dewey 1981). Why is Kekchi subsistence agriculture less diverse and more specialized than cash cropping? In part, different forms of production have been added to existing ones instead of replacing them. Also, farmers plant more varieties of crops in order to replace the wild foods that are scarce in densely settled areas, and they interplant to get more production from less-fertile land. Finally, they experiment with new cash crops, seeking new markets.

The patterns of diversity within settlements are also informative. In Aguacate households planted between five and 34 crop varieties, depending partially on the number of years a farmer had lived in the village and his age. A simple correlation of adult years' residence in the village and number of varieties grown is curvilinear, leveling off at about 20 years ($r = .654$, $p < .001$). In Indian Creek, however, age and years' residence do not have much effect on crop diversity. The number of varieties grown depends on the amount of household labor available, and whether or not the household head is involved in wage labor. Men who worked off-farm averaged 19 crop varieties, while those who did not grew 30.8 ($t = 2.66$, $p < .02$). This suggests that it is not participation in cash crop production, but wage labor that leads to a drop in crop diversity. The reason for lower crop diversity is labor shortage, particularly during the off-season outside the major crop cycle. Flexible small-task labor is hard to account for (or judge the value of) and is most easily shifted from food production into wage work. It is ironic that some cash earned in wages is spent on imported foods to substitute for food that would otherwise have been grown.

The amount of labor and land spent cultivating major crops is also different in Aguacate and Indian Creek (see Table 8.3, which includes information on San Miguel and Crique Sarco.). The differences are striking, showing a tendency for a decline in wet- and dry-season corn

Table 8.3. *Crop Mixtures in Four Kekchi Villages*

	Aguacate	Crique Sarco	Indian Creek	San Miguel
Wet-season corn				
Percentage of farmers	96.2	98.0	80.0	>95.0
Mean field size (in Ha)	2.15	2.21	1.88	1.49
Dry-season corn				
Percentage of farmers	77.3	?	51.0	<50.0
Mean field size (in Ha)	0.99	<0.83	0.09	?
Rice				
Percentage of farmers	39.3	66.6	80.0	>90.0
Mean field size (in Ha)	.76	.82	2.04	1.16
Red kidney beans (cash crop)				
Percentage of farmers	0.0	0.0	40.0	>50.0
Pigs (mean number per farmer)	9.4	9.2	0.5	?
Mean total area in corn and rice (per year per farmer)	3.33	?	3.24	?

SOURCES: Data on Crique Sarco are from Schackt (1986:35, 167–68). Data on San Miguel are from Berte (1983:185). Data on Augacate and Indian Creek are my own.

Table 8.4. Agricultural Income in Two Toledo Villages

	Corn	Rice	Beans	Pigs	All Commodities
Percentage of farmers who sell commodity					
Aguacate	30.0	39.3	0	100.0	
Indian Creek	40.0	80.0	40.0	0	
Average cash return per seller (in U.S. dollars)					
Aguacate	26.30	113.50	0	179.00	
Indian Creek	26.00	298.40	117.00	0	
Average village income[a] per capita (in U.S. dollars)					
Aguacate	7.90	35.20	0	179.00	222.10
Indian Creek	10.50	239.00	46.70	0	296.20

NOTES: These figures are individual farm enterprise income, not household income. Average household income is higher because some households have more than one rice-producing farmer.

[a] Average village income spreads cash receipts over both producers and nonproducers.

production and numbers of pigs in the northern zone, and more rice and bean acreage. The northern zone production system also uses less land. A series of trade-offs and balances are being made within a single system. While Aguacate and Crique Sarco farmers depend on pigs and some rice for cash, Indian Creek families depend on rice and some beans. See Table 8.4 for total annual income in Aguacate and Indian Creek by source; wage labor is not included, nor is income from selling forest products, wild game, or other minor crops.

The totals for cash return per annum are deceptively similar in the two villages. Sale of minor crops in Indian Creek adds an additional average of U.S. $20 per farmer, and wage labor adds an average of $170. The cost of marketing rice in Indian Creek is lower because the rice mill is so close, but the cost of production is also higher because men use more herbicide and pesticide, and the two balance each other out. The low cash income in Aguacate is more evenly distributed than the larger incomes in Indian Creek. The range of total incomes, including wage labor, for 10 Indian Creek farmers was from $103 to $967, while the range for eight Aguacate men was between $28 and $357, not including shopkeepers.

As mentioned above, the agricultural strategy of the Kekchi tends to be accretionary: new crops are added to the existing agriculture cycle, and adjustments are made as necessary to the labor schedule and land resources. The core of subsistence production may be modified a bit, expanded or shrunk, but it always remains. This pattern of agricultural change—adding cash crops as markets and opportunities present themselves—has costs for the farmer. The main problem is the limited flexibility of the household labor supply and the frequency of labor bottlenecks, times when a farmer need to be in two or three places at once. To depict graphically the labor problems faced in expanded cash crop production, I have, in Figure 8.1, compared agricultural calendars for Santa Theresa, Aguacate, and Indian Creek. The flow of work in Santa Theresa is straightforward—most of the annual work goes into producing corn for both humans and pigs. In Aguacate rice has been added to the calendar, creating two periods of conflict during planting and harvesting seasons. Indian Creek adds a conflict between bean production and dry-season corn, as well as other complications. Some Indian Creek farmers try to deal with the labor bottleneck during the short dry season by clearing their wet-season cornfield in low scrubby secondary forest, which takes much less time than cutting the trees in longer-fallowed forest. Other farmers deal with the conflicts through social means to be detailed in Chapter 9.

Agricultural change in Toledo Kekchi villages is following a course of reallocation and differentiation. Farmers are becoming differentiated both regionally and locally. Some are part-time farmers who also keep shops or work seasonally in capitalist agriculture, while others are adopting mixtures of cash and subsistence crops. The system of converting subsistence goods into cash through the medium of pigs remains entrenched in the south, while northern farmers are small-scale cash crop producers. Northern farmers have expanded the variety of crops they produce and have shifted their emphasis more into crops grown specifically for sale. In the process land and labor are reallocated to meet new priorities, and purchased foods are substituted for cultivated and wild ones. Demand for consumer goods, especially improved housing, accompanies changes in production.

In each village, whatever the local circumstances, farmers try to meet their own basic food needs. The transition to a way of life based on the sale of crops and the purchase of food is resisted, as farmers try to maintain their independence from the marketplace. This is part of a strategy for reducing risk over the long term, so they can keep from

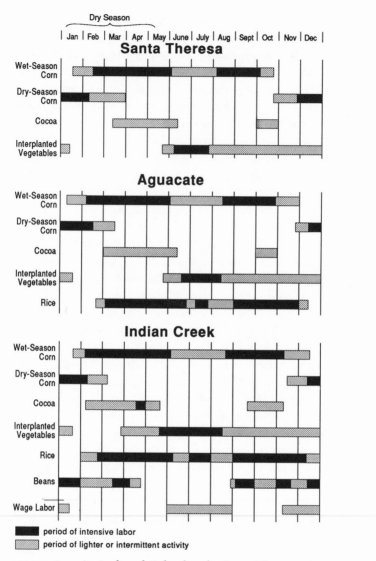

FIGURE 8.1   Agricultural Calendars for Santa Theresa, Aguacate, and Indian Creek

being caught in market fluctuations and retain flexibility in dealing with prices and incentives. In Toledo a family that becomes dependent on cash is at the mercy of a marketplace over which it has no control.

The structure of the market system itself is important. The move away from subsistence production is hindered by the lack of a nearby urban area or a local system for exchanging food. The regional market is of the network type, oriented toward bulking goods out of the area and importing commodities. The lack of a rural peasant marketing system keeps small farmers from specializing (Smith 1977 : 129); their own products are cheap and imports are dear.

Differentiation and reallocation cannot be explained as simply the passive reaction of farmers to population pressure and market structure. The Kekchi move frequently from place to place as they try to balance access to markets and fallow land. They may be drawn to the roadside by increased desire for cash income and participation in the less tangible, but just as real, benefits of communication and contact with Belizean national culture. But once they get to the roadside they find that production is more difficult: they have a greater number of productive cycles to coordinate and poorer access to land. Their lives are encumbered with government organizations, cooperatives, agronomists, census takers, school principals, and even anthropologists. They have to change and adapt their agricultural techniques, at the same time they are finding new ways to organize their families and communities.

Some decide to stay at the roadside, perhaps looking for wage work to tide them over or trying to open a shop or other small enterprise. They might send a bright son or daughter off to high school. Most experiment with intensified production, join agricultural cooperatives, plant citrus and cocoa groves, interplant more densely, and depend more heavily on root crops. Others decide that the costs of living at the roadside outweigh the benefits. They take off northward to the new villages springing up in Stann Creek District, where high forest can still be found. Or they follow the paths of previous generations, turning their back on the roadside and what it represents, heading back to the dwindling refuge of the south where life is not easy or prosperous, but at least seems simpler.

While migration can be measured by relatively simple demographic techniques, decisions about migration are made in the context of the household and kinship group. Agricultural change can also be described through charts and tables of production and crop mixes, but again it must be explained by looking at the decisions made at the level of the household. I have worked upward in this chapter from the microlevel to describe regional patterns and trends; now it is time to move the scale of analysis back to the household and community.

9 The Organization of Labor

The organization of labor is the crucial link between production and social organization. But where is the causal arrow to be drawn? Anthropologists usually assume that social organization has some inherent stability and therefore hold it constant: we start with the idea that a society has a joint family extended household system based on monogamy and patrilocal residence and then look at how production is organized within these constraints. Like Sahlins and Chayanov, we take the social formation (consumer-to-worker ratios, values, goals) and deduce the logic of production from it.

Here and in Chapter 10 I will work in the opposite direction, beginning with the system of production and showing how social life is constrained by it. I do not pretend to break new ground in asking how social organization adapts to systems of production. This is a venerable theme in anthropology, from the vague but prescriptive statements of Murdock (1949), the historical comparative methods of Spoehr (1947) and Eggan (1950), and the optimistic cultural ecology of Steward. But even more-recent writers on this theme (e.g., Medick 1976; Goody 1976; Fricke 1986) have tended to treat the constraints of production by commonsense deduction. Some might think that intensive agriculture suits nuclear families (Goodenough 1955), while others see it as most appropriate to agnatic lineages (Meggitt 1965; Harner 1970). As I will show, categories such as intensive agriculture or swidden farming are far too broad and unspecific to be useful; we need to look at systems of production in far more detail before we can specify the constraints they place on social organization.

I will begin by treating production as a stable system, although it is rarely so. Change will be introduced as a practical matter because the processes through which social groups adapt to productive systems are most visible when production is changing. These situations bring out the complex reality that *neither* production nor social organization are constants, that both are dynamic systems that interact with each other.

Some anthropologists have argued that each culture organizes work according to cultural conventions and norms (see, e.g., Nadel 1947: 54). I assume that people work toward the goal of practical efficiency within a culturally defined framework of rules for mobilizing labor. But I will also stress how rules can change through both active, conscious manipulation and the gradual and mostly unconscious assimilation of ideas and practices (what Bourdieu [1977] calls *habitus*). We need to start with an objective idea of how particular jobs and tasks are most efficiently achieved, regardless of cultural predispositions. Terray (1972:100–26) provides a useful typology of labor processes, and I will use many of his concepts here, although not his terminology.

Labor-intensive tasks, such as raising a roof beam or pulling a log out of the forest, are simply those that require more power than a single person can provide. Every task has a labor restriction as well, a point at which adding more workers will no longer improve efficiency. Only two people at a time can efficiently thresh rice—beyond this number the marginal return to labor is close to zero (see Figure 9.1).

Differentiation and specialization affect the efficiency of different-sized work groups at each task, defining the amounts of return from additional units of labor. Corn harvesting can be done in teams—one breaks ears, another collects and carries them, and another stacks. Specialization matches people to tasks for which they have a special skill or proficiency, as when children stuff corn into sacks, while adults carry the sacks to the corn house.

In agriculture the scheduling of particular tasks has a major effect on optimum work group size and the efficiency of labor. We can break scheduling down into timing, the place of a task in the yearly cycle of work, and sequencing, the order of tasks in relation to each other. Corn must be planted in the first weeks of the rainy season: a timing problem. It can be planted only after the field is burned: a matter of sequence. Timing and sequencing constraints often lead to bottlenecks, times when a number of tasks need to be done simultaneously. Here the concept of schedule elasticity is useful. Some tasks are elastic and can be scheduled flexibly (e.g., harvesting corn), while inelastic jobs must be done within narrow time limits. An agricultural calendar with many elastic tasks and few rigid timing and sequencing constraints is likely to have few bottlenecks.

At a general level productive regimes favor particular kinds of labor groups. At one extreme we have linear systems wherein all tasks are scheduled one after another, each task has a low labor restriction point,

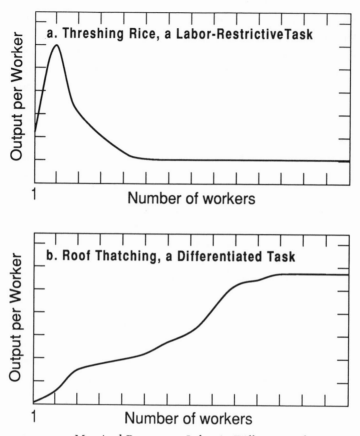

FIGURE 9.1   Marginal Returns to Labor in Different Tasks

and the benefits of differentiation and specialization are small. The intensive hoe farming of the Kofyar in Nigeria is diverse: many crops are grown, but in a linear yearly round, one after another, with little schedule overlap and few sequencing conflicts. The resulting labor demand is therefore elastic, and a nuclear family can meet most of them (Netting 1965a). The other extreme is simultaneous labor scheduling: tasks must be done at the same time in different locations, and differentiation or specialization is important. Moala subsistence (Sahlins 1957, 1962) is highly simultaneous. Each household works several kinds of fields at the same time, fishes, and gathers copra in different parts of the island. The crop sequences conflict at various points, and many tasks are labor-intensive or specialized. A large and flexible work group meets the inelastic and simultaneous demands of the system.

There are a number of different ways people can provide labor in any productive system. There may be many acceptable solutions as well as a few optimal ones. Work can be organized within the household, or nonhousehold labor can be obtained by labor exchange, barter of goods for work, sharecropping, and wages. In discussing some of the ways the Kekchi mobilize labor, we should consider both the cost (what must be exchanged to get labor) and the crucial variables of access and flexibility. In meeting scheduling problems and bottlenecks, the cost of labor is sometimes not as important as the ability to get labor when it is needed (Moore 1975:283).

KEKCHI PRODUCTIVE GROUPS

Working in a group always leads to joking, laughter, gossip, verbal and physical play, and all kinds of learning. Men get to see each other's fields and check the progress of crops. The pace of work is fast, and younger men sometimes compete. The fun is balanced by the solemn quiet ritual of sharing a meal afterward, when religion brings the group together.

Kekchi men consistently say that a group gets a job done in fewer total hours than a single man working alone. I wish I had been able to measure the efficiency of different kinds of groups accurately, since the literature on this issue is contradictory (Foster 1942:35; Moore 1975:278). In the absence of such evidence I am inclined to accept the Kekchi opinion. Another practical reason why group labor is preferred is safety. Tales are told of men who died in accidents because they were alone with nobody to come to their aid.

The Kekchi recognize a number of formal types of labor groups with distinct rules of exchange and reciprocity. The rules are not inflexible because the sphere of labor exchange is not separate from that of kinship: people can often call on alternate standards of behavior. ("We are cousins—you should not treat me like him.") While the rules are presented as timeless, they probably change as people stretch previous precedents and reinterpret old rules to fit new situations (see, e.g., Rosen 1984). I have drawn on Erasmus (1956), Guillet (1980), and Moore (1975) in labeling these labor groups and in comparing them to those in other cultures.

The gender-based division of labor among the Kekchi is similar to that of many Mesoamerican peoples. Many agricultural tasks are exclusively a male province, while many domestic tasks, including food processing and cooking, are exclusively female. In between are a number of tasks for which there are preferences but not prescriptions, where there is room for negotiation and choice. Regrettably, almost all my date were collected with a specific focus on agricultural production and therefore concern male labor. Women do form work groups of various kinds. Several women will rotate child-care duties (for toddlers and older children) so some will be free for other tasks that take them out of the house. Food processing is sometimes intensified, as when two or three women coarse-grind corn for tortillas together. When men gather for a farm work group, women (including some but not all of the wives of the workers) share the job of preparing the evening feast.

Women do a variable amount of agricultural work. There is a clear trend toward less female participation in farming in the northern zone near the highway. In Santa Theresa women visit the fields two or more times a month and help plant vegetables, gather wild food, harvest, and carry firewood and corn, and other food, home. In Aguacate I recorded zero to three visits per month with a mean of slightly less than one. Indian Creek women rarely admitted to visiting fields at all. Nevertheless, even in Indian Creek women's work is crucial in all stages of agriculture. Women specialize in such flexibly scheduled (elastic) tasks as processing and drying grain, tending animals, and growing herbs and other crops around the house.

The majority of all agricultural labor is family labor. The question of whether or not to call this another form of exchange labor is difficult to answer. It is easy to follow Sahlin's (1972) idea of the domestic mode of production and assume that all labor transactions within the family are based on generalized reciprocity, with no reckoning of balances or awareness of specific exchanges. A very different position is found in recent work by economists and formalist social scientists who argue that the household can be treated as a small business (Becker 1981; Blau & Ferber 1986; Barnum & Squire 1979; England & Farkas 1986). But even if we accept that the family is a privileged and separate realm of exchange in all societies, what Cheal (1989) calls a moral economy, surely the rules and rights to labor and property vary from family to family and culture to culture. There is no simple primitive communism found in all families, but instead a complex balance of obligations, duties, strategies, promises, and values, a balance that is achieved through a range of practices from negotiation and bargaining to threats and violence.[1] Among the Kekchi the practice of allocating domestic labor is different in two major types of household.

A dwelling unit is the group of people who regularly live in a single house. This is usually a nuclear family, although it may sometimes be extended to include adopted children and stepchildren, widowed parents, and the nuclear family of a married child. Labor relations are based on a principle of seniority. The labor of any male within the household is at the disposal of the male household head, and female labor is similarly under the control of the female head. Children do not participate fully in domestic labor until they get out of school at age 14, although they may be kept out of school during labor bottlenecks.

By the time a boy is out of school he is used to following his father's direction, working in the fields for no more than food, lodging, an occasional cash gift, and the promise of bearing marriage expenses. If a boy is capable of a man's day of work, his father may borrow labor from other households and send his son to repay the day in his place. Only in rice cultivation is the son allowed some autonomy. The ideal is that when a son's knowledge and experience grows he will play more of a part in farm management, but this is not always a smooth transition.

There is no explicit measurement of balance in the labor relationship between father and son within the dwelling unit, but this does not mean that there is no balance. The father is expected to work at least as hard as his son, and the son expects to get time off to play soccer, visit relatives in search of a wife, and travel to other parts of the country. Today, sons sometimes leave when these expectations are violated. In Aguacate in 1979 one ran off to join the police, and another took a paying job in another village, visiting only on weekends (when his father demanded rent). Of course, older men now muse about the good old days when sons showed more respect.

Household clusters consist of two or more dwelling units. When a couple first marry, they have a number of residence options. It used to be common for the couple to spend one to two years in the wife's parents' house, while the groom did bride service. Today only a small minority still practice uxorilocal postmarital residence, and virilocality is more common. The couple lives in the husband's parents' dwelling unit for one to three years until their first child is born. During this time the son's labor is still at his father's disposal, although he has a bit more autonomy than before. He may have his own dry-season cornfield, and his father may share money from selling pigs.

A household cluster is formed when a couple moves out of the parental house into a new one nearby; the two dwellings retain many economic ties. Clusters of brothers or brothers-in-law may persist after the parents die, and clusters are also formed around other kinship bonds. The rules of labor exchange within clusters are generally the same regardless of membership. (In the following discussion I will use the more common virilocal cluster.) The norms closely resemble Sahlin's (1972) ideal of generalized reciprocity, but practice is different from the norm.

Sons in household clusters have independent agricultural enterprises, although their fields tend to be close or adjacent to their father's. Sons are supposed to give days of labor to their father on request, and he is supposed to reciprocate when asked. No count of days owed is kept, since other forms of cooperation and sharing are supposed to even out the differences. In practice the labor exchanges in clusters do not balance out. Sons give their fathers much more than they get in return. In one cluster where I had complete records a son gave his father 42 days and got back 19. A son-in-law gave 26 and received 11. Exchanges between the son and son-in-law balanced out evenly.

Tension, disagreement, and fission often result from perceptions of long-term imbalances in a household cluster. Still, the ties are flexible and can be renegotiated in a number of ways. And because relationships are so multistranded and long-term, including many things besides agricultural labor, it is hard to know who is ahead or behind at any particular moment.

The most frequent arguments in household clusters are between brothers. Let me give the example of the Cus family. The older, married brother, Pablo, asked his father, Julio, to help him in his rice field. The next day Julio came to work bringing his young unmarried son, Tomas, along to help. Tomas now found himself working for his elder brother, with no return. When he worked for his father he at least shared the food produced, but here he got nothing. The next year young Tomas made his own rice field and asked Pablo to return all the days of work he was owed from the previous year. Pablo said he owed no days, since he is older and since Tomas was working for his father, not for him. Sometimes these kinds of arguments linger on for years and lead younger brothers to leave the cluster.

Above all, labor relations within household clusters should be seen as flexible and pragmatic rather than as rigid products of rules. They can be scaled from the most dependent—those between a father and an unmarried son in a single dwelling, for example—to the most independent—between men who act as if they lived in separate households. Concomitantly, labor exchange between households varies across different sorts of groups, each with its own dynamics.

Labor groups composed of male members of different households range in size from two to the entire adult male population of the village. Permanent labor groups have a fixed membership from year to year, including all the heads of dwelling units. They are formal institutions within the village, and for major tasks they work in each member's field on successive days in rotation. Each person gives and receives a day of labor from the other members. The group works only on such activities as planting corn, when all villagers have the same task to do at the same time. In the larger villages, such as San Miguel, there are too many men for a single group and there may be two or three, which men join as soon as they have their own house (McCaffrey 1967).

Labor circles are a similar form of exchange group that convenes temporarily for a single task. They are not institutional and each one has a different membership, based on who needs a job done and has time to reciprocate. For many jobs during the year—for instance, planting dry-season corn—a man needs only four or five extra workers, so he will try to find men who are also planting at the same time. I call these groups circles because, like permanent groups, each man in the circle exchanges a day of work with every other man.

In both permanent groups and circles a man may need to do additional work before or after the group comes to work for him. His major problem is finding that time, when he is obliged to reciprocate to each man in the group on successive days. Often a circle will agree not to work on Saturdays or Sundays, or both, which gives each man time to work on his own, but this can still make for tricky scheduling.

Individual exchange groups occur when a man borrows labor from several men and pays back that day to each man later, but the men he calls do not exchange labor among each other (see Figure 9.2). These groups are much more flexible than the two types above because the time of repayment of labor can be negotiated. This is also the major reason why men are reluctant to participate; why should they give a day of labor unless they have a specific need for the returned day? And why should they have to organize another group of their own in the future? A circle has the advantage of closing accounts after it is done, while individual exchanges lead to all kinds of hanging labor debts that Kekchi men prefer to avoid. The other problem with this kind of group is that tasks are not really considered equivalent. Chopping low bush for sak'ecwaj is hard "hot" work and is not really equivalent to a day spent building a corn house. There can be resentment when people feel they are not getting back what they have given.

Men get involved in this kind of labor group, despite their lack of enthusiasm, because of need on one side and kinship on the other. It is mostly men who live neolocally, who do not have household cluster labor to draw on, who need this kind of extra labor. Most individual

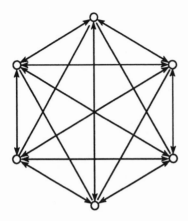
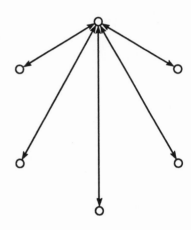

Group Exchange   Individual Exchange

FIGURE 9.2   Two Types of Labor Exchange

exchange groups are among close kin, and the sense of obligation to help one's kin can outweigh the practical problems. And two or three men who call each other frequently for small personal exchange groups build up a continuing relationship of mutual aid that has other benefits.

Kekchi often state that the village should act like a single large extended family. This norm both supports and is reinforced by the community work group, or fagina. The alcalde calls all adult males in the village together for one or two days about four times a year, to clear the village green and to fix and maintain bridges and community buildings. While labor-exchange groups move between villagers, the fagina is a more diffuse kind of exchange in which the beneficiary is an abstract entity, the community, that is made more real by the very act.

The alcalde has, by custom, the right to punish by fine or imprisonment those who avoid fagina. The fagina has become the focus of conflict over the alcalde's authority and role in recent years. Members of minority religions often refuse to participate and take their cases to court in Punta Gorda. Factions may precipitate village fission by refusing to participate in fagina. All of the tensions that surround the necessary sacrifice of community life tend to get focused on the fagina, making it a potent symbol that is linked to ethnicity, something that makes Kekchi different from other Belizeans.

While the fagina works for the community, another form of village labor benefits each dwelling unit in turn. Kekchi houses are rebuilt from the ground up about every 10 years, and rethatched about every five. Each builder organizes the community work group to build and thatch his home, and it is unheard of for a man to refuse to participate. The owner must obtain the wood posts and poles used in construction, but the group gathers leaves for thatching. The size of the group depends on the size of the house. The average in Aguacate was 13 men, with a maximum of 20. This is a form of exchange labor because each man remembers to whom he has given a day of work, but he does not call in that debt until he works on his own house. This is the only kind of labor debt that is metaphorically kept on the books for more than a year. But because people move between villages so often, there are always outstanding debts and credits, and the system often acts like generalized reciprocity.

When a man builds a house from imported materials, concrete blocks and tin roofing, he cuts himself out of this system. This is one reason why people resent it so much when some people change housing styles—it is both symbolically and practically divisive. One man in Aguacate tried to call a labor group to help him build a cut-lumber and tin-roofed shed for his shop. Nobody came, and he ended up hiring an East Indian carpenter to do the job.

Indeed, the only wage labor I observed in Aguacate involved the village shopkeepers. Two of them hired young men, who had no rice of their own, to help them plant and harvest their rice. Another shopkeeper hired several boys for such odd jobs as carrying his supplies and gathering firewood (the latter was considered scandalous by his neighbors). The wages were less than half the going rate on large farms in Toledo, showing that supply and demand do not operate perfectly within the village economy. Instead, prices are "sticky" because of social costs and benefits.

In other Kekchi villages wage labor is slightly more common but is still restricted to specific tasks, especially rice production, and workers are paid less than in the external market. Most wage work in villages is done by young men who have no farms of their own, and they are expected to give their wages to their parents. Berte (1983:203) reports that in San Miguel a shopkeeper who did not pay back labor debts was pressed to make cash payments instead. Shopkeepers tend to prefer to deal in cash and goods instead of labor anyway, and this kind of event will be more common as the labor and cash economies adjust to each other. In large communities, such as San Antonio and San Pedro Columbia, the more diffuse exchange involved in house building has broken down. This task is now done by circles, or even by wage labor.

TASKS AND LABOR STRATEGIES

The use of labor for particular agricultural tasks is not just a matter of cultural convention; it is a product of both the physical and ecological constraints of each job, and the social costs and benefits of each kind of labor. In Table 9.1 the major agricultural cycles in Aguacate and the kinds and amount of labor used, based on census interviews and labor

Table 9.1. Major Agricultural Cycles and Labor Groups in Aguacate

Task	Reciprocal Labor-Exchange Groups			Household Cluster or Dwelling Unit
	Permanent	Circle	Individual	
Wet-season corn				
Finding, marking				1
Chopping, felling	1			2
Planting	1			3
Building the corn house			2	
Harvesting		2	3	1
Transporting				1
Dry-season corn				
Clearing		1	3	2
Planting		1	3	2
Weeding			2	1
Harvesting				1
Transporting				1
Rice				
Finding, marking				1
Chopping, felling		2	3	2
Planting		2	3	2
Weeding			3	1
Harvesting			2	1
Threshing			2	1
Transporting			3	1
Minor crops				
Planting				1
Weeding				1
Harvesting				1

NOTE: 1 indicates that the labor group contributes over 50 percent of the labor needed to complete the task; 2 indicates a significant (30%–50%) contribution; and 3 indicates that the group is a minor, supplementary source of labor (contributing less than 30% of needed input). Data for household clusters and dwelling units are combined because many village residents do not live in clusters.

Table 9.2. Mean Group Size for Major Agricultural Tasks in Aguacate

Task	Total Number of Groups Recorded	Mean Number of People per Group
Wet-season corn	198	5.01
Clearing (with machete)	48	5.10
Felling trees	38	5.90
Planting	15	13.50
Building the corn house	27	3.60
Harvesting	70	3.20
Dry-season corn	53	4.00
Clearing	39	3.70
Planting	14	5.00
Rice	53	3.70
Clearing	17	3.20
Planting	19	4.80
Harvesting	17	3.10

NOTE: Figures are based on records of 330 labor groups called together in 1978–1979. Group size includes immediate household members and the man who called the group together.

records that counted 330 labor groups, are listed. Aguacate men participated in an average of 17.3 labor groups per year (not including the fagina), with shopkeepers working in the fewest and older men working in the most.

In Table 9.2 we see the mean size of labor groups used in each task, including all dwelling unit and household cluster groups, but not the farmer's solitary days. The wet-season corn mean is low because of a single aberrant case. One farmer, who had three unmarried adult sons in his household (a rare and fortunate circumstance), did not use any labor-exchange groups during the agricultural year. Instead he recorded 38 household labor groups consisting of himself and his sons in various combinations. The average size for the rest of the village was 6.7 men for clearing and 8.7 for cutting trees. This mean still does not reflect the size of the community permanent work group, because many farmers start and finish clearing, felling, planting, and harvesting with small groups drawn from their dwelling or household cluster.

That wet-season corn production uses the largest labor-exchange groups, and rice production the smallest, is clear in Table 9.2. Planting groups for all crops tend to be the largest, while harvesting groups are smaller. This reflects the ecological timing and scheduling constraints

Table 9.3. Man-Hours of Labor by Household Members and Labor-Exchange Groups in Aguacate

Status of Farmer and Household Number		Major Productive Cycle			
		Wet-Season Corn		Dry-Season Corn	
		Domestic	Exchange	Domestic	Exchange
Cluster heads	15	1,193	785	0	0
	21	956	303	144	63
	8	954	259	0	0
	17	626	408	129	170
	19	746	422	0	0
Cluster sons	7	234	246	270	99
	13	617	357	0	0
	18	695	530	57	72
	16	343	319	52	82
	12	483	206	48	91
Independents	9	0[a]	0[a]	129	63
	23	776	185	129	125
	11	610	287	65	82
Mean hours for all those working		686	359	114	94
Percentages from domestic and exchange labor		65.7	34.3	54.7	45.3

[a] Farmer grew no wet-season corn because he was ill and unable to work.

of rain and weeds discussed in Chapter 6. There is also a reciprocal relationship between the number of groups and their size; corn planting takes fewer larger groups, while corn harvesting takes many small ones.

So far I have contrasted labor groups of all kinds with solitary labor by individual farmers. Socially, however, the most important distinction is between domestic labor, provided by members of the dwelling and household cluster, and labor provided by nonhousehold members through various forms of exchange; see Table 9.3 for the amount of domestic labor used by 13 households. Two-thirds of annual labor needs were met with domestic labor, but this proportion varied between crops (54.7% to 100%) and among households (53.8% to 78.7%). It is important to note that the one-third of each household's annual labor supply from exchange labor, while quantitatively less, comes at critical times. A lot of the domestic work listed in Table 9.3 was absorbed

| Major Productive Cycle | | | | | |
| Rice | | Minor Crops | | Total Percentage | |
Domestic	Exchange	Domestic	Exchange	Domestic	Exchange
0	0	27	0	60.8	39.2
0	0	15	0	75.0	25.0
360	145	0	0	76.5	23.5
145	80	94	0	60.2	39.8
467	125	5	0	69.0	31.0
0	0	45	0	61.4	38.6
0	0	18	0	64.1	35.9
185	216	14	0	53.8	46.2
94	36	9	0	53.3	46.7
0	0	27	0	65.3	34.7
432	94	18	0	78.7	21.3
383	131	9	0	74.6	25.4
210	118	0	0	64.5	35.5
285	118	26	0		
70.7	29.3	100.0	0	66.0	34.0

by time-consuming but flexible tasks such as carrying sacks of corn from the field or visiting the field to check for animal damage. The crucially timed operations all used large amounts of exchange labor.

Wet-season corn production uses the most man-hours of exchange labor, while (setting aside minor crops) rice production uses the largest proportion of domestic labor. Much dry-season sak'ecwaj labor is provided by exchange groups because clearing and planting the crop conflicts with the wet-season corn harvest. In household clusters one man will make a sak'ecwaj field using exchange labor, freeing the other members of the cluster to finish the corn harvest. This division of labor within the household cluster shows how labor-exchange strategies depend on the composition of individual dwellings and household clusters.

The data on labor groups in Aguacate show that families at each stage of the developmental cycle, in different residential situations, use

Table 9.4. Measures of Labor Recruitment Strategies

	Number of Individuals	Percentage of Annual Labor Borrowed	Diversity Index	Gini Index	Mean Relatedness
Cluster heads	5	31.7	0.288	0.510	1.314
Cluster sons	5	40.4	0.394	0.451	1.100
Independents	3	27.4	0.460	0.337	0.823

variable amounts of exchange labor and obtain that exchange labor through different strategies. To show this, on Table 9.4 I have divided the households into three groups. First are the heads of household clusters and the heads of households having one or more working-age children. These five men can use dwelling or household cluster labor without immediate reciprocity. The second group includes five younger men who are junior members of household clusters headed by their fathers or fathers-in-law. They can get some labor from the head of the cluster, but they receive much less than they give. Third we have three men who are the heads of independent nuclear family households in which there are no working-age male children. If these men want to borrow labor they must participate in a labor-exchange group.

Looking at the percentage of annual labor borrowed through exchange groups outside the household cluster, we see that heads of clusters do not have to borrow as much exchange labor as their sons. Their sons cannot get all the labor they need from their father or brothers and must often use exchange groups. These younger household cluster members also have more flexibility in entering into exchange circles, because they can usually depend on other members of the cluster to do regular tasks that would otherwise constrain them. The third group, the independent household heads, are limited in the amount of exchange labor they can use by these same inflexible tasks. Scheduling labor is very tricky for independent household heads because they do not have the flexibility of men who live in a household cluster, and this restricts the number of labor groups in which they can participate. The obligations on future labor created by an exchange group are difficult for these men to deal with.

The diversity index in Table 9.4 is the total number of different individuals that a man called for all his labor groups divided by the number of days he borrowed from these men. A high score on this index means that a man is spreading out his labor exchanges among a large group, while a low score means that he is exchanging within a small group. The cluster heads score low in diversity—they concentrate on a few other men—while heads of independent households spread out their labor exchanges more widely through the village. The independent household heads therefore borrow less labor than cluster heads, but they borrow from a larger group.

The Gini index is a measure of inequality based on the Lorenz curve, used originally to quantify economic inequality (Allison 1978; Shyrock et al. 1973). Here it measures the unequal contribution of different men to an individual's labor-exchange pool during the year. If a man called each of 10 men to work for him once, the Gini index would be zero. If he called one man 10 times the Gini index would be one. A low Gini shows labor exchanges spread evenly among the men he called, while a high Gini shows a concentration of exchanges with a few men. The Gini index thus supports the inference drawn from the diversity index: cluster heads concentrate their labor exchanges with a small group of men, while independent household heads spread their labor exchanges widely around the village.

An explanation for these differences can be found by looking at the mean relatedness figure (last column of Table 9.4). This figure is based on the consanguineal, affinal, or fictive relationship between each household head and every other adult man in the community. Assigning a numerical value to each kind of relationship (0 = unrelated; immediate lineal = 6) and averaging the value produces a mean measure of how closely an individual is related to all other community members (the range is from 0.44 to 2.03). The mean relatedness between the labor recruiters and those called into exchange groups is shown in Table 9.4. Heads of household clusters have more close kin within the village than cluster sons or the heads of independent households have. This brings us back to the structure of village politics, for the heads of these household clusters are at the core of the village kinship system, while most independent household heads are at the fringe. The members of established founding families in the village concentrate their labor exchanges within their kinship network, while those who do not belong to a household cluster spread their labor exchanges among the entire community. The heads of independent households do participate in permanent and circle exchanges, but they do not have close kinship networks in which they can build a high density of labor exchange.

I have argued in previous chapters that effective sak'ecwaj and rice production depends on careful, continuous scheduling of small labor

Table 9.5. Measures of Productivity by Domestic Group Type

	Number of Indi-viduals	Wet-Season Corn (Mean Kg/ Man-Hr)	Dry-Season Corn (Mean Kg/ Man-Hr)	Rice (Mean Kg/ Man-Hr)	Mean Total Annual Hours Worked
Cluster heads	5	2.84	1.99	2.21	1,724
Cluster sons	5	2.27	1.61	1.07	1,079
Independents	3	2.57	1.96	1.59	1,555

groups of precisely the kind that independent household heads do not have access to. They have their own labor, and the more formal permanent and circle exchange groups, but intermediate-sized groups are difficult for them to manage. In the meantime household cluster heads, and household heads who have adult sons living at home, find it much easier to gather small work groups. The extra hands at their disposal mean they can handle simultaneous tasks—they do not avoid labor debts the way the independent household heads must. A man with extra labor at his disposal knows that if he has to go pay back a day in someone else's field, his son (or father) will still haul corn to his family, or can check his cornfield, or finish cutting his rice before the birds get to it.

The different labor capabilities of different kinds of households are reflected in their productivity. The leaders of large extended household clusters should be farming more effectively, managing complex simultaneous schedules of agricultural work, and ably adding cash cropping to their subsistence farming. While I would like to have a larger and longer-term data base on the efficiency of each farm operation, the consistent trends shown in Table 9.5 support these predictions. Cluster heads had the highest returns to labor, cluster sons the lowest, with independents between. The total number of days of labor used by each dwelling follow a similar pattern; household cluster heads use the most labor (some drawn from their sons in the dwelling or household cluster), while cluster sons use the least, with independent households between. It is important to note, however, that independent households are providing almost all this labor themselves. The mean labor per worker in two household clusters where I could measure it accurately was 1,226 hours (counting only labor on corn, rice, and other field crops, not including hunting, gathering, and marketing), compared with 1,555 hours for independent household heads (173 nine-hour days as opposed to 136).

There are no simple explanations for these patterns of efficiency and labor allocation. The heads of household clusters can act efficiently because they can schedule labor effectively and divide labor among a number of male workers. They are able to take full advantage of the village labor-exchange system in order to specialize and differentiate their work. The junior members of household clusters are the other side of this story, performing relatively poorly because they are being exploited by the father (or father-in-law). Their labor is not entirely their own, but they get other returns: more security and lower work load. An independent household lacks this insurance of pooled labor and products, and the members are under pressure to make every hour count, and every crop a success.

CHANGING AGRICULTURE, CHANGING LABOR

I have shown that different crops require different amounts of labor at different times. The rice cash crop, for example, is farmed mostly with household or cluster labor, as are vegetable and tree crops. Next I showed that within Aguacate there are different strategies for motivating and deploying labor in each crop, and that these strategies are related to household organization. The point is that continual, generalized reciprocal labor exchanges between close kin in household clusters is an advantage in scheduling and sequencing simultaneous operations during the productive cycle. Independent households with a single adult male worker have the most trouble dealing with labor bottlenecks, specialization, and simultaneous tasks, and participate the least in labor exchanges.

So far this has been a synchronic discussion, treating the productive system, the labor group types, and domestic groups as static elements, when in fact all are changing. Now I compare data from other villages to build a more dynamic model of how households, labor groups, and agriculture are related to each other.

Santa Theresa participates in the market mainly by selling pigs fed on corn grown in the wet season. Some households feed so much corn to their pigs that they need to grow a dry-season crop as well. The general labor schedule throughout the year is linear and has few bottlenecks: the two cycles of corn production do not conflict at any time; plantains, vegetables, tree crops, and root crops can all be scheduled elastically and are planted in slack times during corn production.

Hunting and gathering activities fill in any remaining gaps in the calendar.

The wet-season cornfield in Santa Theresa is usually cut from primary forest, which is relatively abundant within 30 minutes of the village. Each farmer is therefore on very much the same schedule for most of the year, and this makes planning large labor groups quite easy. The permanent village work group clears each field, plants it, and then harvests it in rotation, finishing most of the work in each field since they are of quite uniform size. Those households that need more corn either grow a dry-season crop or enlarge the wet-season field. Small circles meet for building corn houses because the task is most efficiently accomplished with five or six men. While most labor for wet-season cultivation comes from permanent groups, the sak'ecwaj cycle uses circle groups. The men in the village who have decided to grow corn in the dry season meet in late September or October and set up a schedule to clear and plant each field in succession.

Outside of the tasks performed by permanent or circle exchange groups, all the labor in Santa Theresa's agricultural year can be provided by a single farmer with no loss of efficiency. The linear scheduling of tasks and the use of exchange labor during the few bottlenecks allows a single farmer to be as efficient as a farmer living in an extended family or a household cluster.

The agricultural calendar in Aguacate is more complex because farmers pursue a wider variety of productive strategies, with different mixes of subsistence and cash crop production. Some farmers use primary forest, others secondary, so their schedules for clearing are different. Some plant very large wet-season fields and no dry-season crop, while others balance the two cycles more evenly and therefore need variable amounts of labor to meet different bottlenecks. Permanent labor groups become clumsy, and a larger proportion of labor is provided by the domestic group or through individual exchanges.

The dry-season crop is more important in Aguacate than in Santa Theresa (partially because population pressure makes yields of wet-season corn lower), so more sak'ecwaj is cleared and farmers must begin earlier. This creates a conflict with the harvest of the wet-season crop. Farmers no longer use permanent group labor for harvest because so many farmers want to start their sak'ecwaj instead. At the same time each farmer's labor sequencing is more complex and difficult, and the diversity of activities within the village is increasing, making it harder for the farmer to coordinate the exchange labor that could help deal with bottlenecks and conflicts.

When the sequencing of corn production becomes more complex households with only one worker have less time. The gaps in the major agricultural cycle that would otherwise be taken up with hunting, gathering, and fishing are now times to catch up on other jobs that were put aside during busy periods, such as planting minor food crops. Household cluster heads, who have the most flexible supply of labor and are troubled by fewer bottlenecks, grow an average of 26.2 varieties, while independent household heads plant only 17.1 varieties (junior members of clusters plant only 15.8).

Population pressure forces some of these changes in the agricultural calendar, but the addition of rice as a cash crop creates scheduling problems. All phases of rice production conflict with some part of wet- and dry-season corn production, or with the tending of other food crops. More scheduling problems, sequencing conflicts, and bottlenecks crop up in the farming year, and because of the diversity of productive strategies, labor is harder to recruit.

Farmers respond by depending more heavily on domestic labor, which can be more flexibly allocated. Household clusters, as opposed to independent households, are able to carry on different enterprises at the same time with their larger, coordinated work force. A household cluster, for example, may clear both primary and secondary forest cornfields in the same year, mixing yield maximization and risk reduction strategies to mutual advantage. The household cluster can coordinate subsistence and cash crop production with less risk. Many of the physical operations in sak'ecwaj and rice are most efficiently performed by a small work group of three to five men instead of by larger groups, and a household cluster can often manage these jobs without having to call on exchange labor at all. In Aguacate the individual nuclear family group is at a disadvantage compared with household clusters.

Villages that are more involved in cash cropping than Aguacate have more-complex production cycles. Indian Creek men who use low forest for their wet-season fields often use circles instead of permanent work groups to clear these fields. On the other hand, almost all rice fields are cleared from primary forest by permanent work groups.

In many northern villages people pursue a wider diversity of ways of life, from itinerant preaching to part-time wage labor. This has made it harder to convene circles or individual exchange groups for anything but the most inelastic tasks (clearing and planting). Farmers in Indian Creek plant more vegetables and tree crops because such crops do not require exchange labor and can be handled by an individual or a domestic group. The total amount of labor per year devoted to agriculture is about 110 hours higher in Indian Creek than in Aguacate, but each farmer borrowed less from other households—about 320 man-hours compared to 470 in Aguacate. This reflects the increased importance of domestic and household labor in place of reciprocal exchange groups. So labor exchange does not in fact decline in Indian Creek, it merely shifts in location from the space between individual households (reciprocal exchange) to the space between individual dwelling units within a household cluster (domestic exchange).

Labor-exchange groups are often considered precapitalist vestiges, doomed to be displaced by capitalist wage labor. This fits well into modernization and acculturation theories of development, which see traditional forms of relationships based on sentiment declining in the face of "the commercialization of agriculture, monetization, increased specialization and division of labor, 'individualization', and the emergence of an agricultural proletariat" (Guillet 1980:157). These models fit well with Sahlins's (1972) argument that in the domestic mode of production, a characteristic of traditional societies, reciprocal exchange between households predominates, and this basis disappears with the rise of more-complex forms of economy (redistributive, market, etc.).

Recasting this argument in more-modern anthropological terms, Collins (1986) argues that in Andean households traditional forms of interhousehold labor cooperation are disrupted and destroyed by the capitalist labor market, and households become increasingly nuclearized and isolated. This may happen in some areas, but in other cases (see, e.g., Netting 1965a; Abrams 1973) the monetarization of traditional economies and the commercialization of agriculture have increased the importance and frequency of reciprocal labor exchange. The decline in exchange labor is therefore not some invariant product of macroeconomic forces and abstract processes but is instead the result of very specific, local characteristics of agricultural ecology.

What particular aspects of agrarian transformations lead to the advance or decline of exchange labor as opposed to wage labor (though it is not at all clear that the two are incompatible)? Guillet (1980) argues that the persistence of agricultural labor in the Andes is a result of a lack of cash in the rural economy, and of local ecological circumstances that make reciprocal labor economically sensible. Moore (1975:283–84) lists a number of positive advantages of labor exchange and suggests that population pressure, unequal land distribution, and the intensification of labor all make exchange labor less efficient, militating for the substitution of wages. His most intriguing suggestion is that the basis of exchange labor breaks down when some people begin to value their labor more highly than others' because they are more productive, having better access to capital, land, or technology.

This line of argument leads in some interesting directions. It suggests that exchange labor can be seen as part of the village political economy, the structure of inequality. We are wrong to counterpose the inequality of festive labor groups or wage labor against the egalitarian labor-exchange system. Each is a different structure of inequality for a different kind of community. The Kekchi system is certainly founded on the concept of the equivalence of all labor, and custom says that any person's work on a particular job is the same as any other's. There are few ways to manipulate this system to advantage, unlike wage labor and festive labor where the employer can come out ahead. The only inequities built into the system are those that support the existing inequalities within the village, based on age, gender, and length of residence.

Labor-exchange groups keep women completely out of the arena of agricultural production and exclude them from the economy of labor. When labor itself is the main instrument of production, the rules of male labor equivalence mean that women have no currency, no ability to motivate production, no power over the ultimate source of all food and wealth. Young men are not excluded, but they are exploited because they work harder. A 60-year-old man participates in the labor-exchange group and does perhaps half the work of an 18-year-old, but when the group comes to his field he gets back in return the labor of many young men. This is a form of village social security that keeps energy flowing from young to old in each generation. It also restricts the productive abilities of young men, who must always include their elders in the groups of workers they assemble. The exchange system also brings benefits to those long-term residents of the community who are well embedded in the kinship network. These big men (who mostly head household clusters) make the timing and scheduling decisions for the permanent labor groups, and they use their network of kinship obligations to draw on the labor of young relatives in a network of circle and personal exchange groups.

But let us return to the historical question and ask if labor-exchange systems are in fact primordial and precapitalist among the Kekchi. Unfortunately we just do not know what kinds of labor organization existed in pre-Hispanic and colonial times. If the indigenous Kekchi states were like those of other Maya peoples, various kinds of communal labor served the state and nobility. This is hardly exchange labor but is rather a form of tribute. If the Kekchi were indeed intensive horticulturalists, living in scattered farmsteads rather than in nucleated villages (the towns were another matter), then it is unlikely that they practiced exchange labor on any large scale. Instead, dispersed intensive horticultural production seems most congruent with the use of household labor.

The colonial government continued and intensified the pre-Hispanic practice of taking tribute in labor and services as well as commodities. Through independence into the coffee era, it was common practice for church, government, and capitalist forcibly to recruit labor teams from Kekchi communities. And the communities themselves were artificial entities created by the colonial regime. I suspect that this was the environment in which the Kekchi pattern of exchange labor originated, in an era when the subsistence economy was subject to unprecedented stress. People were forced to live in villages, commute to their farms, and produce more surplus. All this increased their need for labor at a time when they were subject to being taken away from their fields without warning for weeks and months at a time. The continuance of individual farm units would have been close to impossible, and the village itself must have become a corporate unit crucial to survival (Wolf 1957). The organization of communal labor-exchange groups would ensure at least the subsistence needs of individual households, even if the men in those households were dragged off to carry a priest's baggage for a week at corn-planting time. The communal labor organization was therefore an adaptation to predatory capitalism. As people escaped to the lowlands and colonized new areas, these forms of exchange labor became essential in pioneering and founding new villages.

I offer this possibility as no more than a likely scenario, but one that shows that exchange labor can be a product of outside pressure on the subsistence economy rather than a precursor to it. And what of the future of exchange labor? These institutions have shown surprising vitality and adaptability to new forms of production. In Indian Creek the permanent village groups are now registering as agricultural cooperatives, entitling them to rent government agricultural equipment and buy other supplies at subsidized rates. The government Agriculture Department, after years of failure in extension, has now made the permanent work groups the main unit for education and training. And recently the government has granted two blocks of land, off the reservations, to work groups. At the same time, through such organizations as the Toledo Maya Cultural Council, exchange labor of all types is becoming an important symbol of traditional identity. The fagina and the permanent work group are both practical and symbolic means of promoting solidarity and resistance in the face of threatening change.

Politicizing exchange labor in this new way is potentially a two-edged sword, and on strictly economic grounds the prognosis is mixed. As long as exchange is a cheaper and socially convenient means of procuring labor, farmers are likely to continue using it at specific times. But as Moore (1975) points out, wage labor tends to exclude exchange when differences in wealth and property become large, and when growing numbers of landless workers are willing to accept less and less for their work. This is not likely to occur in the Kekchi area in the near term, but there is another form of competition for exchange labor that is an immediate threat. For some farmers domestic labor, the work of sons and sons-in-law, is cheaper and more convenient than exchange labor.

10 Households as Adaptive Groups

Anthropology has traditionally viewed domestic groups as the products of kinship systems. If households in a community are not the same, variations are attributed to their being at different stages of the developmental cycle (Goody 1958) or to alternative residence rules (Goodenough 1956; Korn 1975). From this point of view it makes the most sense to classify and analyze households on the basis of the kinship connections between members (see, e.g., Keesing 1958; Bohannon 1963; Harter & Bertrand 1977). But the resulting classifications and lists of genealogical types of households and their frequency lack explanatory power. They tell us little about the economic and social significance of domestic groups and their responses to economic change (Wilk & Netting 1984).

An alternative methodology is to view households as adaptive groups, in which a large number of different economic, reproductive, and social activities are performed.[1] What households do is logically prior to what they look like, and while kinship relations may provide a framework for the composition of household groups, kinship does not determine residence.

As activity groups, households are flexible and versatile analytical units, but defining the boundaries of the domestic unit becomes more difficult. Living under a single roof is no longer a sufficient defining characteristic, for coresidence is only one of many possible activities that take place within households. Instead the household must be defined as the minimal social group with the maximum number of intersecting and overlapping activities (Hammel 1980; Wilk & Netting 1984).

The Kekchi are a good example of a group for whom a traditional definition of the household does not work very well. Often the significant economic and social unit lives in a single building, but in other cases the cooperating unit lives in two or more dwellings. Others who have found similar flexible multihousehold economic units have called them "domestic groups" (Ashcraft 1966), "mutual aid clusters" (Brown 1977), and "nonresidential extended families" (Nutini 1968; Taggart 1975). I refer to these multiple dwelling units as household clusters, distinct from independent households living in a single dwelling. My first goal here is to describe the economic and social composition of the two forms of household.

HOUSEHOLD FUNCTIONS

I have already discussed the role of the household as a labor group in agriculture. Households play important roles in other aspects of Kekchi society, including rearing and socializing children, maintaining houses, redistributing goods and food among members, and transmitting rights and property between generations through marriage settlements and inheritance.

Inheritance is an important organizing principle and a basic factor in residence decisions in many societies where access to land or other basic productive means is limited (see, e.g., Wheaton 1975; Goody 1972, 1976; Collier 1975). Given the reservation system in Toledo, however, village residence is the major avenue of access to land, not inheritance or household membership. There are only a few other limited goods that are owned and transmitted through ties of kinship in Kekchi villages. The best sak'ecwaj land, cacao groves, orchards, and stands of copal trees are individually owned and are transmitted to children through gifts or inheritance. Other goods such as draft animals, shotguns, radios, musical instruments, and pigs also move between generations.

The Kekchi have no strict rules or norms of transmission or inheritance, perhaps an indication of the relatively low value of inheritable goods in a mobile society. No adults died in Aguacate while I lived there, but informants' statements were consistent on two points: a child who solely cares for aged parents should inherit the bulk of the parents' goods; and all children who have stayed in their parents' household cluster should share evenly when the parents die. There was also consensus (voiced loudly by younger people) that the groom's parents should pass on some property—a couple of pigs, a few chickens, and basic household goods—to a couple when they marry. Older men felt that these gifts should be given gradually during the years following marriage, if the couple remains in the parents' household cluster. While marriage prestations were quite small in Aguacate, Berte (1983) found that grooms' parents in San Miguel spent an average of U.S. $182. Most of this went for the wedding feast and should not be counted as transmission of wealth. It is interesting that wedding expenditures in San Miguel were much higher when the couple married virilocally and joined the groom's parents' household cluster (mean of $215) than when the couple lived neolocally ($66) or matrilocally ($41).

In practice, inheritance follows a fairly orderly pattern, the product of circumstances and pragmatic choice more than normative rules. When one of a couple dies, the surviving spouse has rights to dispose of the property however she or he wants. The survivor brings the possessions into whatever household is willing to offer support or keeps them pending remarriage. Aged widowed persons of either sex often have a hard time finding a child who will take them in, even with this incentive.

If a single survivor dies while living in a household cluster, the goods are often held in common by the heirs for some time. Only when the household cluster later breaks up will the property be divided, and quarrels over the division are part of the general ill will a fission generates. I did not observe any of these inheritance quarrels, but I heard of three cases in which the eldest sons ended up with the lion's share, and the daughters who had married outside the village were excluded. In one case a daughter who lived in the village was still fighting with her brothers and their wives about some cooking equipment, two years after the breakup.

When gifts or inheritance are not very valuable, their prospect has little influence on the residential decisions of young couples. But when land is hard to find and cacao groves are high in value, people take property into account when they decide whether or not to live with parents. Joint ownership of businesses and capital goods among fathers and sons also affects residence, often changing the balance of relationships in subtle ways. Where property and land are scarce and valuable, we may expect to see that parents who possess them will be able to keep one or more of their children attached to their households after marriage (Collier 1976; Klapisch 1972; Smith 1959; Collomp 1984). Parents have a means of attracting and holding their children by offering the use of land and resources, and by holding out the prospect of inheritance.

There is no a priori reason why male children should be held in their natal households after marriage more often than female children. In practice, however, men hold and transmit goods of increasing value and scarcity. While women can give or transmit household goods and chickens to their daughters or daughters-in-law, men can offer pigs, land rights, and draft animals to their sons or sons-in-law. In the competition for the father's goods, a son who has grown up in the household has a head start over a son-in-law who comes in at age 18 or later (average age of first marriage is 14.8 for women, 17.8 for men in Aguacate). A son-in-law is therefore at a disadvantage and may have to give more than a son to get the same access to property. Fathers-in-law are notorious for placing heavy labor demands on sons-in-law who live in their household clusters. I found that sons-in-law lived in a household cluster only when the father-in-law had no coresident sons of his own, or when the son-in-law's natural father had died or left his mother. So the increasing value of land and goods has imparted more patrilocal bias to residence, although there is no stated conscious rule of patrilocality.

Cross-culturally one of the most constant activities within the household group is child rearing. Fosterage, child sharing, and forms of day care are the major exceptions and seem to be most common when there are conflicts between household labor schedules and child care (Brown 1970; González 1961; Pasternack, Ember & Ember 1976). Membership in a multiple-family household can ease the burden of child care by spreading out the work among a larger group. Among the Kekchi, early marriage and high birth rate used to be balanced by very high infant mortality. Older children did a lot of child care too. Although infant mortality remains very high (between 80 and 200 per 1,000 in the first two years, varying from village to village), it has decreased in the last decade and today the population pyramid in Aguacate shows the bottom-heaviness typical of the developing world. Meanwhile mandatory primary schooling has removed a major source of child care labor.

These two changes have increased the burden on mothers and have left less time for farm work. The only way Kekchi women can reduce this constant work load is to share child care with other women. But women living in independent households do not have many opportunities for sharing. Cooking, caring for domestic animals, and housework require them to spend most of their day in their own dwellings and also make them reluctant to take on the burden of harboring someone else's children for the day. Women who live in household clusters have more opportunities to share child care. Cooking does not become a proportionately more time-consuming task when a larger group is fed; it does not take three times as long to cook for three times as many people. Three woman living in a single household cluster can divide cooking and child care and do less total work. In household clusters cooking duties are often rotated, or all women may work together, cooking several times a week.

These economies account for the preference most women express for living in a household cluster. Close bonds often develop between women and their mothers-in-law, although many women would prefer to live close to their mothers and sisters, and want their husbands to move into their fathers' household clusters. Women do sometimes get along badly with their mothers-in-law and want to return to their mothers; the classic Kekchi marital conflict is between a husband who wants to reside patrilocally and a wife who wants to live matrilocally. It is hard to tell how much this conflict causes marriages to break up, as opposed to serving merely as a focus for other discontents. Divorce rates are moderately high—out of 56 marriages recorded in Aguacate personal histories, 13 were dissolved by death of a spouse and eight by divorce.

I use the term *distribution* for exchange, consumption, and use of goods and consumables within the household. Households share and own many goods as a group, and often the rules for exchange within households differ from those for exchange between them. Households often handle distribution by pooling, creating a common fund of goods and foodstuffs from which all members can freely draw in a form of generalized reciprocity (Wallerstein 1984). The household economy is usually so complex and multistranded—including exchanges of like and unlike goods and services over very long periods of time—that any attempt to balance these pooled exchanges would be fruitless. This is not to say that members do not try to achieve some kind of long-term equity, but that this equity will always be subject to negotiation, doubt, and interpretation, as immaterial factors are weighed against the visible and measurable. As I point out elsewhere (Wilk 1987), pooling takes many forms in different cultures, and not all households pool.

Kekchi households pool in different ways, but the most important pooling is always of food. In independent households all members contribute to, and eat from, the same pot. All of the cash income of members, except part of what unmarried males earn from rice farming and most of what women get from selling chickens or eggs, goes into a pool managed unilaterally by the male household head. In a household cluster pooling is more complex and variable. Clusters can be scaled between extremes that I label "loose" and "tight."

In a tight household cluster the corn grown separately by each head of a dwelling unit is usually stored in separate corn houses, but each nuclear family has access to all the granaries. Corn is freely lent and borrowed between members according to need, reflecting the men's close cooperation in producing this food. Each adult male in a tight cluster may have his own rice field, but all the men harvest and market together, and the eldest male divides up the proceeds. In tight clusters pigs are penned communally and fed with corn provided by all the members. Profits from the sale of pigs are divided among the other men by the eldest male. The loosening of a cluster is marked when the younger cluster members get to their mid-twenties and the pig herd is divided. There is continuous sharing of food in tight clusters. Meat, gathered food, and minor crops are evenly distributed to each kitchen; the cluster may share a single orchard and vegetable plot. Sharing also takes place at communal meals. More than half the meals in a week are taken together in one house.

In loose household clusters there is still a great deal of sharing, but it is more formal and more attention is paid to balance on a shorter term. Men's cornfields are not adjacent, a count is kept of the number of ears loaned, and repayment is expected. Pigs are tended, penned, fed, and sold separately. Fewer meals are taken communally (as few as five shared meals a month). Garden crops and fruit trees are planted in several places, and they are distributed less evenhandedly.

Pooling has obvious advantages. People are cushioned from short-ages by the common fund of corn, the economic penalty of illness or injury is reduced, and dietary diversity in each dwelling is greater. The converse of these advantages has been, perhaps unjustly, the prevailing theme of most anthropological discussions of extended family groups (see, e.g. Pasternack, Ember & Ember 1976; Shah 1974). There are more possibilities for inequities in distribution that can lead to quarrels, hostility, and eventually, fission. From my limited knowedge of Kekchi cluster fission, it is rarely a difference over distribution that lies at the core of the quarrel; it is far more common for dissatisfaction with labor-exchange balances to begin the dissolution of a household cluster. We should be wary, however, of assuming that the social overhead, the inherent stress of cooperation, is always greater in a larger household than in smaller ones, as many authors do.

The importance of pooling tends to increase from south to north in Toledo District. When the subsistence activities of cluster members increase in diversity with more cash crops, pooling allows household cluster members access to a wider range of subsistence and manufactured goods, especially through shared use of radios, shotguns, tools, and luxury foods. Pooling also allows some entrepreneurial activities for which an independent householder rarely has the capital. All the shops in Aguacate are owned and operated by household cluster members, and in Indian Creek four men in a cluster have pooled their money to purchase an old truck they use to haul pigs and produce.

There is a close relationship between settlement patterns and the economic and social relationships that exist within and among domestic groups. There has been a tendency, especially among archaeologists, to regard settlements as products of large-scale economic or political formations (see, e.g., Plog 1974; Marcus 1976) or as simple products of a subsistence type (see, e.g., MacNeish 1964; Sanders 1962). The Kekchi show that patterns of dwellings on the landscape are best understood as the products of choices and decisions by households, balancing a changing variety of social, economic, and symbolic variables (see, e.g., Sutlive 1978; Brown 1977; Ross 1973).

Tight household clusters that have a high frequency of reciprocal exchange and interaction tend to be physically more densely grouped, and individual houses sometimes touch. Distance between houses is greater in loose clusters, and the constant rebuilding of houses allows rapid realignment in response to changes in interpersonal relationships (cf. Turnbull 1962). In 1974 the head of an Aguacate multiple-household cluster quarreled with his two sons over their lack of respect for him, and he rebuilt his new house on top of a steep hill 60 meters away. In 1979, with his advancing age and the burden of the alcalde office, he patched up his differences with his sons and built his new house at the bottom of the slope about 10 meters from his eldest son's.

When a young man has lived with his father or father-in-law for a year or more after marriage, building his own house with the older man's help is a part of his growing maturity and autonomy in other matters. This is the time of major decisions about future economic relationships with the parental household, and everyone in the village keeps a close eye on the distance between the new house and the parents' house. A distance of more than about 60 meters is a claim to independence.

We have seen that a household cluster can cope with a diversified subsistence system better than an independent household. The larger cluster can both concentrate on a single task when extra labor is needed and specialize in different tasks at the same time, later pooling the products. There is one aspect of production, however, that I have not yet discussed—coordination and leadership. In Sahlins's (1957, 1962) functional analysis of large extended family households on Moala, he argues that a strong leadership role is needed to coordinate and apportion work and redistribute goods among members. While in Moala the leadership of the household head is complemented by a system of ranking of junior members, the argument could be applied to the Kekchi. A large labor group can be more effective than a small group, but without leadership and coordination it can quickly degenerate and become very inefficient (see, e.g., Taggart 1975).

Sahlins seems to argue that the emergence of a status hierarchy and leader is inevitable, given the need for coordinating widely spaced activities and planning in advance. But just how inevitable is this? Younger members, those on the bottom of the hierarchy, must perceive that the rewards (present or future) of their subordination outweigh the disadvantages. They must also be convinced that their security and opportunities are better than they would be if they set up house on their own. And what about women, who accept subordination with only the prospect of acquiring indirect authority over their daughters and daughters-in-law in the future?[2]

Roles, rights, and duties within the household are not necessarily a structure into which people either mechanically fit themselves or face the consequences of their deviance. The household system is a product of negotiation in a context of economic rationality, in which such notions as proper behavior or respect are as much in dispute as they are labels to be avoided or used. The authority of Kekchi household cluster heads is related to the balance of costs and benefits they can offer to younger members, and to the difference between the benefits of living in a household cluster or in an independent household. This difference is called surplus or economic rent by economists (England & Farkas 1986:54). Balance between factors changes drastically when the subsistence–cash production balance changes from being like that of Santa Theresa to being like that of Indian Creek.

In Santa Theresa there is no great disadvantage to living in an independent household. Most productive tasks can be accomplished with the village labor group or by the single household head. The village is the important social and economic unit above the level of the individual conjugal family household. A household cluster still has some advantages in child care and distribution, but these are not strong attractions for young men who have more power in making residence choices than their wives have.

In Santa Theresa relations between men and their sons tend to be brittle after the sons are married. Most young men are happy to be free of the burden of their fathers' authority, and fathers are angry because their sons no longer pay them the respect they feel they are due even after their economic relationship has changed. Mother-daughter dyads are not nearly as brittle, and the benefits of continued cooperation in child care, cooking, and distribution tend to be more directly perceived by women in southern villages. It is therefore not surprising that neolocal and matrilocal residence is more common in southern villages, as husbands agree to move to their wife's village, if not their in-laws' residence.[3]

In Aguacate and the northern zone the balance of power between parents and children is more complex and leads to a very different result. Young men can easily see that in a household cluster they can have more flexible work groups and grow more cash crops. They see that men in independent households work harder and have a more difficult time managing diverse production. There are other benefits too: the prospect of setting up a business; the status of being allied with one of the big men of the community; and the protection he offers in disputes. Older men have something real to offer their grown sons, something to bargain with. This is not to say that there is less conflict between fathers and sons in these circumstances. Fathers still ask too much, and sons decide they would rather be independent or think they can make better bargains elsewhere (as in-laws are now in greater competition). This is why we find some household clusters of different composition than fathers and sons. Some young men find their father's authority too strong and leave for a more equitable cluster.

VARIATIONS IN HOUSEHOLD STRUCTURE

My conclusions about residence choice have been at an analytical level to this point. Statements from two young men who were making decisions about postmarital residence provide a useful emic complement. Table 10.1 is a translated list of reasons for why a man would want to leave his father's household after his first child is born, contrasted with reasons for wanting to stay in the father's household cluster.

I was told that sometimes a man moves away from his father because he wants to live in another village. This points out that processes of household formation and fission (mobility) cannot be separated from processes of migration in response to political, economic, and environmental forces. Table 10.2 is a list of reasons for moving to a new village, reasons that become important only if there is already trouble with a father.

These emic explanations are important because they show that the Kekchi themselves differentiate between movements motivated by the domestic or interpersonal and those motivated by regional differences in markets, land, and other resources. They recognize that the two are linked, but that the effects are sometimes different, as domestic problems can often be solved by moving around within a village.

Table 10.1. Postmarital Residence: Young Men's Emic Perspective

Reasons for Leaving the Natal Household Cluster	Reasons for Staying in the Natal Household Cluster
1. Your wife's father has no one to help him; maybe he will give you more respect than your father does	1. You help each other with your work, you can call on your father anytime you want: a friend may be busy, but your father will help you when you need it
2. You want to go live with your friends in another village, or maybe you have compadres there you want to be with	2. It is better for growing rice or beans, because your father always helps you and you split the money with him; if he gives you a lot of help then you give him half or a quarter of the rice
3. Your wife does not get along with your mother or your sister, or wants to be with her mother (maybe you can just move away from your father but stay in the same village)	3. Your father might give you things from his house—comal, *coxtal* (woven bag), *ka* (mano and metate), *sec* (bowls)—things to help you start your home, and pigs; this makes you close with him and shows he loves you, but some men leave their father as soon as he stops giving them things
4. You argue with your brothers	4. You can share corn for food and hogs with your father, and take from each other's field—this is good if your own corn is not so good that year; you also share meat with him
5. Your father is always drunk, and you get tired of that	5. It is easier to start a shop if your father has money, as long as he does not want the money back right away
6. You want to get your wife away from other men who want her	

Table 10.2. Reasons for Moving to Another Village:
Young Men's Emic Perspective

1. You want to be somewhere closer to the road so you can sell your crops better

2. You are sick, so you may want to be near the road so you can go to town to see the doctor [older people sometimes move for this reason and try to drag their children's families along with them]

3. It is easier to buy things if you live close to the road

4. You may want to move someplace where you can live closer to your plantation

5. You want to move where there is better hunting or fishing

6. You quarrel with someone in the village, because they steal, fight, hurt someone's animals, or fool around with your wife—things that happen if you drink too much

By now the reader should have a clear idea of why household clusters should increase in frequency as we move from the isolated southern zone to the northern roadside villages. In Table 10.3 some evidence for this trend is provided. Moving from Santa Theresa to Indian Creek there are fewer independent households, more household clusters, and larger dwelling units. Four villages are not a conclusive sample, but visits to other villages (and reports by other ethnographers) confirm that wherever there is population pressure on land, direct access to markets by road or river or both, there is a higher proportion of household clusters and fewer independent households (see Table 10.4).

Independent households usually include a nuclear family, and sometimes a widowed parent, a stepchild, or a half brother. After divorce young children and older girls usually stay with their mothers, but sometimes upon remarriage a husband refuses to allow the stepchildren to stay, and they are sent to their mother's parents or to more-distant relatives. In Indian Creek I found one child living with his godparents after being thrown out by his stepfather.

Two circumstances lead two or three nuclear families to live together in a single dwelling. The first is the practice of bride service, whereby a woman's parents require a prospective husband to live and work in their house for a year or more. This custom is now rarely followed, and cash payments have largely taken the place of bride service in the northern villages. Parents in southern villages, who often want their daughter to marry someone from the north, have had to drop their demands for bride service and accept cash. The common practice today is

Table 10.3. Frequencies of Different Household Types in Four Villages

	Santa Theresa	Aguacate	Crique Sarco	Indian Creek
Total population	101	159	222	54[a]
Number of dwelling units[b]	21	30	43	10
Mean number of persons per dwelling unit	4.81	5.30	5.16	5.40
Number of independent households	17	10	12	1
Percentage of independent households[c]	81.0	33.3	27.9	10.0
Mean number of persons per independent household	5.0	5.7	unknown	8.0[d]
Number of independent households with two nuclear families	0	2	2	0
Number of household clusters	2	8	13	5
Two-dwelling clusters[e]	2	5	9	4
Three-dwelling clusters	0	2	3	1
Four-dwelling clusters	0	1	1	0
Mean number of dwellings per cluster	2.0	2.5	2.4	2.2
Mean cluster size[f] (no. of persons)	8.0	11.9	unknown	

SOURCES: Schackt (1986) and my surveys.

NOTES: [a]The actual total population of Indian Creek is about 320. The listed figure is the total for the 10 censused households.

[b]Dwelling units are individual houses, whether clustered or not.

[c]This figure is merely the number of independent households divided by the number of dwelling units. Schackt (1986) did not define household clusters in Crique Sarco; I have done so using his map of the village.

[d]This is based on a single case.

[e]This is the number of household clusters composed of two dwelling units. Indian Creek figures are inconsistent with the total number of dwelling units because in that village I censused only one dwelling unit in each household cluster.

[f]Only one cluster in Indian Creek was completely counted, so I have no meaningful figure for this village.

postmarital residence of one or two years with the groom's parents. The couple stay until they have their first child and then build their own house. One young married man in Aguacate, who was living in his father's house when I first moved into the village, had a first child after 18 months of patrilocal residence, but every time the subject of build-

Table 10.4. Cash Cropping, Population Pressure, and Household Form

	Santa Theresa	Agua-cate	Crique Sarco	Indian Creek
Percentage of independent households	81.0	33.3	27.9	10.0
Percentage of farmers growing rice	0.0	39.3	55.8	80.0
Usable soil per household in catchment (in Ha)	218	110	167	70

SOURCES: Schackt (1986) for Crique Sarco; my surveys for Santa Theresa, Aguacate, and Indian Creek.

ing a house came up his father put him off. When the baby was six months old the young man's wife increased her complaints about not having a house and kitchen of her own. The husband took a week-long trip to San Pedro Columbia (a northern zone village) and announced on his return that his compadre there was going to help him build a house. A week later his father began to build him one in Aguacate.

Multiple nuclear families sometimes share one house if they are recent immigrants to a village and have not yet had time to build a second dwelling. In newly settled villages an entire household cluster often lives uncomfortably in a single house for a year or two. In Xanilha I found 19 people in four conjugal families living in a single house.

The developmental cycle of independent households starts with a couple and young children. Expansion begins when sons marry and bring in their wives for a year or two, but the household is denuded when they have children and leave. If either spouse dies in the later stages, the remaining member must either seek to join another household or try to find another person in a similar situation to remarry. Remarriage seems the commoner alternative—an Aguacate woman who was widowed in her late forties went all the way to Otoxha to marry a recently widowed man in his fifties.[4]

Two common types of household cluster have already been discussed: patrilocal clusters including a married son's dwelling and his parents'; and matrilocal clusters including a married daughter's nuclear family. There are other, less-frequent kinds, including:

- Patrimatrilocal: a married couple, their married son's dwelling, and their married daughter's dwelling
- Fraternal: two brothers and their wives in adjacent dwelling units; sometimes two half brothers
- Sororal: two sisters and their husbands in adjacent dwellings

- Extended sororal: a sororal cluster that also contains the dwelling of one husband's mother and stepfather (one case observed)
- Unrelated or compadrazgo: two or more dwellings of people connected by friendship, very distant kinship ties, or fictive kinship

This list does not exhaust the possibiliities, many of which may be found in villages I did not visit. After all, composition is a matter of pragmatics and circumstance rather than just rules and norms.

The domestic cycle of household clusters is considerably more complex than that of independent households, although the two are closely interrelated. Most people live in an independent household at some stage in their life, as well as in different types of household clusters. One 25-year-old Aguacate man had already lived in a matrilocal cluster, an independent household of his own, and an unrelated cluster; in 1979 he lived in a patrimatrilocal cluster but was planning on moving out to form a cluster with his mother's brother. This is an extreme case, but it should cast doubt on any attempt to define a normal developmental cycle for all clusters. Flexible membership is a more constant characteristic of clusters than any partticular sequence of structural development. Given the high mobility of the population and the speed with which economic changes are taking place in the district, developmental cycles of any kind are an analytical illusion.

About half the household clusters in Aguacate can still be ordered into a sequence of stages. The sequence begins with an independent household containing a nuclear family. Internal expansion begins when a son marries and brings his spouse into the house with him, followed by external expansion when this son builds his house nearby to form a household cluster. External expansion is regulated by the sex ratio of the household head's children and their birth spacing. The head's dwelling unit will expand and contract as more children are born, daughters leave, sons bring in wives, and sons leave to set up their own dwellings. The son's dwellings will expand as more children are born.

Early marriage means that women have long reproductive lives, and it is not unusual for 20 years or more to separate a woman's oldest from her youngest child. This could lead to complex multigenerational household clusters if extension were continued indefinitely. Household fission, migration, and short life span limit these possibilities, and I found no four-generation household clusters.

When the sons in a household cluster themselves have sons old enough to work, they are no longer dependent on their father or brothers for labor exchange. Instead they use their sons' labor without the burden of reciprocity. The relationships between brothers become increasingly strained during the expansion phase, and the eldest brother usually leaves first to start his own independent household. The largest patrilocal cluster I recorded in any village had three married sons and seemed to retain its stability because it was extremely loose—ties of obligation and shared ownership were minimal—and because the head was exceptionally rich in cacao groves, political power, cash, and possessions. This implies that property and "cultural capital" are an effective glue for binding clusters together past the point at which elder sons have their own household labor to draw on. In the absence of significant property, clusters do not endure.

When the eldest son departs (often following a quarrel with his father), a phase of decline begins. If the household head dies soon after, a fraternal cluster is left. The end result of the decline phase may be a single household, as the parents are left behind by their children, but usually the household head is dead by the time his youngest son has working-age children. If we take this sequence of development from an individual's point of view we would expect a typical first son's residence to follow this sequence: about one year living with parents in grandparent's dwelling; 12 to 15 years with parents in a separate dwelling within the household cluster; four to six years with parents in an independent household; two years in father's house after marriage; 12 to 15 years in a separate dwelling within the household cluster, beginning tight and ending loose; five to 13 years in an independent household with unmarried working-age sons: two years with married son living in dwelling; nine to 24 years in household cluster with married sons, depending on number of sons and birth order; a variable period living in an independent household after all sons have left the cluster.

What of the other household clusters that are not organized on this patrilocal pattern? In Table 10.5 we find some clues to the reasons for cluster information by breaking down cluster types within three villages. While the majority of Aguacate clusters fit into the patrilocal cycle, and the matrilocal clusters in Santa Theresa are explained above, the clusters in Indian Creek are much more varied in composition. This is in part simply because Indian Creek is a new village composed of distantly related or unrelated households drawn from all over the district—people live with whomever they can find; and in part because patrilocal clusters tend to be tight, while other clusters—especially those formed around distant kin, nonkin, or siblings—tend to be quite loose and involve little common property holding and less distribution of crops and money. In the villages close to the road, where cash crops are more important, a loose household cluster is often more attractive.

Table 10.5. Household Cluster Types in Three Villages

	Santa Theresa	Aguacate	Indian Creek
Patrilocal	1	7	1
Matrilocal	1	0	0
Patrimatrilocal	0	1	1
Fraternal and unrelated	0	0	3

The balance of labor exchange is more even, pooling less complete, and a nuclear family can accumulate more cash instead of sharing it. The advantages of sharing child care and flexible labor exchange are still there, but there is more autonomy in consumption.

Because Indian Creek is a new, expanding settlement, there is still equal access to land, and there is little heritable property, so transmission is not a major organizing principle for household clusters. Given time, and property worth enough, there should be more tight patrilocal clusters and fewer loose clusters organized on other principles. This has already happened in the Kekchi-Mopan village of Pueblo Viejo where lineal groups have become more important in recent years (Howard 1977a:47–75).

Many anthropologists use the ratio of consumers to workers in the household as a basic index of economic performance through the developmental cycle. However, the importance of CW ratios within the household depends on how permeable the economic boundaries of the household really are (Sahlins 1972). If exchanges and transactions between households also change with the developmental cycle, then the CW ratio may have little significance as a static measure. In the Kekchi case CW ratios mean much more to independent households than they do to dwelling units within a household cluster.

First let us look at how CW ratios change during the growth and decline of independent households.[5] On Figure 10.1a, we see that independent households start out with high CW ratios—they have a lot of young children—but as the children grow up the CW ratio declines. Aging couples see the CW ratio go up again as their productivity declines relative to their consumption. The age of the household head and CW ratio for the conjugal dwelling units within household clusters (see Figure 10.1b) fall into two clear groups—young couples whose CW ratio is rising as they have young children, and the older heads of clus-

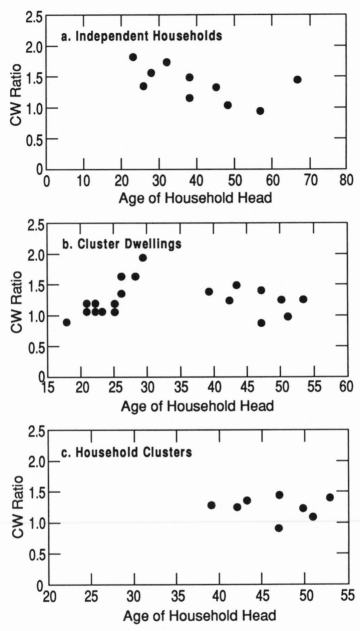

FIGURE 10.1   Age of Household Head and CW Ratio

ters who maintain a relatively balanced ratio into late middle age. Living in a cluster clearly has advantages for those young households on the steep early curve after marriage, with lots of mouths to feed and limited work power. But individual CW ratios say little about these dwelling units, for they are merged into the larger economy of the household cluster. There is much less variability in CW ratios between clusters (see Figure 10.1c), implying that these groups have more stability. While members of a household cluster may never get to enjoy living in an independent household with three or four grown sons working up a storm, they are also never stuck alone with six school-age children to feed.

MOBILITY AND KINSHIP

The developmental cycles of domestic groups must be understood in relation to patterns of mobility and migration. Just as there are regularities in the growth and development of domestic groups, patterns exist in the timing of movements between villages during the life course. Based on residence histories collected in Aguacate and Santa Theresa, the first point in the life cycle at which mobility becomes a matter of choice is marriage. While there is no rule of exogamy in Kekchi villages, the small size and high interrelatedness of most settlements often require that a person seek a mate outside the village (incest prohibition extends to all who share a grandparent).

Therefore, at marriage a decision is made between living in the husband's or wife's village. But opportunities are not equal in each village. Suppose the man is from Aguacate and his wife is from Santa Theresa. In Santa Theresa membership in a household cluster is not particularly important or vital to agriculture, and the couple could easily set up an independent household. In Aguacate the couple would have strong economic incentives to live with the groom's parents. The choice is not just between places and forms of residence, but between economic contexts. Most men in Aguacate would be reluctant to give up the security and access to resources they enjoy at home for the prospect of an independent household in a place like Santa Theresa. But if the husband comes from another southern zone village where independent households are common, residence in the wife's village is a more attractive option.

The result of these delicate balances is that residence patterns vary widely from village to village and from year to year, and generalizing on the basis of a single village is dangerous. In Table 10.6 the histori-

Table 10.6. Postmarital Residence and Exogamy in Aguacate by Marriage Cohort

	Number of Marriages	Percentage of Exogamous Marriages	Percentage of Patrilocal Residence	Percentage of Matrilocal Residence	Percentage of Neolocal Residence
1930–1939	1	0	0	100	0
1940–1949	9	89	50	25	25
1950–1959	8	100	71	14	14
1960–1969	12	67	67	8	25
1970–1979	17	76	75	19	6

NOTE: Postmarital residence refers to the village the couple chose to live in after marriage if the marriage was exogamous, and the household the couple chose to live in if the marriage was endogamous. In some cases locality could not be determined; percentages were then calculated on the basis of known cases.

cal variability in exogamy and postmarital residence among Aguacate residents is shown. As the size of the village and the local economy has changed, so have these choices. The recent decrease in neolocality, for example, is related to the increasing frequency of household clusters.

Another mobility decision point in the domestic cycle is when bride service ends, or at the birth of a couple's first child. The couple then chooses between joining the husband's parents' household cluster, setting up an independent household in the parents' village, or joining another household cluster. This choice is again between different domestic situations on one hand and different villages and opportunities for access to land and roads on the other. Yet in both this and the preceding stage of marriage the couple's resources are few and their needs are great. Therefore they tend to put the interpersonal above the regional, opting to live in the cluster or village where they have the greatest number of kin and the securest network of aid and support.

When a nuclear family has older, productive children they no longer depend heavily on other households for labor and aid, and their choices change. By this point their household has accumulated property and resources, and they can move to new communities quite easily. New villages are usually pioneered by households at this stage of development. The parents have also established ties of compadrazgo in other villages, and their children's marriages can extend affinal networks to other villages. A household that wants to be closer to the road or farther into the forest will try to marry a son into the target village and then follow and set up a patrilocal household cluster with that son. A daughter may also be used in this way if the son-in-law can be persuaded to join a household cluster.

When children are married the household again becomes stabler in location. Political power and community responsibility are now important considerations. The cultural ideal is to become so enmeshed in kinship ties within the village that one acquires the status of big person. One is surrounded by a tight and interconnected fabric of relationships that provide both security and power, based ideally on the respect of the community. There is less reason to move once this process has begun.

As mentioned previously, some households remain part of the mobile fraction of the population. Three of the independent households in Aguacate were headed by men who had no close male kin with whom they could affiliate to form a household cluster. All three had moved to Aguacate because they had affinal kin there. They were not taken into their wives' sisters' household clusters, but they did reside nearby and cooperate closely with their affinal male kin in labor exchanges. For these men the range of residence choices is curtailed, and therefore they are freer to respond to regional factors in their residence choice. Many of the households that gravitated to new roadside villages came from this fraction. These households' problems are often due to simple accidents—premature deaths, long illness, few living affines or consanguines, or skewed sex ratios among kindred. Ties of fictive kinship are inadequate substitutes (Howard 1977a:76–81). Where economy and polity is built on the fabric of kinship, those without kin find the economic frontier of the roadside village a cloth as yet unwoven.

Kinship has always presented something of a problem in studies of Mesoamerican societies. As Nutini (1976:5–6) sees it, anthropologists have tended to dismiss kinship in Mesoamerica as historically derivative of Spanish bilateral patterns imposed during the conquest (in other words, it is not traditional enough for them). Fixed on African unilineal kinship systems with explicit jural norms and political functions, ethnographers found Mesoamerican bilateral and cognatic systems uninteresting. They turned instead to the putatively traditional exotica of civil-religious hierarchy and compadrazgo.

Hawkins (1984:241) has recently suggested that the fault does not lie entirely on the shoulders of anthropologists; the ethnographer has ignored kinship because the Indians themselves pay little attention to it. Throughout the region (and certainly among the Kekchi) kinship has little importance beyond the level of the household. Hawkins can then ask a very interesting question: why is kinship not important in most Indian communities? Although I do not agree with his answer, he does look for it in the right place—the colonial past and ethnic and economic relations between Indians and the dominant Europeanized culture.

In pre-Hispanic times kinship was an important organizing principle in most small states and chiefdoms in Mesoamerica. Everywhere people reckoned descent as the key to political power and legitimacy, and larger states used and adapted clan systems in administration and government. As in the East African chiefdoms beloved of anthropology, the political order was built on a framework of (often unilineal) kinship relations or perhaps kinship metaphors. The Spaniards' assault on the native states was therefore also an attack on kinship systems, and they destroyed both. To eliminate Indian polities, the Spanish undercut their economic and social bases.

Amerindians have mostly reconstructed extended kinship systems in new forms after the conquest. In pre-Hispanic times kinship systems rarely had much to do with local systems of daily production and distribution of goods. Kinship played its main role in allocation of land and resources and in mediation of jural disputes over inheritance, property, and political rights. After the conquest, with little property to inherit, none of the ritual autonomy necessary to sanctify kinship authority, and with no rights to mediate important disputes or wage war, lineages and clans were rarely reconstructed. Instead kinship has remained submerged, or even hidden, within the corporate community, which has taken on many of these functions.

But as Nutini (1976) points out, there are some parts of Mesoamerica where clans and unilineal kinship systems do exist, where they have reemerged (rather than having survived, as some would have it; see Edmonson 1979; Colby 1976). Collier (1975) suggests, based on study of several Maya groups, that the existence and strength of patrilineages can be directly tied to the availability of land. When land is short patrilineages become important landholding units. Multigenerational corporate patrilineal groups cluster near the family land, and true lineages emerge. The Kekchi do not disprove Collier's hypothesis, and I have pointed out several ways that transmission between generations seems to increase patrilocal residence clustering. But I have also shown that cooperation in production plays an important role in structuring residence groups. Even in Aguacate, where land is not scarce, household clusters based on kinship ties are an important part of village social structure. Economic cooperation to cope with diversified crop production and entrepreneurial opportunities can also lead to the growth of new social groups at levels between the individual nuclear family and the whole village.

The Belizean Kekchi are something of a special case because the reservation system and abundance of land have made inheritance relatively unimportant in forming domestic groups. A similar case are highland Maya craft producers who also depend on household labor rather than property (Loucky 1979). They also expand their domestic groups to meet the demands of diversified production. Usually, however, systems of transmission and of production interact in complex ways that seem to vary with the local history, ecology, and economy. Does this mean that we cannot draw any useful generalizations from the Kekchi that can be applied to other cases of culture change?

HOUSEHOLDS AND CULTURE CHANGE

Attempts to equate household types with stages of cultural evolution produce only weak and uninformative correlations (see, e.g., Nimkoff & Middleton 1960). As I argued in Chapter 2, the household cannot be deduced from the world system, and we should reject moralistic or political agendas that seek to equate a social or economic stage with a household type. A better way to move from the specific case to more-general insights is to use the concept of niche. A niche is not a place or a resource, nor is it a mode of production or a particular social formation. For a household a niche is a combination of different resources and techniques for production and consumption with which members survive and reproduce. This is not a kind of historical particularism, but it does require close attention to the ecological setting of households on a case-by-case basis. Seemingly minor changes in an economic or ecological setting can have major effects on households.

For this reason, such gross categories as peripheral capitalism or simple commodity production simply will not do. What has been called the capitalist world system is temporally and spatially variable, "polymorphous," to use Chevalier's (1983:155) term. Capitalism presents many different niches, and historical phases of political and mercantile change create new niches and sweep old ones away (see Cancian, Goodman & Smith 1979). In much of the Third World today, capitalism provides many insecure and short-term niches that present special challenges to individuals and households. Households often respond to this variability by diversifying to occupy wide niches, broadening their resource base. They may also become more mobile in order to occupy a spatially dispersed niche. In the Third World many households have members in both rural and urban areas, in factories in California or shops in Germany. Flexibility and diversification have their own costs and structural problems that affect other parts of the household system. Household membership may become very fluid, and a single individual may belong, in different roles, to a number of households.

As households diversify to occupy different niches, they become more varied. In some places households change niches serially as they go through developmental cycles and have different resources and problems. Sometimes, however, households at the right stage of development are able to catch particular short-lived economic opportunities to accumulate rather than consume. Kekchi households that managed to occupy the shopkeeping–subsistence farming niche in the 1970s are reinvesting profits as capital, moving them completely out of the cycles of growth and decline that characterize their neighbors' households.

The key economic role of households in a developing country such as Belize, then, is that they bring together and integrate the fragmented and disarticulated local, regional, national, and even international economies. While economists and anthropologists argue about how modes of production are related to each other—articulated—the members of households bring together different modes of production every day. "Households frequently develop . . . strategies involving members in qualitatively different relations of production, both capitalist and noncapitalist. In fact, it is only through the combining of these various forms of economic activity that households sustain continuity. . . . Also, there is a great deal of variation among households as to their adaptive capabilities and performance" (Long & Richardson 1978 : 186–87). If these are very general statements about how households adapt, it is because our models of the environment presented by the expansion of the world system remain general. Netting and I (Wilk and Netting 1984) have suggested a number of ways that households adapt to specific characteristics of different economic niches by showing how different constellations of household activities can affect household organization and size. I will apply some of these concepts here to sketch some possible futures for the Kekchi household.

Anthropologists, like science fiction writers, predict the near future only if they are willing to be embarrassed. Any projection of the Kekchi future faces several imponderables: the future of land tenure and the reservation system on which it depends; the Belizean government's policies on agriculture and the development of Toledo; the resulting mix of development assistance and foreign capital that will affect it; and the amount of large-scale capitalist farming in Toledo and the resulting demand for farm labor. I should mention, too, the increasing ability of the Kekchi to affect their own future through such organizations as the Toledo Maya Cultural Council and various cooperatives. Perhaps most important of all will be the ability of some Kekchi to survive the poor rural primary school system and go on for higher education.

As wages and money become a larger part of Kekchi household income, distribution will become more problematic. When exchanges between household members consist mainly of intangibles they are complex and multistranded (including promises for the future), and it is hard for individuals to draw short-term balances. But when labor can be valued on a market, when commodities can be converted into cash values, relationships can be more accurately judged in economic terms, and cohesive productive units with several adults are harder to maintain. Younger people with better education can make much more money than their parents, and they no longer want to contribute their entire income to a common fund (cf. Martin 1984). Household clusters may still be important, but they will be looser and less stable. When some households begin to specialize in cash crop production, buying a majority of their food instead of growing it, they can hire labor instead of using kin or labor exchange and will seek neolocal residence. If they cannot hire labor, they may still live in household clusters, although this will depend on the labor-scheduling demands of their cash crop.

The response to shortage of land will depend on wage rates, the alternatives for rural employment, patterns of rural credit, land tenure, and marketing. Skewed ownership of land creates a high effective population density for the poor, even when overall population density is relatively low (Durham 1979). Several responses by households are possible. In early stages of land shortage households become important institutions for holding land and transmitting holdings to the next generation. In such a stable peasantry rules are developed for restricting inheritance to a few household members, while ineligibles who stay in the household contribute labor and share in consumption without hope of a share of the household's capital (see, e.g., Netting 1981; Smith 1959). This restriction on who will inherit, while preserving the farm as an economic unit, promotes outmigration of noninheritors. Resultant households tend to be large, but internally differentiated, and their fission and morphology may be more a product of property management than of efforts at efficient production. In any case, there is always tension between the need to manage property restrictively and the need to procure as much labor as possible.

Collier (1975) sees a second phase of land shortage in which the size of holdings becomes so small that property relations no longer hold households together. Individuals and couples break off to seek niches in the wage economy, in crafts or small-scale trading. As the rural economy is squeezed, households may change niches several times during the developmental cycle, or they may resort to mobility. While households may have very high fertility in order to provide labor, they have trouble keeping children home because the prospects for the future are poor and other niches beckon (Birdwell-Pheasant 1984).

Collier, however, worked in a fairly unusual situation where very few economic options were open to households because of ethnic and political discrimination. This keeps households equally poor, creating a uniform *minifundista* class that serves as a reserve labor pool for capitalist agriculture. In most cases when pressure on land increases, households become differentiated and then stratified by wealth (Stone, Stone & Netting 1984; Netting 1982). Households that accumulate capital are able to expand the breadth of their operations, pooling from diverse sources and investing in productive enterprises. Often members are recruited from poorer households, and the group takes on aspects of a small capitalist firm. Such large prosperous family businesses can achieve local political dominance that bolsters their economic power. These household firms, integrating complex productive, trading, and distributive activities and managing corporate capital, are found in towns and urban areas in settings as diverse as medieval Genoa and modern Mexico (Hughes 1975; Hunt 1965).

Groups who become involved in rural artisanry and crafts, like Guatemalan rope makers (Loucky 1979), may have large complex households that superficially resemble those of kulaks. But functionally these households are organized almost exclusively around the production process; as Medick (1976:303) says of protoindustrial cloth producers in Europe, "inherited property as the 'tangible' determinant of household formation and family structure receded in the face of the overwhelming importance of the family as a unit of labor." The retention of some part of a subsistence economy in such a unit allows capitalists to pay less then a living wage for the labor of the household members or the products of that labor. At best such an artisanal economy can develop into the kinds of independent rural small industry described in Italy by Conrad (1984), and at worst it presents one of the most exploitative faces of capitalism.

The poorest sector of the rural population, the landless workers, have households like those of craftspeople, organized around pooling resources. But it is important to distinguish what is being pooled and why. Richer peasant and merchant households not only pool labor, but pool income for investment. While craft-producing households pool their labor in the production process and may then put their incomes into a common pool of goods, the purpose is consumption rather than investment. As Medick (1976:295) says, they are pooling to redistribute their poverty. By concentrating on household pooling, we obscure the pooling between households and kin groups, which can be of equal or greater importance (see Segalen 1984). Rapp (1978) discusses circulation of food, furniture, clothing, appliances, money, and children among urban households, and others highlight the importance of such networks in times of crisis. Rapp stresses that these networks of sharing and pooling can be a leveling device, preventing anyone from accumulating the resources needed to escape poverty.

When property becomes less important in household strategies because of poverty and land shortage, mobility of all kinds tends to increase dramatically, and the boundaries of household membership become difficult to define. Certainly it is to the advantage of the rural household to keep its boundaries as fluid and open as possible and to assert its rights over the income of distant members. But household maintenance activities (housework) and petty production remain vitally important activities in households even when most wage earners are absent and their remittances are the major source of cash income (Palacio 1985). Fluid boundaries and membership allow the household to take advantage of new niches, especially in an economic setting where income opportunities are scattered and short-lived. As Rubenstein (1975:320) says of the poor in St Vincent,

> bounded corporate units on the domestic level would not permit individuals to easily change residential affiliation, mating behavior, or the organization of domestic and extra-domestic tasks when external socioeconomic conditions and opportunities (market prices for agricultural produce grown by villagers, wage labor prospects, migration outlets, etc.) fluctuate in an unpredictable fashion. A form of domestic organization in which domestic group and family functions are either independent or loosely associated with each other produces considerable scope for flexibility and maneuverability in domestic life.

As I have mentioned previously, individuals' interests sometimes counter those of households. When income is variable and unreliable, individual interests seem to come to the fore because most niches are too small for more than a single adult. Multiple household membership (like that described by Stack [1974] in modern U.S. urban black households), single-person households, institutional residence, consensual or communal sharing of dwellings, and even transient living without a residence are all viable alternatives. The deciding issue is what household membership can offer the individual, and what it requires in return, although these balances and decisions are complex.

In many ways the poorest rural households being squeezed off the land are similar to the poorer households in Third World cities. In the urban environment many niches are in the informal sector, and differences among those niches have a direct effect on household organization and strategy (Hackenburg, Murphy & Selby 1984). As income increases there is a tendency for greater structural stability in household organization. Certainly those with higher income have the resources to invest in educating children, and in the tools, equipment, or stock needed to open a microenterprise to broaden the niche. The full variety of urban niches has not been adequately described to date, but I suspect that the security and variability of niches is just as important as their wage rates.

I hope that it will be some time before the Kekchi have to deal with urban problems. But even in a relatively stable rural economy we are likely to see a kind of adaptive radiation as households, individuals, and communities cut new and diverging trails through the wilderness of the Belizean economy. The household is the nexus where individuals and groups confront their possibilities and make choices. I cannot agree with Fricke (1986) that the dynamics of the domestic economy determine the trajectory of the future. It is too easy to oppose the logic of household production to the impersonal grand mechanism of capitalist expansion. A collision of opposing principles is a nice dramatic theme, but it is inaccurate and historically naive. The household economy and the world economy are merely the two ends of a continuum that extends in temporal, spatial, and conceptual dimensions. We should not try to force Kekchi households to represent some primordial principle or reduce them to the capitalist logic of the firm. The power to determine the shape of the future does not lie at one extreme or the other but is always itself in dispute. As anthropologists acknowledge people's power to build cultures, invent traditions, and make their own histories, we should also accept (and praise) their ability to craft social structure.

11 Household History and Ecology

All anthropology is work-in-progress: no ethnography has a convenient end. Along the way, the choice of topics and issues is sometimes fortuitous, accidental, or arbitrary. Only reflection and hindsight find an ending, organize the wandering track into a direct road, and clean up the comfortable mess in the workroom so visitors feel welcome. This brief conclusion will draw out and tie together some of the threads that have been woven into the narrative so far.

Anthropologists have written a great deal about history lately, but in the daily grind of work, sweat, and food; the difficult business of getting along with family, kin, and community, is often lost. In this new literature history often appears as something verbal, as stories, tales, discourse, speeches, accounts, and debates about issues, people, and memorable events. The past is a series of contradictory interpretations and alternative explanations.

It is nice that history has become an object for anthropology. It is certainly an advance to find alternatives to writing history as timeless truth or as naive empirical description; it is important to allow a number of voices to disrupt an otherwise oppressive and self-serving enterprise. But from the standpoint of the household, history must be more than discourse and interpretation. Household history is a rich mix of events, labor, struggle, blood, argument, negotiation, decision, agreement, satisfaction, and every emotion from hatred to bliss. Sometimes individuals act on their own, sometimes with the group. Their contradictory interests are always weighed and balanced in both the short and long terms. Often a household can change its circumstances through calculated action, but just as often it faces narrow constraints and problems that are far beyond its control.

This fragile mote in the world certainly has a history, individual and collective, as intricate and important as its role in holding up the rest of the social world. For all that anthropologists write of history and social organization, this domestic world is still an unknown land, perceived dimly if at all (Wilk 1989). As to why this terra incognita, this cavernous black box, exists right in the middle of our analytical map of the world, I fear the answer is not very pleasant: households have no history because they have tradition instead.

Households have been sunk in our deepest preconceptions about the nature of traditional society—communitas, shared values, continuity with the past, structures of rules and norms. As the firm structural-functional order of lineage, clan, village, and tribe has melted away, we have often let the household and family remain as an untouched bedrock of social life. We assume the household is a communal unit with firm corporate boundaries, a place where individual goals and interests are submerged in a harmonious corporate group. Traditional social organization is thereby kept as a structural category, which is then opposed to the active individual goal-seeking strategies that make up history. In reality the household is no different from any other social field. Tradition and adaptation never exist without each other, and though they may be presented as opposed principles, they are actually two sides of an ongoing dialectic of change.

Another obvious problem in writing household history is that there are just so many households out there. How can we ever write meaningful histories for more than a tiny fraction? But this question confuses the real issue; history is not a life story, a sequence of events or a tale with a beginning and ending. The business of surviving and adapting in a group with other people is common shared experience in any community. We do not face our family with an empty slate. Household history is a composite of the perceptions, knowledge, and tools for survival as well as the pragmatic actions and decisions that they inform.

While I have not considered the discourse and perception of Kekchi household life in full detail, I have sketched the framework of pragmatic action and economic behavior at a few critical junctures. The best household histories weave the economic pragmatics of individual and group action together with the structure of knowledge and sentiment. This weave often becomes most visible in the discourse of family life, of discussions, arguments, bargaining, and even violence (see, e.g., Medick & Sabean 1984; Gaskins & Lucy 1986; Watson-Gegeo & Gegeo 1983; Rutz 1989). With hindsight the texture of domestic experience seems more important than it did during my original fieldwork. The cultural and expressive history of the household should complement and strengthen the economic history that I have focused on here. This is another reason why fieldwork is never finished.

HOUSEHOLDS AND ETHNICITY

A Kekchi household history or household ecology cannot be written without attention to ethnicity. In Mesoamerican ethnology ethnicity and domesticity have been linked in a number of ways. Many of the elements of Indian identity—consumption styles in clothing and cooking, patterns of domestic production in crafts and farming, rituals of curing, the life cycle and religious worship—have their locus in the domestic group (Friedlander 1975: 83–100; Annis 1987: 60–75).

But there is a great deal of controversy about where this ethnic identity came from, about its current transformations and ultimate fate. Some argue that it originated in the pre-Columbian era, others that it was produced by historical events during the early colonial period (Sherman 1979; Martínez Pelaez 1971) or in the commercial expansion of the late nineteenth century (Stavenhagen 1978; Wasserstrom 1983). Some ethnographers argue that Indian ethnic identity survives tenaciously as a source of central cultural values (Tedlock 1982), others that Indian ethnicity is an oppositional mirror image of the oppressive ladino culture (Hawkins 1984). Some see ethnic identity as a vehicle of resistance to economic and cultural domination (Warren 1978), and some go further to cast ethnicity as an overdetermined reaction to capitalist encroachment.

As with their approaches to the household, both modernization and dependency theorists tend to see ethnicity as a precapitalist vestige, doomed by the spread of modern instrumental and contractual relationships based on capitalism or class (or both). They see the dynamics of both domestic life and ethnicity as determined by the rhythms of global political economy. A much more sophisticated view of ethnicity is now emerging in anthropology. Just as some scholars now acknowledge that households are constantly constructed, negotiated, contested, and reinterpreted, others now argue that ethnicity is also a matter of practice and process (see, e.g., Isbell 1978; Herzfeld 1987). And one of the major means by which people invent and contest alternative traditions is through the construction of alternative histories.

The best history I have been able to write for the Kekchi in Belize is incomplete and uneven, but it shows that there was no simple long-term transition from a static and isolated culture to a dynamic and open one (cf. Gregory 1987). Instead there have been cycles of changing challenges and circumstances, through which the Kekchi have built cultural continuity and created an identity that they define as their traditional culture. I suspect that tradition was the most important focus of political identity, resistance, and group action at those times when economic surivival and political autonomy were most in question. Tradition crystalized and was codified in times of maximum stress. The two main episodes when traditional cultural identity was built include the Spanish pacification of Alta Verapaz and the German coffee era from 1860 to 1890. These crises were the context in which present Kekchi culture was formed: the civil-religious hierarchies; communal land tenure; mixed subsistence and cash crop farming; folk Catholicism; flexible bilateral kinship and the mobile household.

Today in Belize there is a new episode of culture building, as the Kekchi face new political and economic challenges. As they are drawn more deeply into market production and wage labor, traditional Indian identity is being rebuilt around the alcalde system, communal landholding on reservations, village labor groups, swidden farming, corn monoculture, and pig production, defined in opposition to the Belizean government and foreign business. While these practices are represented as timelessly rooted in the past, they are all relatively recent innovations.

But what role do households play in the construction of ethnic and historical tradition? In the first few chapters of this book I rejected many of the larger evolutionary models of traditional societies and economic development that provide conventional answers to this question. Without the evolutionary vocabulary, without the concept of timeless static tradition changing into dynamic and differentiated modern society, moving from structural transformation in the economy to the level of individual households means breaking an untrodden path. It is hard to think about the place of households in historical change without falling into an evolutionary idiom.

I have suggested that the best way around this problem is to concentrate on local economic, cultural, and ecological factors contained in the concept of an economic niche. But this metaphor does not help us understand the role that households play in constructing those niches. Part of our difficulty is a kind of cultural lag in anthropology. We have transformed the way we look at such people as the Kekchi, accepting that they have a long history in our modern world rather than existing in some isolated bubble of the ethnographic present. But we have not been able to bring these ethnographic insights to bear on the macroscale of regional and global systems and patterns. The problem is not one of articulating different modes of production, but one of articulating different levels of analysis.

HOUSEHOLDS AND THE FUTURE

Ethnography and ethnohistory are being rewritten partially in response to the increased self-awareness of previously isolated, downtrodden, and uneducated people, as a result of their struggles for economic and political power. Ethnographers and archaeologists have been, until very recently, the willing accomplices of the Maya in creating tradition. We have worked just as diligently as these people without history themselves, to create an image of stability and harmony, of culture rooted in the past. Now that many Maya are reading and writing their own history, their relationship with anthropologists is likely to become more complex and difficult, although also more interesting and productive. We will have to wait a bit longer for them to get around to building new theories of political economy and social evolution that go beyond both conservative and Marxist evolutionism.

The Toledo Maya Cultural Council began in the early 1980s as an ethnic-awareness group, composed of both conservative and progressive people concerned about economic, linguistic, and cultural issues, although motivated most urgently by the issue of land and the future of the reservations. Today they include representatives from a number of Mopan and Kekchi villages and are actively using history and tradition to further their economic and political goals. In 1988 the council petitioned the national government for a homeland of half a million acres in southern Belize. This area, almost the entire Toledo District, would replace the reservations and allow each village to decide on a mixture of communal and private tenure. To establish their rights to the land, the council emphasizes ancestry from the ancient Maya and identity with the people who built the ancient ruins of Toledo. They have worked at self-representations of Maya life in videotapes of dance and ritual performance, and are promoting the use of Mopan and Kekchi languages in education and radio programming.

In interviews with various government officials about the homeland issue in 1988, I was told a number of times (with reference to my own writings) that the Mopan and Kekchi were recent immigrants to Belize and therefore had no ancestral rights to a homeland. The Indians, it was said, should be treated like other Belizeans when it comes to landownership—why should they be protected or given special privileges? Perhaps it is special pleading, but I think the Kekchi and Mopan do deserve special treatment, if that is what we are to call the right to self-determination. If Amerindian history has taught us (and the Kekchi and Mopan) anything, it is that land, and the control of land, is vital to cultural and economic survival. Nobody, except the ghosts of the Manche Chol, has a better claim to the interior of Toledo District than the Mopan and Kekchi, and that claim should include the right to determine how that territory is to be divided and administered in the future. But the government continues to deny any such claim.

In 1988 the International Fund for Agricultural Development, in cooperation with USAID, began an agricultural development project in Toledo. They plan to divide up Crown Land (and eventually the reservations) into 50-acre parcels on which Indian families will be resettled before they receive assistance in planting cocoa and citrus (USAID 1986). Nobody consulted those labeled "project beneficiaries" in advance, nobody demonstrated that it is possible to survive and make a living on parcels arbitrarily limited to this size. Nobody has told the Kekchi and Mopan that if the price of cocoa falls and they default on their crop loans, they lose their land. Nobody has made provision for female landowners or for the next generation of farmers who are going to find themselves hedged in on all sides by private farms in foreign hands. How will local farmers—Indian, East Indian, or Garifuna—ever be able to compete with rich foreign farmers for land to expand their farms? The cocoa boom in Toledo is beginning just like the coffee boom in Alta Verapaz, and it could end up having the same result.

I have some very direct things to say about the way this development is going to affect Kekchi domestic life. It is easy to predict, for example, that in established villages larger household clusters will be able to take advantage of new opportunities for diversified production much more easily than independent nuclear family households. It is also clear that unattached independent households in the floater faction of village politics are more likely to move to new communities in the Crown Lands that are parceled out. But the establishment of permanent private land tenure will also have subtler, more pervasive and disruptive, effects that can only be understood by looking at the economic basis of the Kekchi household.

Kekchi households do not manage significant amounts of property. They are organized around labor exchanges and around the complementarity of male and female production. The whole basis of the relationships between spouses in marriage, between parents and children, between siblings, is negotiated and balanced without the issue of property entering the equation. The enduring ties among kin are not built on the expectation of inheritance or the joint use or ownership of property and capital. The household budgetary process, that intricate explicit and implicit balancing of contradictory and common interests, is a flow of food, cash, labor, and attention, but not of ownership and investment. When valuable property, such as 50 acres of cocoa, enters this economic system, the foundation of the household will change. Agrarian societies in which land is the crucial productive resource have dramatically different kinds of households, relationships between generations, and even demographic regimes (see, e.g., Collier 1975; Collomp 1984; Segalen 1984). Marriage becomes a strategy for managing property instead of labor (Lofgren 1974). The prospect of inheritance builds more lasting ties between parents and children. And in the process the nature of kinship, sentiment, and security are transformed.

Left to themselves, population growth would lead the Kekchi gradually into a system of restricted land tenure and private ownership. The household system would have time to adapt and adjust, as generations renegotiated their implicit and explicit contracts with each other—their elders and their children. But when private ownership is instituted suddenly by government action, contracts and agreements are more likely to be broken than renegotiated. The social disruption that ensues is not the result of some vague cultural anomie, hopelessness, or disorientation. It is the direct result of having the rules changed in the middle of the game, without warning. Suddenly losing the security of the most basic relationships in human life—the tacit agreements and contracts shared with one's closest kin—is more than an emotional shock. These relationships form the basis of economic security and even of survival. They are the fabric of political action and group solidarity, and people are often defenseless without them. It can take many years to find a new basis for trusting each other, as new agreements and forms of cooperation are found.

To end my dire predictions about the future, I want to make a final observation about the rate of economic change in Belize. The cycles of boom and bust in different industries and markets seem to be increasing in pace, and this effect is compounded by a bombardment of short-term programs, projects, initiatives, and incentives by a welter of government agencies, private voluntary organizations, and foreign-funded assistance programs. The economic environment within which rural people make their decisions and choices is changing so rapidly that they have little basis for predicting the future. And the future is the essence of the household. Generalized exchanges depend on a continuous relationship, on the knowledge that others can be depended on when they are needed, on a life cycle of growth and development that has some regularity, that can be foreseen. We may soon find that the kind of change is not as important to households as the pace of change. And extremely rapid economic change may undermine the bases of exchange that make it possible for households to perform their daily miracle of bringing together many activities under a single (metaphorical) roof.

Notes

1. The accepted orthography (Sedat 1971) writes the name of the language as *K'ekchi'*, marking the two glottalizations. For convenience, and following modern usage in Belize, I have eliminated the glottals in this book, but only from this word. Other Kekchi words are rendered accurately.

CHAPTER I. INTRODUCTION

1. Burkhofer's *The White Man's Indian* (1978) is an excellent example from U.S. history. Herzfeld (1987) discusses the "structural nostalgia" both within modern Greek society and in outsiders' views of that society.

2. Will Baker's interesting and challenging *Backward* (1983) is a prolonged meditation on just how that barrier is created and maintained.

CHAPTER 2. HOUSEHOLDS AND SOCIAL EVOLUTION

1. So-called primitive people may themselves become convinced that their way of life is a doomed relic and may therefore be willing to give it up more easily. Consider, too, the self-claimed scientific agricultural economist whose recommendations, based on the perception of African (for example) agriculture as backward and primitive, lead to the destruction of that system (and the substitution of putatively modern techniques), whatever its objective merits.

2. It is interesting that Le Play, like many before and after, equated rural life with the past and urban life with the future, drawing evolution out of geography. He left the countryside at an early age and never returned except to do fieldwork.

3. This point about typological errors preceding evolutionary errors also draws on Leach's (1961) criticism of British social anthropology.

CHAPTER 3. THE HOUSEHOLD AS A UNIT OF ANALYSIS

1. The middle-class North American ideology of the independent, self-reliant household is perhaps a reaction to, and mask for, an unprecedented amount of state domination of, and interference in, the household.

CHAPTER 4. THE HISTORICAL AND ETHNOGRAPHIC SETTING

1. This was presumably because in high population density areas there were fewer places for the Indians to run away to, and also because they were already

practicing land-intensive agricultural production techniques that could be successfully adapted to crowded areas around new towns. For those used to more-land-extensive agriculture, especially those in lowland areas, an entirely new agricultural system (one that was probably much less productive in terms of return to labor) had to be learned in order to survive in a reducción town.

2. Cambranes (1985:128) mentions that forced labor, in the form of groups called militias composed of Indians pressed from their farms to perform public work with minimal pay, was common in the 1700s as well. We do not know to what extent the Dominicans used this technique in the Verapaz, although Hawkins (1984:56) says that all Indians on church lands in Guatemala were required to give labor tribute.

3. There is unfortunately no room here to discuss the similarities between the schemes proposed today for developing the lowland tropics and those of over a century ago. There is something curiously timeless about the encounter between capitalism and the rain forest.

4. This pattern of land speculation's financing agricultural projects, or of speculators touting agriculture to foreign investors, continues in Belize today. This is one reason why over 90 percent of private land in the country was owned by foreigners in the early 1970s.

5. It is interesting that the 1891 census already lists 63 persons living on the Moho River, most of whom were probably loggers, but 10 are called "small planters" and may have been Kekchi or Mopan from Pueblo Viejo.

6. There were Carib Reserves on lines identical to those of the Indian system. A similar system was set up for the Mopan in San Antonio in 1897 (Bolland 1987:55).

7. Belize has become a relay point in international labor flows. Belizeans migrate to the United States, sending money home to support children and relatives. Hondurans and Guatemalans migrate to Belize for higher wages, and also send the money home.

CHAPTER 5. THE PHYSICAL SETTING

1. The Koeppen classification is *AFw*.

2. Most of this information is taken from Romney (1959), and the reassessment of this work by the same author (Charles Wright) in Nicolait et al. (1984).

CHAPTER 6. LAND TENURE AND CROPS

1. Most of these data were gathered in Aguacate, a village lying on the border between the northern and southern zones, and so sharing aspects of both. Whenever the discussion is couched in general terms it refers to practices in Aguacate. Additional information was obtained during visits to Otoxha and Santa Theresa in the southern zone and Indian Creek in the north. A single agricultural survey form was used with a small sample in Otoxha, Santa Theresa, and Indian Creek. In Aguacate basic quantitative data came from four separate questionnaire surveys of the entire village and a set of 15 eight-month daily work diaries kept by randomly selected paid male informants. Three one-month activity diaries were obtained from the three literate adult women in the community. Spot checks and resurveys were done constantly in order to

improve the reliability of the data. This was especially important with the recall survey, which recorded the number of workdays expended during the six months prior to the beginning of daily labor recording. Surveyed measurement of field sizes proved impossible—fields were just too scattered, irregular, and impassable. Three fields were measured, and the results proved close to the farmers' estimates. I have therefore used the farmers' estimates in each case, converted to hectares from the native measures, which are *tasks* (Spanish *mecates*) of 25 by 25 yards, and *manzanas* of 16 tasks.

2. Survey costs are a barrier to many poor Belizeans who want title to land. Government surveyors are overburdened with work, and the first person who pays a private surveyor will get the best piece. Not knowing the law is also a major problem for Kekchi.

3. Literally, sak'ecwaj means "sun field," meaning that it grows during the sunny dry season. The local Creole term is the Spanish *matahambre*, meaning "kills hunger."

4. Work groups are always fed corn tortillas and dumplings along with pork or chicken. The ceremonial meal that follows the calling of a work group has a fixed and rigid grammar that allows no substitutions. A farmer who has no corn to feed the work group must buy it.

CHAPTER 7. DOMESTIC ANIMALS, HUNTING
AND GATHERING

1. It was especially easy for this male fieldworker to deemphasize some parts of the diet because I spent most of my time following men around, and while I saw them hunt and fish a bit, I had less chance to work with women and children to see how much they were involved in tending livestock and gathering wild plants.

CHAPTER 8. ECONOMIC CHANGE

1. Some important recent studies include those by Mintz (1979, 1985), Bourdieu (1984), Appadurai (1986), McCracken (1988), and Orlove and Rutz (1989). Consumer researchers are increasingly interested in basic theoretical and cultural issues (see Belk 1983; Wallendorf & Arnould 1988; Roberts & Wortzel 1984). Social historians, too, have contributed insightful studies of consumer culture (see, e.g., Hobsbawm & Ranger 1983; Csikszentmihalyi & Rochberg-Halton 1981; Williams 1985; Wilson 1987).

2. One village shop owner has completely stopped farming. His father and his two brothers continue, and he gives them goods in exchange for corn. This household cluster has encapsulated a portion of the capitalist economy within the domestic mode of production.

3. This figure does not include expenses of production; for rice farmers this is about U.S. $40 for transport and weed killer. Household incomes sometimes include cash from two individual farmers.

4. These figures are consistent with a TRDP (1984 : 113) estimate of U.S. $460 annual gross cash revenue for upland Mopan farming. Berte (1983) gives no figures for annual cash income in San Miguel but estimates gross individual proceeds from rice farming at about U.S. $180, excluding income from other

sources. Schackt (1986:43–45) estimates incomes in Crique Sarco at U.S. $108 to U.S. $216 from the sale of pigs. Twenty-five households also made an average of $176 from rice, for a total of about $280 per household.

5. In the remotest villages only trees, shotguns, and items of clothing and personal adornment are considered private property; everything else is the communal property of the household. These notions of individual property are extended to bicycles, guitars, pens, watches, and a whole range of other goods, but not without a struggle. Arguments often ensue when a visitor asks, "Whose bicycle is this?"

6. Officially the fire remains a mystery; it may, however, have been personal or organized revenge. Fear of witchcraft is pervasive though public accusations are extremely rare. While the fear sometimes acts as a social control, some men with reputations as sorcerers (*aj tuul*) are subject to no sanctions at all because everyone is afraid of them. Some curers (*ilonel*) are respected and sought out for their medicinal skills at the same time they are feared.

CHAPTER 9. THE ORGANIZATION OF LABOR

1. Recent consumer research has begun to look carefully at how households balance demand and resources in making complex decisions (Wilk 1987). Anthropological interest in the topic has come through the debate about the economic value of children (Caldwell 1981) and through feminist anthropology for which the division of labor within the household is an important focus (Young, Wolkowitz & McCullagh 1981; Oppong 1983; Moock 1986).

CHAPTER 10. HOUSEHOLDS AS ADAPTIVE GROUPS

1. Barth (1967) laid the groundwork for this approach to household organization in an important paper on social change.

2. The issue of authority in households has been tackled seriously by feminist writers concerned with patriarchy, but rarely with long-term data or an ecological approach. Olivia Harris (1981:51), for example, argues that it is state policy and law that leads to strong patriarchal household headship, and makes interesting observations about the variable power of household heads in different situations.

3. I use the terms *matrilocal* and *patrilocal* in the most general sense to mean a choice to live closer to the wife's or husband's parents. The Kekchi believe that residence proximity is a matter of degree, and their praxis evades the standard anthropological terminology.

4. Marriage is rarely legal or Catholic at first but instead follows traditional forms that are more flexible. Traditional betrothal (see Schackt 1986) is far commoner in the south of the district. Church and legal weddings are considered luxuries, and most couples live together for some time and have children first.

5. I have calculated CW ratios according to the following schedule (see Chibnik 1987 for comparisons). I count women as full producers, as the work they do is just as essential as that of men. The rest of the figures were worked out with a Kekchi informant.

Age	Production		Age	Consumption	
	Female	Male		Female	Male
0–9	0	0	0–4	0.3	0.3
10–13	0.2	0.3	5–13	0.6	0.6
14–54	1	1	14–54	0.8	1
>55	0.5	0.5	>55	0.7	0.8

Bibliography

Abrams, Ira
1973 Cash crop farming and social and economic change in a Yucatec Maya community in northern British Honduras. Ph.D. diss., Harvard University, Cambridge, Mass.
Adams, John, and Alice Kasakoff
1984 Ecosystems over time: The study of migration in "long run" perspective. In *The ecosystem concept in anthropology*, ed. Emilio Moran, Boulder, Colo.: Westview Press.
Adams, R. E. W.
1972 Maya highland prehistory: New data and implications. In *Studies in the archaeology of Mexico and Guatemala*, ed. John Graham. Berkeley: Contributions of the University of California Archaeological Research Facility.
Adams, Richard N.
1965 *Migraciones internas en Guatemala: Expansión agraria de los indígenas Kekchies hacia el Petén.* Guatemala City: Centro Editorial José de Pineda Ibarra and Ministerio de Educación.
Aguilar, David
1984 National perspectives on land pressure in the Toledo uplands. In *Upland Workshop, Proceedings,* ed. Toledo Rural Development Project. Punta Gorda: Belize Ministry of Natural Resources.
Allison, Paul
1978 Measures of inequality. *American Sociological Review* 43:865–80.
Amin, Samir
1976 *Unequal development.* New York: Monthly Review Press.
Annis, Sheldon
1987 *God and production in a Guatemalan town.* Austin: University of Texas Press.
Appadurai, Arjun
1986 Introduction: Commodities and the politics of value. In *The social life of things: Commodities in cultural perspective,* ed. Arjun Appadurai. New York: Cambridge University Press.
Arcury, Thomas
1984 Household composition and economic change in a rural community, 1900–1980: Testing two models. *American Ethnologist* 11:677–98.

Arnould, Eric
1984   Marketing and social reproduction in Zinder, Niger Republic. In *Households: Comparative and historical studies of the domestic group*, ed. R. Netting, R. Wilk, and E. Arnould. Berkeley: University of California Press.
Ashcraft, Norman
1966   The domestic group in Mahogany, British Honduras. *Social and Economic Studies* 15:266–74.
1973   *Colonialism and underdevelopment: Processes of political economic change in British Honduras.* New York: Teacher's College Press.
Baer, Phillip, and William Merrifield
1971   *Two studies of the Lacandones of Mexico.* Publication no. 33. Mexico City: Summer Institute for Linguistics.
Bailey. F. G.
1969   *Stratagems and spoils.* New York: Schocken.
Baker, Will
1983   *Backward: An essay on Indians, time, and photography.* Berkeley, Calif.: North Atlantic Books.
Baran, Paul
1957   *The political economy of growth.* New York: Monthly Review Press.
Barlett, Peggy
1980   Cost-benefit analysis: A test of alternative methodologies. In *Agricultural decision making*, ed. Peggy Barlett. New York: Academic Press.
1982   *Agricultural choice and change.* New Brunswick, N.J.: Rutgers University Press.
Barnet, Richard, and Ronald Muller
1974   *Global reach.* New York: Simon & Schuster.
Barnum, Howard, and Lyn Squire
1979   An econometric application of the theory of the farm household. *Journal of Development Economics* 6:79–102.
Barth, Fredrik
1956   Ecological relationships of ethnic groups in Swat, North Pakistan. *American Anthropologist* 58:1079–89.
1967   On the study of social change. *American Anthropologist* 69:661–69.
Becker, Gary S.
1981   *A treatise on the family.* Cambridge, Mass.: Harvard University Press.
Beckerman, Stephen
1979   The abundance of protein in Amazonia: A reply to Gross. *American Anthropologist* 81:533–60.
1983   Does the swidden ape the jungle? *Human Ecology* 11:1–12.
Befu, Harumi
1968   Ecology, residence and authority: The corporate household in central Japan. *Ethnology* 7:25–42.
Belize Agriculture Department
1978   Agriculture Department annual report, Toledo District 1977. Internal memorandum, January, on file with Toledo Agricultural Station.
Belize.   Archives of Belize, Belmopan (BAB)
1916   Minute papers 1454-16, 1472-16.

1928   Minute paper 1279-28.
1932   Minute paper 249-32
1936   Minute paper 397.
Belize.   Public Records Office (BPRO)
n.d.   Deed Book 2, entry 883.
n.d.   Deed Book 4, entry 67.
n.d.   Deed Book 6, entries 470, 498.
n.d.   Deed Book 12, entry 128.
1886–1894   Plan Book.
n.d.   Register of titles, bk. 2.
1948   Probate and administration boxes, no. 24.
Belk, Russell
1983   Worldly possessions: Issues and criticisms. *Advances in Consumer Research* 10:514–19.
Beneria, Lourdes, and Gita Sen
1981   Accumulation, reproduction and women's role in economic development: Boserup revisited. *Signs* 7:279–98.
1982   Class and gender inequalities and women's role in economic development: Theoretical and practical implications. *Feminist Studies* 8:157–76.
Bennett, J.
1969   *Northern plainsmen: Adaptive strategies and agrarian life.* Chicago: Aldine.
Bennett, J., and D. Kanel
1983   Agricultural economics and ecological anthropology: Confrontation and accommodation. In *Economic anthropology: Topics and theories,* ed. Sutti Ortiz. Lanham, Md.: University Press of America.
Berardo, Donna, Constance Shehan, and Gerald Leslie
1987   A residue of tradition: Jobs, careers, and spouses' time in housework. *Journal of Marriage and the Family* 49:381–90.
Berk, R. A., and S. F. Berk
1979   *Labor and leisure at home: Content and organization of the household day.* Beverly Hills, Calif.: Sage.
Berkhofer, Robert F.
1978   *The white man's Indian.* New York: Alfred A. Knopf.
Berkner, Lutz K.
1972   Rural family organization in Europe: A problem in comparative history. *Peasant Studies Newsletter* 1:145–54.
Berte, Nancy
1983   Agricultural production and labor investment strategies in a K'ekchi' village, southern Belize. Ph.D. diss., Northwestern University, Evanston, Ill.
Bertrand, Michel
1982   Demographic study of the Rabinal and El Chixoy regions of Guatemala. In *The historical demography of highland Guatemala,* ed. Robert Carmack, John Early, and Christopher Lutz. Albany State University of New York at Albany Institute for Mesoamerican Studies.

Birdwell-Pheasant, Donna
1984   Personal power careers and the development of domestic structure in a small community. *American Ethnologist* 11:699–717.
Blau, Francine, and Marianne Ferber
1986   *The economics of women, men, and work.* Englewood Cliffs, N.J.: Prentice-Hall.
Boeke, J. H.
1942   *The structure of the Netherlands Indies economy.* Washington, D.C.: Institute for Pacific Relations.
Bohannon, Paul
1963   *Social anthropology.* New York: Holt, Rinehart & Winston.
———, and Laura Bohannon
1968   *Tiv economy.* Evanston, Ill.: Northwestern University Press.
Bolland, O. Nigel
1977   *The formation of a colonial society.* Baltimore, Md.: Johns Hopkins University Press.
1981   Systems of domination after slavery: The control of land and labor in the British West Indies after 1838. *Comparative Studies in Society and History* 23:591–619.
1987   Alcaldes and reservations: British policy towards the Maya in late nineteenth-century Belize. *América Indígena* 47:33–76.
———, and Assad Shoman
1977   Land in Belize, 1765–1871. Mona, Jamaica: University of the West Indies Institute of Social and Economic Research.
Boserup, Esther
1965   *The conditions of agricultural growth.* Chicago: Aldine.
Boster, James
1973   K'ekchi' Maya curing practices in British Honduras. B.A. thesis, Harvard University, Cambridge, Mass.
Bourdieu, Pierre
1977   *Outline of a theory of practice.* Cambridge: Cambridge University Press.
1984   *Distinction: A social critique of the judgment of taste.* Cambridge, Mass.: Harvard University Press.
Bradby, Barbara
1982   "Resistance to capitalism" in the Peruvian Andes. In *Ecology and exchange in the Andes,* ed. D. Lehman. Cambridge: Cambridge University Press.
Braudel, Fernand
1982   *The wheels of commerce.* New York: Harper & Row.
British Honduras (BHAR)
1891   *British Honduras annual report.* Belize City: Government Printing Office.
———   (BHBB)
1901   *Blue book.* Belize City: Government Printing Office.
1914   *Blue book.* Belize City: Government Printing Office.
Bronson, Bennet
1966   Roots and the subsistence of the ancient Maya. *Southwestern Journal of Anthropology* 22:251–79.

Brown, Judith K.
1970 A note on the division of labor by sex. *American Anthropologist* 72:1073–78.
Brown, M. W., and M. Salam
1985 *Report on a survey of red kidney bean farmers in Toledo, Belize, 1984/5.* Punta Gorda: Toledo Research and Development Project.
Brown, Susan E.
1977 Household composition and variation in a rural Dominican village. *Journal of Comparative Family Studies* 3:257–67.
Brush, Stephen
1977 *Mountain, field and family: The economy and human ecology of an Andean valley.* Philadelphia: University of Pennsylvania Press.
1987 Who are traditional farmers? In *Household economies and their transformations,* ed. Morgan Maclachlan. Lanham, Md.: University Press of America.
Burdon, J. A.
1934 *Archives of British Honduras.* Vol. 2: *1801–1840.* London: Sifton Praed.
Burkitt, Robert
1905 A Kekchi will of the sixteenth century. *American Anthropologist* 7:271–94.
Cabarrus, Carlos
1974 *La cosmovisión K'ekchi' en proceso de cambio.* Cobán, Guatemala: Centro San Benito.
Caldwell, John
1981 *The theory of fertility decline.* Homewood, Ill.: Irwin Publishers.
Cambranes, J. C.
1985 *Coffee and peasants in Guatemala.* Stockholm: Plumsock Foundation.
Cancian, Francesca, Louis Goodman, and Peter Smith
1979 Capitalism, industrialization, and kinship in Latin America: Major issues. *Journal of Family History* 26:319–36.
Cancian, Frank
1972 *Change and uncertainty in a peasant economy: The Maya corn farmers of Zinacantán.* Stanford, Calif.: Stanford University Press.
1979 *The innovator's situation.* Stanford, Calif.: Stanford University Press.
Caporaso, James A., and Behrouz Zare
1981 An interpretation and evaluation of dependency theory. In *From dependency to development,* ed. Heraldo Muñoz. Boulder, Colo.: Westview Press.
Cardoso, Fernando, and Enzo Faletto
1979 *Dependency and development in Latin America.* Berkeley: University of California Press.
Carneiro, Robert L.
1960 Slash and burn agriculture: A closer look at its implications for settlement patterns. In *Man and cultures: Selected papers of the Fifth International Congress of Anthropological and Ethnological Sciences,* ed. A. Wallace. Philadelphia: University of Pennsylvania Press.
Carter, Anthony
1984 Household histories. In *Households: Comparative and historical stud-*

ies of the domestic group, ed. R. Netting, R. Wilk, and E. Arnould. Berkeley: University of California Press.

——, and William Merrill

1979   *Household institutions and population dynamics.* Washington, D.C.: U.S. Agency for International Development.

Carter, William E.

1969   *New lands and old traditions: Kekchi cultivators in the Guatemalan lowlands.* Gainesville: University of Florida Press.

Cayetano, M., S. Hickman, and M. Brown

1986   *Lowland programme.* Proceedings of Final Workshop. Blue Creek, Belize: Toledo Research and Development Project.

Chance, John K., and William Taylor

1985   Cofradías and cargos: An historical perspective on the Mesoamerican civil-religious hierarchy. *American Ethnologist* 12:1–26.

Chapin, Mac

1988   The seduction of models: Chinampa agriculture in Mexico. *Grassroots Development* 12:8–17.

Charter, C. F.

1941   *The soil of British Honduras.* Port-of-Spain, Trinidad: University of the West Indies Press.

Chayanov, A. V.

1966   *The theory of the peasant economy.* Homewood, Ill.: Richard Irwin.

Cheal, David

1989   The social organization of the family economy: Political economy or moral economy. In *The household economy: Rethinking the domestic mode of production,* ed. R. Wilk. Boulder, Colo.: Westview Press.

Chevalier, Jacques

1983   There is nothing simple about simple commodity production. *Journal of Peasant Studies* 10:153–86.

Chibnik, Michael

1987   The economic effects of household demography: A cross-cultural assessment of Chayanov's theory. In *Household economies and their transformations,* ed. Morgan Maclachlan. Lanham, Md.: University Press of America.

Chirot, Daniel

1981   Changing fashions in the study of the social causes of economic and political change. In *The state of sociology: Problems and prospects,* ed. James Short. Beverly Hills, Calif.: Sage.

Christiansen, Sofus

1981   Shifting cultivation—Survey of recent views. *Folk* 23:12–23.

Clarke, William C.

1976   Maintenance of agriculture and human habitats within the tropical forest ecosystem. *Human Ecology* 4:247–60.

Clegern, Wayne

1968   *Maudslay's Central America: A strategic view in 1887.* Studies in Middle American Economics, no. 29. New Orleans La.: Tulane University Middle American Research Institute.

Coe, Michael, and Richard Diehl
1980   *In the land of the Olmec.* Vol. 2:*People of the river.* Austin: University of Texas Press.

Cohen, Abner
1981   *The politics of elite culture.* Berkeley: University of California Press.

Cohen, Mark
1977   *The food crisis in prehistory: Overpopulation and the origins of agriculture.* New Haven, Conn.: Yale University Press.

Colby, Benjamin
1976   The anomalous Ixil—Bypassed by the Postclassic? *American Antiquity* 41, no. 1:74–80.

Collier, George
1975   *Fields of the Tzotzil.* Austin: University of Texas Press.

Collins, Jane
1986   The household and relations of production in southern Peru. *Comparative Studies in Society and History* 28:651–71.

Collomp, Alain
1984   Tensions, dissensions and ruptures inside the family in seventeenth- and eighteenth-century Haute Provence. In *Interest and emotion,* ed. Hans Medick and David Sabean. Cambridge: Cambridge University Press.

Conklin, Harold C.
1954   An ethnoecological approach to shifting agriculture. *Transactions of the New York Academy of Sciences* 17:133–42.

Conrad, Jane
1984   Family structure and micro-industrial development in central Italy. Paper presented at the eighty-third meeting of the American Anthropological Association, November 14–18, Denver, Colo.

Conzemius, Eduard
1928   Ethnographical notes on the Black Carib. *American Anthropologist* 30:183–205.

Coombs, Gary
1980   Decision theory and subsistence strategies: Some theoretical considerations. In *Modeling change in prehistoric subsistence economies,* ed. T. Earle and A. Christenson. New York: Academic Press.

Covich, Alan P., and Norton Nickerson
1966   Studies of cultivated plants in Choco dwelling clearings, Darien, Panama. *Economic Botany* 20:285–301.

Cowgill, Ursula M.
1962   An agricultural study of the southern Maya lowlands. *American Anthropologist* 64:273–86.

Creighton, Colin
1980   Family, property and relations of production in Western Europe. *Economy and Society* 9:129–64.

Csikszentmihalyi, Mihaly, and Eugene Rochberg-Halton
1981   *The meaning of things: Domestic symbols and the self.* Cambridge: Cambridge University Press.

Culbert, T. P., P. Magers, and M. Spencer
1978   Regional variability in Maya lowland agriculture. In *Prehispanic Maya*

agriculture, ed. Peter Harrison and B. L. Turner. Albuquerque: University of New Mexico Press.

Denevan, William H.

1982   Ecological heterogeneity and horizontal zonation of agriculture in the Amazon floodplain. Paper presented at the Conference on Frontier Expansion in Amazonia, February 8–11, University of Florida, Gainesville.

Denton, Jeremiah, with Ed Brandt

1982   *When hell was in session.* Lake Wylie, S.C.: Robert E. Hopper & Associates.

Desieux, Dominique

1981   Development as an acculturation process. *Development: Seeds of Change*: 33–38.

Deutsch, Karl

1973   Social and political convergence in industrializing countries—Some concepts and evidence. In *Social science and the new societies,* ed. Nancy Hammond. East Lansing, Mich.: Social Science Research Bureau.

Dewey, Kathryn

1981   Nutritional consequences of the transformation from subsistence to commercial agriculture in Tabasco, Mexico. *Human Ecology* 92: 151–87.

Diamond, J. M.

1978   Niche shifts and the rediscovery of interspecific competition. *American Scientist* 66: 322–31.

Diener, Paul, Kurt Moore, and Robert Mutaw

1980   Meat, markets and mechanical imperialism: The great protein fiasco in anthropology. *Dialectical Anthropology* 5: 171–92.

Dieseldorff, Erwin P.

1909   [Untitled]. *Zeitschrift für Ethnologie* 41: 862–76.

Dillon, Brian

1977   *Salina de los Nueve Cerros, Guatemala: Preliminary archaeological investigations.* Socorro, N.M.: Ballena Press..

1985   Preface to the English edition. In Karl Sapper, *The Verapaz in the sixteenth and seventeenth centuries.* Occasional Paper, no. 13. Los Angeles: University of California Institute of Archaeology.

Douglas, Mary, and Baron Isherwood

1979   *The world of goods.* New York: Basic Books.

Dow, James

1981   The image of limited production: Envy and the domestic mode of production in peasant society. *Human Organization* 40: 360–64.

Dunk, Herbert

1921   *Report of the census of 1921.* Belize City, British Honduras: Government Printing Office.

Durham, William H.

1979   Scarcity and survival in Central America: Ecological origins of the soccer war. Stanford, Calif.: Stanford University Press.

Eachus, Francis, and Ruth Carlson

1966   Kekchi. In *Languages of Guatemala,* ed. Marvin Mayers. The Hague: Mouton.

Edmondson, Munro
1979 Some Postclassic questions about the Classic Maya. *Estudios de Cultura Maya* 12:157–78.

Eggan, Fred
1950 *Social organization of the western Pueblos*. Chicago: University of Chicago Press.

Ellen, Roy
1982 *Environment, subsistence, and system*. Cambridge: Cambridge University Press.

Engels, Friedrich
1942 *The origin of the family, private property, and the state, in the light of the researches of Lewis H. Morgan*. New York: International Publishers.

England, Paula, and G. Farkas
1986 *Households, employment and gender*. Chicago: Aldine.

Erasmus, Charles
1956 The occurrence and disappearance of reciprocal farm labor in Latin America. *Southwestern Journal of Anthropology* 12:444–69.

Escobar, A. de
1841 Account of the province of Vera Paz in Guatemala and the Indian settlements or pueblos established therein communicated by Don Carlos Meaney. *Journal of the Royal Geographic Society* 11:89–97.

Evers, H., W. Clauss, and D. Wong
1984 Subsistence reproduction: A framework for analysis. In *Households and the world economy*, ed. J. Smith, I. Wallerstein, and H. Evers. Beverly Hills, Calif.: Sage.

Ewel, John J.
1976 Litter fall and leaf decomposition in a tropical forest succession in eastern Guatemala. *Journal of Ecology* 64:293–308.

Ewen, Stuart
1976 *Captains of consciousness: Advertising and the social roots of consumer culture*. New York: McGraw-Hill.

Fabian, Johannes
1983 *Time and the other: How anthropology makes its object*. New York: Columbia University Press.

Falcón, G.
1970 Erwin Paul Dieseldorff, German entrepreneur in the Alta Verapaz of Guatemala, 1889–1937. Ph.D. diss., Tulane University, New Orleans.

Farriss, Nancy
1978 Nucleation versus dispersal: The dynamics of population movement in colonial Yucatán. *Hispanic American Historical Review* 58:187–216.
1984 *Maya society under colonial rule*. Princeton, N.J.: Princeton University Press.

Feldman, Lawrence
1975 *Riverine Maya*. Brief no. 15. Columbia: University of Missouri Museum.

Ferguson, James
1988 Cultural exchange: New developments in the anthropology of commodities. *Cultural Anthropology* 3:488–513.

Flandrin, Jean-Louis
1979 *Families in former times: Kinship, household and sexuality.* Cambridge: Cambridge University Press.
Flannery, Kent V.
1982 Preface. In *Maya subsistence,* ed. Kent Flannery. New York: Academic Press.
Flores, Anselmo
1967 Indian population and its identification. In *Handbook of Middle American Indians,* ed. Robert Wauchope. Vol. 6. Austin: University of Texas Press.
Folan, W., L. Fletcher, and E. Kintz
1979 Fruit, fiber, bark and resin: Social organization of a Maya urban center. *Science* 204:697–701.
Foster, George
1942 *A primitive Mexican economy.* Monograph no. 5. New York: American Ethnological Society.
1965 Peasant society and the image of limited good. *American Anthropologist* 67:293–315.
Foster-Carter, Aiden
1978 Can we articulate "articulation"? In *The new economic anthropology,* ed. John Clammer. The Hague: Mouton.
Fox, James J.
1977 *Harvest of the palm: Ecological change in eastern Indonesia.* Cambridge, Mass.: Harvard University Press.
Fox, John W.
1981 The Late Postclassic eastern frontier of Mesoamerica: Cultural innovation along the periphery. *Current Anthropology* 22:321–46.
Frank, Andre Gunder
1967 *Capitalism and underdevelopment in Latin America.* New York: Monthly Review Press.
1969 *Latin America: Underdevelopment or revolution.* New York: Monthly Review Press.
Freeman, J. D.
1955 *Iban agriculture: A report on the shifting agriculture of hill rice by the Iban of Sarawak.* London: Her Majesty's Stationery Office.
Fricke, Thomas
1986 *Himalayan households: Tamang demography and domestic processes.* Ann Arbor, Mich.: UMI Research.
Friedlander, Judith
1975 *Being Indian in Hueyapan.* New York: St. Martin's Press.
Friedman, Kathie
1984 Households as income-pooling units. In *Households and the world economy,* ed. J. Smith, I. Wallerstein, and H. Evers. Beverly Hills, Calif.: Sage.
Frykman, Jonas, and Orvar Lofgren
1987 *Culture builders: A historical anthropology of middle-class life.* New Brunswick, N.J.: Rutgers University Press.
Furley, P. A.
1975 The significance of the cohune palm, *Orbignya cohune* (Mart.) on the nature and development of soil profiles. *Biotropica* 7:32–36.

Furnivall, J. S.
1948   *Colonial policy and practice.* Cambridge: Cambridge University Press.
Furtado, Celso
1970   *Economic development in Latin America.* Cambridge: Cambridge University Press.
Gaskins, S., and J. Lucy
1986   Passing the buck: Responsibility and blame in the Yucatec Maya household. Paper presented at the Annual Meeting of the American Anthropological Association, December 3–7, Philadelphia, Pennsylvania.
Geertz, Clifford
1963   *Agricultural involution.* Berkeley: University of California Press.
Godelier, Maurice
1977   *Perspectives in Marxist anthropology.* Cambridge: Cambridge University Press.
Golley, F., et al.
1975   *Mineral cycling in a tropical moist forest ecosystem.* Athens: University of Georgia Press.
Gómez-Pompa, A., et al.
1982   Experiences in traditional hydraulic agriculture. In *Maya subsistence,* ed. Kent Flannery. New York: Academic Press.
González, D.
1961   Memorias sobre el Departamento del Petén. *Guatemala Indígena* 1:75–102.
Gonzalez, Nancie S.
1969   *Black Carib household structure.* Monograph no. 48. Seattle: American Ethnological Society.
1986   Garifuna traditions in historical perspective. *Belizean Studies* 14:11–26.
Goode, William J.
1963   *World revolution and family patterns.* Glencoe, Ill.: Free Press.
Goodenough, Ward
1955   A problem in Malayo-Polynesian social organization. *American Anthropologist* 57:71–83.
1956   Residence rules. *Southwestern Journal of Anthropology* 12:22–37.
Goody, Jack
1958   *The developmental cycle of domestic groups.* Cambridge: Cambridge University Press.
1972   The evolution of the family. In *Household and family in past time,* ed. Peter Laslett and Richard Wall. Cambridge: Cambridge University Press.
1976   *Production and reproduction.* Cambridge: Cambridge University Press.
Greenhalgh, Susan
1985   Is inequality demographically induced? The family cycle and the distribution of income in Taiwan. *American Anthropologist* 87:571–95.
Gregory, James
1972   Pioneers on a cultural frontier: The Mopan Maya of British Honduras. Ph.D. diss., University of Pittsburgh, Pittsburgh, Penn.
1975   Image of limited good, or expectation of reciprocity? *Current anthropology* 16:73–93.
1976   The modification of an interethnic boundary in Belize. *American Ethnologist* 3:683–709.

1984   Cooperatives: "Failure" versus "success." *Belizean Studies* 12 : 1–15.
1987   Men, women and modernization in a Mayan community. *Belizean Studies* 15 : 1–32.
Griffith, William J.
1965   *Empires in the wilderness*. Chapel Hill: University of North Carolina Press.
1972   Attitudes towards foreign colonization: The evolution of 19th century Guatemalan immigration policy. *Middle American Research Publications* 23 : 73–110.
Grigg, David
1980   *Population growth and agrarian change: An historical perspective*. Cambridge: Cambridge University Press.
Gross, Daniel R.
1975   Protein capture and cultural development in the Amazon Basin. *American Anthropologist* 77 : 526–49.
Gudeman, Stephen
1978   *The demise of a rural economy*. London: Routledge & Kegan Paul.
Guillet, David
1980   Reciprocal labor and peripheral capitalism in the central Andes. *Ethnology* 19 : 151–69.
Gusfield, J.
1967   Tradition and modernity: Misplaced polarities in the study of social change. *American Journal of Sociology* 62 : 351–62.
Guyer, Jane
1981   Household and community in African studies. *African Studies Review* 24 : 87–137.
1984   Naturalism in models of African production. *Man* 19 : 371–88.
Hackenburg, Robert
1974   Ecosystemic channeling: Cultural ecology from the viewpoint of aerial photography. In *Aerial photography in anthropological field research*, ed. Evon Vogt. Cambridge, Mass.: Harvard University Press.
————, Arthur D. Murphy, and Henry A. Selby
1984   The urban household in dependent development. In *Households: Comparative and historical studies of the domestic group*, ed. R. Netting, R. Wilk, and E. Arnould. Berkeley: University of California Press.
Hames, Raymond
1983   Monoculture, polyculture, and polyvariety in tropical forest swidden cultivation. *Human Ecology* 11 : 13–34.
Hammel, Eugene A.
1980   Household structure in fourteenth-century Macedonia. *Journal of Family History* 5 : 242–73.
1984   On the * * * of studying household form and function. In *Households: Comparative and historical studies of the domestic group*, ed. R. Netting, R. Wilk, and E. Arnould. Berkeley: University of California Press.
Hammond, Norman
1975   *Lubaantun: A Classic Maya realm*. Cambridge, Mass.: Peabody Museum.
1978   Cacao and cobaneros: An overland trade route between the Maya highlands and the lowlands. In *Mesoamerican communication routes and*

culture contacts, ed. Thomas Lee and Carlos Navarette. New World Archaeological Foundation Paper, no. 40. Provo, Utah: NWAF.

Hanks, L. M.
1972 *Rice and man: Agricultural ecology in southeast Asia.* Chicago: Aldine.

Hardesty, Donald L.
1977 *Ecological anthropology.* New York: John Wiley & Sons.

Hareven, Tamara
1982 *Family time and industrial time.* Cambridge: Cambridge University Press.

Harner, Michael
1970 Population pressure and the social evolution of agriculturalists. *Southwestern Journal of Anthropology* 26:67–86.

Harris, David
1969 Agricultural systems, ecosystems, and the origins of agriculture. In *The domestication and exploitation of plants and animals*, ed. P. J. Ucko and G. W. Dimbleby. London: Duckworth.
1972 Swidden systems and settlement. In *Man, settlement and urbanism*, ed. P. Ucko, R. Tringham, and G. W. Dimbleby. London: Duckworth.

Harris, Olivia
1981 Households as natural units. In *Of marriage and the market*, ed. K. Young, C. Wolkowitz, and R. McCullagh. London: CSE Books.
1982 Labour and produce in an ethnic economy, northern Potosí, Bolivia. In *Ecology and exchange in the Andes*, ed. D. Lehman. Cambridge: Cambridge University Press.

Harrison, Peter, and B. L. Turner, ed.
1978 *Prehistoric Maya agriculture.* Albuquerque: University of New Mexico Press.

Harrison, Robert
1976 Hamlet organization and its relationship to productivity in the swidden rice communities of Ranau, Sabah, Malaysia. In *The societies of Borneo: Explorations in the theory of cognatic social organization*, ed. G. N. Appel. Washington, D.C.: American Anthropological Association.

Harter, Carl, and William Bertrand
1977 A methodology for classifying household family structures. *Journal of Comparative Family Studies* 8:401–13.

Hawkins, John
1984 *Inverse images: The meanings of culture, ethnicity and family in postcolonial Guatemala.* Albuquerque: University of New Mexico Press.

Hawkesworth, Dorrit P.
1981 Variations in jointness within the Indian family. *Folk* 23:235–50.

Hayami, Akira, and Nobuko Uchida
1972 Size of household in a Japanese county throughout the Tokugawa era. In *Household and family in past time*, ed. Peter Laslett and Richard Wall. Cambridge: Cambridge University Press.

Hayden, Brian
1975 The carrying capacity dilemma. In *Population studies in archaeology and biological anthropology*, ed. Alan Swedlund. Washington, D.C.: Memoirs of the Society for American Archaeology.

Helms, Mary
1976   Domestic organization in eastern Central America: The San Blas Cuna, Miskito and Black Carib compared. *Western Canadian Journal of Anthropology* 6, no. 3:133–63.

Herlihy, David
1984   Households in the early Middle Ages: Symmetry and sainthood. In *Households: Comparative and historical studies of the domestic group,* ed. R. Netting, R. Wilk, and E. Arnould. Berkeley: University of California Press.

Herzfeld, M.
1987   *Anthropology through the looking-glass: Critical ethnography on the margins of Europe.* Cambridge: Cambridge University Press.

Hobsbawm, Eric, and Terrence Ranger, eds.
1983   *The invention of tradition.* Cambridge: Cambridge University Press.

Holdridge, Desmond
1940   Toledo: A tropical refugee settlement in British Honduras. *Geographic Review* 30:376–93.

Howard, Michael
1973   Political leadership in a Mayan village in southern British Honduras. M.A. thesis, Memorial University of Newfoundland, St. John's.

1974   Agricultural labor among the Indians of the Toledo District. *National Studies* 2:1–13.

1975   *Ethnicity in southern Belize.* Museum Brief, no. 21. Columbia: University of Missouri.

1977a   *Political change in a Mayan village in southern Belize.* Katunob Occasional Publications in Mesoamerican Anthropology, no. 10. Greeley: University of Northern Colorado.

1977b   Social stratification and development in a Kekchi village in southern Belize. Paper presented at the Annual Meeting of the American Anthropological Association, November 17–21, Houston, Texas.

Hughes, Diane
1975   Urban growth and family structure in medieval Genoa. *Past and Present* 66:13–17.

Hunt, Robert
1965   The developmental cycle of the family business in rural Mexico. In *Essays in economic anthropology,* ed. June Helm. Seattle: University of Washington Press.

Hyden, Goran
1986   The invisible economy of smallholder agriculture in Africa. In *Understanding Africa's rural households and farming systems,* ed. Joyce Moock. Boulder, Colo.: Westview Press.

IFAD (International Fund for Agricultural Development)
1985   *Toledo Small Farmers Development Project: Project preparation report—Climate annex.* Rome: International Fund for Agricultural Development.

Isbell, Billie J.
1978   *To defend ourselves: Ecology and ritual in an Andean village.* Austin: University of Texas Press.

Janvry, Alain de
1981 *The agrarian question and reformism in Latin America.* Baltimore, Md.: Johns Hopkins University Press.
Janzen, D. H.
1973 Tropical agroecosystems. *Science* 182:1212–19.
Jochim, M.
1981 *Strategies for survival: Cultural behavior in an ecological context.* New York: Academic Press.
Johnson, D. E.
1986 TRDP land pressure survey, 1984. In *Proceedings of final workshop.* Blue Creek, Belize: Toledo Research and Development Project.
Johnsons, Patricia L.
1988 Women and development: A highland New Guinea example. *Human Ecology* 16:105–23.
Jones, Grant
1971 *The politics of agricultural development in northern British Honduras.* Developing Nations Monograph Series. Winston-Salem: University of North Carolina.
1985 Maya-Spanish relations in sixteenth-century Belize. *Belcast Journal of Belizean Affairs* 1:28–40.
Jones, Grant, ed.
1977 *Anthropology and history in Yucatán.* Austin: University of Texas Press.
Kashiwazaki, Hiroshi
1983 Agricultural practices and household organization in a Japanese pioneer community in lowland Bolivia. *Human Ecology* 113:283–319.
Keesing, Felix
1958 *Cultural anthropology.* New York: Rinehart.
Kellman, M. C.
1969 Some environmental components of shifting cultivation in upland Mindanao. *Journal of Tropical Geography* 28:40–56.
———, and C. D. Adams
1970 Milpa weeds of the Cayo District, Belize. *Canadian Geographer* 14, no. 4:323–43.
Kelsey, Vara, and L. Osborne
1952 *Four keys to Guatemala.* New York: Funk and Wagnall.
King, Arden
1974 *Cobán and the Verapaz: History and culture process in northern Guatemala.* Middle American Research Institute Publication, no. 37. New Orleans, La.: Tulane University.
Klapisch, Christine
1972 Household and family in Tuscany in 1427. In *Household and family in past time,* ed. Peter Laslett and Richard Wall. Cambridge: Cambridge University Press.
Korn, Shulamit R. D.
1975 Household composition in the Tonga Islands: A question of options and alternatives. *Journal of Anthropological Research* 31:235–60.

Kroshus, Laurie
1987   Belizean citrus politics: Dialectic of strategy and structure. M.A. Thesis in Anthropology, University of California, Los Angeles.

Kunstadter, Peter
1984   Household composition and socioeconomic change: Lua' and Karen in northwestern Thailand. In *Households: Comparative and historical studies of the domestic group*, ed. R. Netting, R. Wilk, and E. Arnould. Berkeley: University of California Press.

Lambert, J., and J. Arnason
1980   Nutrient levels in corn and competing weed species in a first-year milpa, Indian Church, Belize, C.A. *Plant and Soil* 55:415–27.
1982   *Traditional milpa agriculture in Belize.* Ottawa: University of Ottawa International Development Studies Group, Institute for International Development and Cooperation.

————, and J. Gale
1980   Leaf-litter and changing nutrient levels in a seasonally dry tropical hardwood forest, Belize, C.A. *Plant and Soil* 55:429–43.

Laslett, Barbara
1981   Production, reproduction, and social change. In *The state of sociology,* ed. James Short. Beverly Hills, Calif.: Sage.

Laslett, Peter
1972   Introduction: The history of the family. In *Household and family in past times,* ed. Peter Laslett and Richard Wall. Cambridge: Cambridge University Press.
1984   The family as a knot of individual interests. In *Households: Comparative and historical studies of the domestic group,* ed. R. Netting, R. Wilk, and E. Arnould. Berkeley: University of California Press.

————, and Richard Wall, eds.
1972   *Household and family in past time.* Cambridge: Cambridge University Press.

Leach, E. R.
1961   *Rethinking anthropology.* London: University of London, Athlone Press.

Lehman, David, ed.
1982   *Ecology and exchange in the Andes.* Cambridge: Cambridge University Press.

Le Play, Frederic
1879   *Les ouvriers européens.* 2d ed. Paris: n.p.
1982   *On family, work, and social change,* ed., trans., and intro. C. B. Silver. Chicago: University of Chicago Press.

Levy, Marion, Jr.
1972   *Modernization: Latecomers and survivors.* New York: Basic Books.

Lewis, W. Arthur
1955   *The theory of economic growth.* London: Allen & Unwin.

Linares, Olga
1976   "Garden hunting" in the American tropics. *Human Ecology* 44:331–50.
1984   Households among the Diola of Senegal: Should norms enter by the front or the back door? In *Households: Comparative and historical studies of the domestic group,* ed. R. Netting, R. Wilk, and E. Arnould. Berkeley: University of California Press.

1985   Cash crops and gender constructs: The Jola of Senegal. *Ethnology* 242:83–94.

Lofgren, Orvar
1974   Family and household among Scandinavian peasants: An exploratory essay. *Ethnologia Scandinavica* 74:702–23.
1984   Family and household: Images and realities: Culture change in Swedish society. In *Households: Comparative and historical studies of the domestic group,* ed. R. Netting, R. Wilk, and E. Arnould. Berkeley: University of California Press.

Logan, Michael, and William Sanders
1976   The model. In *The Valley of Mexico,* ed. Eric Wolf. Albuquerque: University of New Mexico Press.

Long, Norman, and Paul Richardson
1978   Informal sector, petty commodity production, and the social relations of small-scale enterprise. In *The new economic anthropology,* ed. John Clammer. New York: St. Martin's Press.

Loucky, James
1979   Production and patterning of social relations and values in two Guatemalan villages. *American Ethnologist* 6:702–23.

Lovell, W. George
1988   Surviving conquest: The Maya of Guatemala in historical perspective. *Latin American Research Review* 23:25–58.

Lundell, Cyrus
1937   *The vegetation of Petén.* Publication no. 478. Washington, D.C.: Carnegie Institution.

McBryde, Felix
1945   *Cultural and historical geography of southwestern Guatemala.* Social Anthropology Publication, no. 4. Washington, D.C. Smithsonian Institution.

McCaffrey, Colin
1967   Potentialities for community development in a Kekchi Indian village in British Honduras. Ph.D. diss., University of California, Berkeley.

McClelland, David
1961   *The achieving society.* Princeton, N.J.: Princeton University Press.

McCloskey, Donald N.
1975   The persistence of English common fields. In *European peasants and their markets,* ed. W. Parker and E. Jones. Princeton, N.J.: Princeton University Press.

McCracken, Grant
1988   *Culture and consumption.* Bloomington: Indiana University Press.

McCreery, David
1983   *Development and the state in Reforma Guatemala, 1871–1885.* Latin America Series, no. 10. Ohio University Center for International Studies.

Macfarlane, Alan
1977   *Reconstructing historical communities.* Cambridge: Cambridge University Press.

MacNeish, Richard S.
1964   Ancient Mesoamerican civilization. *Science* 143:531–37.

Madge, D. S.
1965   Leaf fall and litter disappearance in a tropical forest. *Pedobiologia* 5: 273–88.
Malefijt, A. deWaal
1974   *Images of man: A history of anthropological thought.* New York: Alfred Knopf.
Marcus, Joyce
1976   *Emblem and state in the Classic Maya lowlands.* Washington, D.C.: Dumbarton Oaks.
1982   The plant world of the sixteenth- and seventeenth-century Lowland Maya. In *Maya subsistence,* ed. Kent Flannery. New York: Academic Press.
Martin, William G.
1984   Beyond the peasant to proletarian debate: African household formation in South Afirca. In *Households and the world economy,* ed. J. Smith, I. Wallerstein, and H. Evers. Beverly Hills, Calif.: Sage.
Martínez Pelaez, Severo
1971   *La patria del criollo.* Guatemala City: Editorial Universitaria.
Medick, Hans
1976   The proto-industrial family economy: The structural function of the household during the transition from peasant society to industrial capitalism. *Social History* 3:291–315.
————, and David Sabean, eds.
1984   *Interest and emotion.* Cambridge: Cambridge University Press.
Meggers, Betty
1971   *Amazonia: Man and culture in a counterfeit paradise.* Chicago: Aldine.
Meggitt, M. J.
1965   *The lineage system of the Mae Enga of New Guinea.* New York: Barnes & Noble.
Meillassoux, Claude
1981   *Maidens, meal and money.* Cambridge: Cambridge University Press.
Mintz, Sidney
1979   Time, sugar and sweetness. *Marxist Perspectives* 2:56–73.
1985   *Sweetness and power: The place of sugar in modern history.* New York: Penguin.
Mitterauer, Michael, and Reinhard Sieder
1979   The developmental process of domestic groups: Problems of reconstruction and possibilities of interpretation. *Journal of Family History* 4:257–84.
Moberg, Mark
1987   How determinant is the world system? Dependency and agency in rural Belize. Paper presented at the eighty-sixth Annual Meeting of the American Anthropological Association, November 18–22, Chicago.
Moock, Joyce, ed.
1986   *Understanding Africa's rural households and farming systems.* Boulder, Colo.: Westview Press.
Moore, M. P.
1975   Co-operative labor in peasant agriculture. *Journal of Peasant Studies* 2:270–91.

Moran, Emilio
1982 *Human adaptability.* Boulder, Colo.: Westview Press.
1984 Limitations and advances in ecosystems research. In *The ecosystem concept in anthropology,* ed. E. Moran, AAAS Selected Symposium, no. 92. Boulder, Colo.: Westview Press.
Moynihan, Daniel P.
1965 *The Negro family—The case for national action.* Washington D.C.: U.S. Department of Labor.
Murdock, George P.
1949 *Social structure.* New York: Macmillan.
Murphy, Robert F., and Julian H. Steward
1956 Tappers and trappers: Parallel process in acculturation. *Economic Development and Social Change* 4 : 335–53.
Myrdal, Gunnar
1957 *Rich lands and poor.* New York: Harpers.
Nadel, S. F.
1942 *A black Byzantium: The kingdom of the Nupe in Nigeria.* London: Oxford University Press.
1947 *The Nuba: An anthropological study of the hill tribes in Kordofan.* London: Cohen & West.
Nash, June
1983 *Implications of technological change for household-level rural development.* Women in Development Working Paper, no. 37. East Lansing: Michigan State University.
Nations, James, and Ronald Nigh
1980 The evolutionary potential of Lacandón Maya sustained-yield tropical forest agriculture. *Journal of Anthropological Research* 36 : 1–30.
Netting, Robert McC.
1965a Household organization and intensive agriculture: The Kofyar case. *Africa* 35 : 422–29.
1965b A trial model of cultural ecology. *Anthropological Quarterly* 38 : 81–96.
1969 *Ecosystems in process: A comparative study of change in two West African societies.* Bulletin no. 230. Ottawa: National Museum of Canada.
1977 Maya subsistence: Mythologies, analogies, possibilities. In *The origins of Maya civilization,* ed. R. E. W. Adams. Albuquerque: University of New Mexico Press.
1981 *Balancing on an Alp: Ecological change and continuity in a Swiss mountain community.* Cambridge: Cambridge University Press.
1982 Some home truths on household size and wealth. *American Behavioral Scientist* 25 : 641–62.
1987 Population, permanent agriculture, and polities: Unpacking the evolutionary portmanteau. Paper presented at the Development of Political Systems in Prehistoric Sedentary Societies Seminar, School of American Research, April 20–24, Santa Fe, New Mexico.
———, Richard Wilk, and Eric Arnould, eds.
1984 *Households: Comparative and historical studies of the domestic group.* Berkeley: University of California Press.

Nicolait, Robert, et al., eds.
1984   *Belize country environmental profile.* San José, Costa Rica: Trejos. Hermanos S.A. and USAID.

Nietchmann, B.
1973   *Between land and water.* New York: Seminar Press.

Nimkoff, M. F., and R. Middleton
1960   Types of family and types of economy. *American Journal of Sociology* 68 : 215–25.

Nisbet, Robert A.
1966   *The sociological tradition.* New York: Basic Books.

Nunes, Frederick
1977   Administration and culture: Subsistence and modernization in Crique Sarco, Belize. *Caribbean Quarterly* 23 : 17–46.

Nutini, Hugo
1968   *San Bernardino Contla: Marriage and family structure in a Tlaxcalan municipio.* Pittsburgh, Penn.: University of Pittsburgh Press.
1976   Introduction: The nature and treatment of kinship in Mesoamerica. In *Essays on Mexican kinship,* ed. Hugo Nutini, Pedro Carrasco, and James M. Taggart. Pittsburgh, Penn.: University of Pittsburgh Press.

Nye, P. H., and D. J. Greenland
1960   *The soil under shifting cultivation.* Harpenden, England: Commonwealth Bureau of Soils.

Olien, Michael
1988   After the slave trade: Cross-cultural trade in the Western Caribbean rimland, 1816–1820. *Journal of Anthropological Research* 44 : 41–66.

Oppong, Christine, ed.
1983   *Female and male in West Africa.* London: George Allen & Unwin.

Orlove, Benjamin
1977   Against a definition of peasantries: Agrarian production in Andean Peru. In *Peasant livelihood,* ed. Rhoda Halperin and James Dow. New York: St. Martin's Press.
1980   Ecological anthropology. *Annual Review of Anthropology* 9 : 235–73.
———, and Henry Rutz
1989   Thinking about consumption: A social economy approach. In *The social economy of consumption,* ed. Henry Rutz and Benjamin Orlove. Lanham, Md.: Society for Economic Anthropology and University Press of America.

Orozco-Segovia, Alma, and Stephen Gliessman
1979   The Marceño in flood-prone regions of Tabasco, Mexico. Paper presented at the Symposium on Mexican Agroecosystems, forty-third International Conference of Americanists, August 11–17, Vancouver, B.C.

Osborn, Anne
1982   *Socio-anthropological aspects of development in southern Belize.* Punta Gorda, Belize: Toledo Rural Development Project.

Painter, Michael
1984   Changing relations of production and rural underdevelopment. *Journal of Anthropological Research* 40, no. 2 : 271–92.

Palacio, Joseph O.
1985 Food, kin ties, and remittances in a Garifuna village in southern Belize. Paper prepared for a symposium at the University of West Indies, Mona, Jamaica.

Parsons, Talcott
1959 The social structure of the family. In *The family: Its function and destiny*, ed. R. N. Anshen. New York: Harpers.

Pasternack, Burton, C. Ember, and M. Ember
1976 On the conditions favoring extended family households. *Journal of Anthropological Research* 35:109–24.

Plakans, Andrejs
1984 Serf emancipation and the changing structure of rural domestic groups in the Russian Baltic provinces: Linden estate, 1797–1858. In *Households: Comparative and historical studies of the domestic group*, ed. R. Netting, R. Wilk, and E. Arnould. Berkeley: University of California Press.

Pleck, Joseph
1985 *Working wives/working husbands.* Beverly Hills, Calif.: Sage.

Plog, Fred
1974 *The study of prehistoric change.* New York: Academic Press.

Pohl, Mary
1977 Hunting in the Maya village of San Antonio Río Hondo, Orange Walk District, Belize. *Journal of Belizean Affairs* 5:52–63.
1985 An ethnohistorical perspective on ancient Maya wetland fields and other cultivation systems in the lowlands. In *Prehistoric Lowland Maya environment and subsistence economy*, ed. Mary Pohl. Papers of the Peabody Museum, vol. 77. Cambridge, Mass.: Harvard University Press.
n.d. Maya hunters. Unpublished manuscript on file with the Arizona State Museum Library, Tucson.

Popenoe, Hugh
1960 Effects of shifting cultivation on natural soil constituents in Central America. Ph.D. diss. Department of Agronomy, University of Florida, Gainesville.

Preiswerk, Roy
1981 Cultural identity, self-reliance, and basic needs. *Development: Seeds of Change* 83–91.

Rambo, A. T.
1962 The Kekchi Indians of British Honduras: An ethnographic study. *Katunob* 3:40–48.
1964 The ethnohistory of the Kekchi Indians of Belize. Unpublished manuscript.

Ranis, Gustav
1977 Development theory at three-quarters century. In *Essays on economic development and social change in honor of Bert F. Hoselitz*, ed. Manning Nash. Chicago: University of Chicago Press.

Rapp, Rayna
1978 Family and class in contemporary America: Notes towards an understanding of ideology. *Science and Society* 42:278–300.

Rappaport, Roy
1968   *Pigs for the ancestors.* New Haven, Conn.: Yale University Press.
Redfield, Robert
1941   *The folk culture of Yucatán.* Chicago: University of Chicago Press.
1956   *Peasant society and culture.* Chicago: University of Chicago Press.
————, and Alfonso Villa Rojas
1934   *Chan Kom, a Maya village.* Chicago: University of Chicago Press.
Reina, Ruben
1967   Milpas and milperos. *American Anthropologist* 69:1–20.
————, and Robert Hill
1980   Lowland Maya subsistence: Notes from ethnohistory and ethnography. *American Antiquity* 45:74–79.
Remesal, A. de
1966   *Historia general de las Indias occidental y particular de la gobernación de Chiapas y Guatemala,* no. 91. Guatemala City: Biblioteca Guatemalteca de Cultura Popular.
Richards, P. W.
1952   *The tropical rainforest.* Cambridge: Cambridge University Press.
1955   The secondary succession in the tropical rain forest. *Science Progress* 43:45–57.
Roberts, Mary, and Lawrence Wortzel, eds.
1984   *Marketing to the changing household.* Cambridge, Mass.: Ballinger.
Robinson, St. John
1985   German migration to Belize: The beginnings. *Belizean Studies* 13:17–40.
Rodman, Margaret
1985   Contemporary custom: Redefining domestic space in Longana, Vanuatu. *Ethnology* 24:269–79.
Romney, D., ed.
1959   *Land in British Honduras.* Colonial Research Publication, no. 24. London: Her Majesty's Stationery Office.
Roosevelt, Anna
1980   *Parmana.* New York: Academic Press.
Roseberry, William
1976   Rent, differentiation and the development of capitalism among peasants. *American Anthropologist* 78:45–58.
Rosen, Lawrence
1984   *Bargaining for reality: The construction of social relations in a Muslim community.* Chicago: University of Chicago Press.
Rosenberger, D. G.
1958   An examination of the perpetuation of southern U.S. institutions in British Honduras by a colony of ex-Confederates. Ph.D. diss., New York University.
Ross, Eric
1980   Patterns of diet and forces of production: An economic and ecological history of the ascendancy of beef in the United States diet. In *Beyond the myths of culture,* ed. Eric Ross. New York: Academic Press.
Ross, Harold
1973   *Baegu: Social and ecological organization in Malaita, Solomon Islands.* Urbana: University of Illinois Press.

Rostow, Walt W.
1960   *The stages of economic growth.* Cambridge: Cambridge University Press.

Roys, Ralph
1931   The ethno-botany of the Maya. Publication no. 2. New Orleans, La.: Tulane University Department of Middle American Research.
1972   *The Indian background of colonial Yucatán.* Norman: University of Oklahoma Press.

Rubenstein, Hymie
1975   The family as a non-group: Domestic organization in an eastern Caribbean village. *Proceedings of the Congress of the Canadian Ethnology Society* 2:311–23.

Ruddle, Kenneth
1974   *The Yukpa cultivation system.* Ibero-Americana, no. 52. Berkeley: University of California Press.

Rudie, Ingrid
1970   Household organization: Adaptive process and restrictive form: A viewpoint on economic change. *Folk* 12:185–200.

Ruthenberg, Hans
1971   *Farming systems in the tropics.* London: Clarendon Press.

Rutz, Henry
1989   Culture, class and consumer choice: Expenditures on food in urban Fijian households. In *The social economy of consumption,* ed. Henry Rutz and Benjamin Orlove. Lanham, Md.: Society for Economic Anthropology and University.

Sahlins, Marshall
1957   Land use and the extended family in Moala, Fiji. *American Anthropologist* 59:449–62.
1962   *Moala: Culture and nature on a Fijian island.* Ann Arbor: University of Michigan Press.
1972   *Stone Age Economics.* Chicago: Aldine.

Saint-Lu, André
1968   *La Verapaz, esprit évangélique et colonisation.* Paris: Centre de Recherches Hispaniques.

Sánchez, P. A.
1976   *Properties and management of soils in the tropics.* New York: J. Wiley & Sons.
———, and S. Buol
1975   Soils of the tropics and the world food crisis. *Science* 188:598–603.

Sánchez, Rodrigo
1982   The Andean economic system and capitalism. In *Ecology and exchange in the Andes,* ed. D. Lehman. Cambridge: Cambridge University Press.

Sanders, William T.
1962   Cultural ecology of nuclear Meso-America. *American Anthropologist* 64:34–44.
———, J. Parsons, and R. Santley
1979   *The Basin of Mexico: Ecological processes in the evolution of a civilization.* New York: Academic Press.

Sanjek, Roger
1982 The organization of households in Adabraka: Toward a wider comparative perspective. *Comparative Studies in Society and History* 24: 57–103.
Sapper, D. E.
1926 Costumbres y creencias religiosas de los indios Queckchi. *Annales de Geografía e Historia* 2: 189–97.
Sapper, K. T.
1897 *Das nördliche Mittel-Amerika nebst einem Ausflug nach dem Hochland von Anahuac.* Braunschweig: Druck und Verlag von Friederich Vieweg und Sohn.
1936 *Die Verapaz im 16. und 17. Jahrhundert.* Munich: Abhandlungen des Bayerischen Akademie der Wissenschaften, Mathematischnaturwissenschaftliche Abteilung.
1985 The Verapaz in the sixteenth and seventeenth centuries. Occasional Paper, no. 13. University of California, Los Angeles: Institute of Archaeology.
Schackt, Jon
1986 One God—Two temples. Occasional Publications in Social Anthropology, no. 13. Oslo: University of Oslo.
n.d.   Unpublished field notes on research in Crique Sarco, Belize.
Schiel, Tilman
1984 Development and underdevelopment of household-based production in Europe. In *Households and the world economy,* ed. J. Smith, I. Wallerstein, and H. Evers. Beverly Hills, Calif.: Sage.
Scholes, France, and J. E. S. Thompson
1977 The Francisco Pérez probanza of 1654–1656 and the Matrícula of Tipu (Belize). In *Anthropology and History in Yucatán,* ed. Grant Jones. Austin: University of Texas Press.
Schultz, Theodore
1977 On economic history in extending economics. In *Essays on economic development and social change in honor of Bert F. Hoselitz,* ed. Manning Nash. Chicago: University of Chicago Press.
Schwartz, Norman
1987 Colonization of northern Guatemala: The Petén. *Journal of Anthropological Research* 43: 163–83.
Seager, P. J.
1983a *Rice production in southern Toledo: Farming system report.* Punta Gorda, Belize: Toledo Research and Development Project.
1983b *Toledo farming system report: Bean enterprise report.* Punta Gorda, Belize: Toledo Research and Development Project.
1983c *Toledo farming system report: Corn enterprise report.* Punta Gorda, Belize: Toledo Research and Development Project.
1983d *Toldeo farming system report: Livestock production report.* Punta Gorda, Belize: Toledo Research and Development Project.
Sedat, S. Guillermo
1955 *Nuevo diccionario de las lenguas K'ekchi' y Español.* San Juan Chamelco, Guatemala: Instituto Lingüístico del Verano en Guatemala.

Segalen, Martine

1983 *Love and power in the peasant family.* Chicago: University of Chicago Press.

1984 Nuclear is not independent: Organization of the household in the Pays Bigouden Sud in the nineteenth and twentieth centuries. In *Households: Comparative and historical studies of the domestic group,* ed. R. Netting, R. Wilk, and E. Arnould. Berkeley: University of California Press.

1986 *Historical anthropology of the family.* Cambridge: Cambridge University Press.

Shah, A. M.

1974 *The household dimension of the family in India.* Berkeley: University of California Press.

Sherman, William

1979 *Forced native labor in sixteenth-century Central America.* Lincoln: University of Nebraska Press.

Shyrock, Henry, et al.

1973 The methods and materials of demography. Washington, D.C.: U.S. Department of Commerce.

Siemens, Alfred

1983 Oriented raised fields in central Veracruz. *American Antiquity* 48, no. 1:85–102.

Silver, Catherine

1982 Introduction. In *Frédéric Le Play on family, work, and social change,* ed. Catherine Silver. Chicago: University of Chicago Press.

Singer, Hans

1964 *International development: Growth and change.* New York: McGraw-Hill.

Smelser, Neil

1963 Mechanisms of change and adjustment to change. In *Industrialization and society,* ed. B. F. Hoselitz and W. E. Moore. The Hague: UNESCO-Mouton.

1967 Toward a theory of modernization. In *Tribal and peasant economies,* ed. George Dalton. Garden City, N.J.: Natural History Press.

Smith, Carol

1977 How marketing systems affect economic opportunity in agrarian societies. In *Peasant livelihood: Studies in economic anthropology and cultural ecology,* ed. R. Halperin and J. Dow. New York: St. Martin's Press.

Smith, Eric A.

1984 Anthropology, evolutionary ecology, and the explanatory limitations of the ecosystem concept. In *The ecosystem concept in anthropology,* ed. E. Moran. AAAS Selected Symposium, no. 92. Boulder, Colo.: Westview Press.

Smith, Joan

1984 Nonwage labor and subsistence. In *Households and the world economy,* ed. J. Smith, I. Wallerstein, and H. Evers. Beverly Hills, Calif.: Sage.

Smith Joan, I. Wallerstein, and H. Evers, eds.

1984 *Households and the world economy.* Beverly Hills, Calif.: Sage.

Smith, Robert E.
1952   *Pottery from Chipoc, Alta Verapaz, Guatemala.* Contributions to American Anthropology and History, no. 56. Washington, D.C.: Carnegie Institute of Washington.
Smith, Thomas C.
1959   *The agrarian origins of modern Japan.* Stanford, Calif.: Stanford University Press.
Spoehr, A.
1947   *Changing kinship systems.* Anthropological Series, vol. 33, no. 4. Chicago: Field Museum of Natural History.
Stack, Carol B.
1974   *All our kin: Strategies for survival in a black community.* New York: Harper & Row.
Stadelman, Raymond
1940   Maize cultivation in northwestern Guatemala. *Carnegie Institute of Washington Contributions to American Anthropology and History* 33:83–263.
Standley, Paul C., and Samuel J. Record
1936   The forests and flora of British Honduras. Botanical Series, vol. 12. Chicago: Field Museum of Natural History.
Stauth, Georg
1984   Households, modes of living, and production systems. In *Households and the world economy,* ed. J. Smith, I. Wallerstein, and H. Evers. Beverly Hills, Calif.: Sage.
Stavenhagen, R.
1978   Capitalism and the peasantry in Mexico. *Latin American Perspectives* 5:27–37.
Stoll, O.
1884   *Zur ethnographie der republik Guatemala.* Zürich: Prell Fussli.
1958   *Etnografía de Guatemala.* Guatemala City: Publicaciones del Seminario de Integración Social.
Stone, Doris
1932   Some Spanish entradas. *Middle American Research Institute Publication* 4:213–96.
Stone, Glenn D., Priscilla Stone, and Robert Netting
1984   Household variability and inequality in Kofyar subsistence and cash-cropping economies. *Journal of Anthropological Research* 40:90–108.
Stout, Donald
1947   *The San Blas Cuna.* New York: Viking Fund Studies in Anthropology.
Sutlive, V. H., Jr.
1978   *The Iban of Sarawak.* Arlington Heights, Va.: AHM Publishers.
Swett, Charles
1868   *A trip to British Honduras and to San Pedro, Republic of Honduras.* New Orleans: n.p.
Taggart, James N.
1975   "Ideal" and "real" behavior in the Mesoamerican nonresidential extended family. *American Ethnologist* 2:347–57.

Taylor, Douglas
1951 *The Black Carib of British Honduras.* Publication no. 17. Chicago: Viking Fund.
Tedlock, Barbara
1982 *Time and the highland Maya.* Albuquerque: University of New Mexico Press.
Terray, Emmanuel
1972 *Marxism and "primitive" societies.* New York: Monthly Review Press.
Thompson, J. Eric S.
1930a *Ethnology of the Mayas of southern and central British Honduras.* Anthropology Series, vol. 17. Chicago: Field Museum of Natural History.
1930b *Notes on the plants cultivated by the San Antonio Mayas.* Anthropological Series, vol. 17, no. 274. Chicago: Field Museum of Natural History.
1938 Sixteenth- and seventeenth-century reports on the Chol Maya. *American Anthropologist* 40:584–604.
1972 *The Maya of Belize: Historical chapters since Columbus.* Belize City: Benex Press.
1977 A proposal for constituting a Maya subgroup, cultural and linguistic, in the Petén and adjacent regions. In *Anthropology and history in Yucatán,* ed. Grant Jones. Austin: University of Texas Press.
Thompson, Lanny
1984 State, collective and household: The process of accumulation in China, 1949–1965. In *Households and the world economy,* ed. J. Smith, I. Wallerstein, and H. Evers. Beverly Hills, Calif.: Sage.
Thunen, J. H. von
1966 *Von Thunen's isolated state,* ed. P. Hall. Chicago: University of Illinois Press.
Topsey, Harriot
1987 The ethnic war in Belize. In *Belize: Ethnicity and development,* ed. SPEAR. Belize City: SPEAR.
TRDP (Toledo Research and Development Project)
1984 *Upland workshop, proceedings.* Punta Gorda, Belize: Toledo Research and Development Project.
1986 *Toledo Research and Development Project: Proceedings of Final Workshop.* Blue Creek, Belize: TRDP.
Turnbull, Colin
1962 *The forest people.* Garden City, N.J.: Anchor Books.
Turner, B. L.
1985 Issues related to subsistence and environment among the ancient Maya. In *Prehistoric Lowland Maya environment and subsistence economy,* ed. Mary Pohl. Papers of the Peabody Museum, vol. 77. Cambridge, Mass.: Harvard University Press.
——, and W. E. Doolittle
1978 The concept and measure of agricultural intensity. *The Professional Geographer* 30:297–301.

Urrutia, Victor M.
1967   Corn production and soil fertility changes under shifting cultivation in Uaxactun, Guatemala. M.A. thesis, University of Florida, Gainesville.
USAID (U.S. Agency for International Development)
1986   Toledo Agricultural Marketing Project, project identification document. Bureau for Latin America and the Caribbean, U.S. Agency for International Development, project 505-0016.
Valenzuela, J. Samuel, and Arturo Valenzuela
1981   Modernization and dependency: Alternative perspectives in the study of Latin American underdevelopment. In *From dependency to development*, ed. Heraldo Muñoz. Boulder, Colo.: Westview Press.
Vasey, Daniel E.
1979   Population and agricultural intensity in the humid tropics. *Human Ecology* 7:269–85.
Vayda, A. P., and B. McCay
1975   New directions in ecology and ecological anthropology. *Annual Review of Anthropology* 4:293–306.
Vayda, A. P., and R. A. Rappaport
1968   Ecology, cultural and non-cultural. In *Introduction to cultural anthropology*, ed. J. S. Clifton. Boston: Houghton Mifflin.
Viana, Francisco Prior de, Lucas Gallego, and Guillermo Cadena
1955   Relación de la provincia de la Verapaz hecha por los religiosos de Santo Domingo de Cobán, 2 de diciembre de 1574. *Anales de la Sociedad de Geografía e Historia de Guatemala* 27:18–31.
Villagutierre Soto-Mayor, Juan de
1983   *History of the conquest of the province of the Itza*, trans. Robert Wood, ed. F. Comparato. Culver City, Calif.: Labyrinthos.
Villa Rojas, Alfonso
1967   Maya lowlands: The Chontal, Chol and Kekchi. In *Handbook of Middle American Indians*. vol. 7: *Ethnology*, ed. Evon Vogt. Austin: University of Texas Press.
Vita-Finzi, C., and E. S. Higgs
1970   Prehistoric economy in the Mt. Carmel area of Palestine: Site catchment analysis. *Proceedings of the Prehistoric Society* 36:1–37.
Wallendorf, M., and E. Arnould
1988   "My favorite things": A cross-cultural inquiry into object attachment, possessiveness, and social linkage. *Journal of Consumer Research* 14:531–47.
Wallerstein, Immanuel
1976   *The modern world-system*. New York: Academic Press.
1980   *The modern world-system II: Mercantilism and the consolidation of the European world-economy, 1600–1750*. New York: Academic Press.
1984   Household structures and labor-force formation in the capitalist world-economy. In *Households and the world economy*, ed. J. Smith, I. Wallerstein, and H. Evers. Beverly Hills, Calif.: Sage.
Warren, Kay
1978   *The symbolism of subordination*. Austin: University of Texas Press.

Wasserstrom, Robert
1983   *Class and society in central Chiapas.* Berkeley: University of California Press.
Watson-Gegeo, K., and D. Gegeo
1983   Shaping the mind and straightening out conflicts: The discourse of Karawa'ae family counselling. Paper presented at the Talk and Social Inference Conference, October, Pitzer College, Claremont, Calif.
Wheaton, Robert
1975   Family and kinship in Western Europe: The problem of the joint family household. *The Journal of Interdisciplinary History* 5, no. 4:601–29.
Wilk, Richard
1981a Agriculture, ecology, and domestic organization among the Kekchi Maya of Belize. Ph.D. diss., University of Arizona, Tucson.
1981b Pigs are a part of the system: A lesson in agricultural development. *Belizean Studies* 9:122–29.
1983   Little house in the jungle: The causes of variation in house size among modern Kekchi Maya. *Journal of Anthropological Archaeology* 2, no. 2:99–116.
1984   Rural settlement change in Belize, 1970–1980: The effects of roads. *Belizean Studies* 12, no. 4:1–10.
1985   Dry season agriculture among the Kekchi Maya and its implications for prehistory. In *Prehistoric Lowland Maya environment and subsistence economy*, ed. Mary Pohl. Papers of the Peabody Museum, vol. 77. Cambridge, Mass.: Harvard University Press.
1986   Mayan ethnicity in Belize. *Cultural Survival Quarterly* 10:73–78.
1987   The Kekchi and the settlement of Toledo District. *Belizean Studies* 15:33–50.
1988   Maya household organization: Evidence and analogies. In *Household and community in the Mesoamerican past*, ed. Richard Wilk and Wendy Ashmore. Albuquerque: University of New Mexico Press.
1989   Decision making and resource flows within the household: Beyond the black box. In *The household economy*, ed. R. Wilk. Boulder, Colo.: Westview Press.
1990   Consumer goods as dialogue about development. *Culture & History* 7:79–100.
———, and Robert McC. Netting
1984   Households: Changing form and function. In *Households: Comparative and historical studies of the domestic group*, ed. R. Netting, R. Wilk, and E. Arnould. Berkeley: University of California Press.
Wilk, Richard R., and William L. Rathje
1982   Household archaeology. *American Behavioral Scientist* 25:617–40.
Williams, Rosalind
1985   *Dream worlds: Mass consumption in late nineteenth-century France.* Berkeley: University of California Press.
Wilson, Elizabeth
1987   *Adorned in dreams: Fashion and modernity.* Berkeley: University of California Press.

Wilson, Fiona
1982   Property and ideology: A regional oligarchy in the central Andes in the nineteenth century. In *Ecology and exchange in the Andes*, ed. D. Lehman. Cambridge: Cambridge University Press.
Wisdom, Charles
1940   *The Chorti Indians of Guatemala.* Chicago: University of Chicago Press.
Wolf, Arthur P.
1984   Family life and the life cycle in rural China. In *Households: Comparative and historical studies of the domestic group*, ed. R. Netting, R. Wilk, and E. Arnould. Berkeley: University of California Press.
Wolf, Eric
1957   Closed corporate communities in Mesoamerica and central Java. *Southwestern Journal of Anthropology* 13:1–18.
1982   *Europe and the people without history.* Berkeley: University of California Press.
Wolf, Margery
1968   *The house of Lim.* New York: Appleton-Century-Crofts.
Woodford-Berger, Prudence
1981   Women in houses: The organization of residence and work in rural Ghana. *Antropologiska Studier* 30/31:3–35.
Woodward, Ralph
1972   Social revolution in Guatemala: The Carrera Revolt. In *Applied enlightenment: Nineteenth-century liberalism*, ed. M. Harrison and R. Wauchope. New Orleans, La.: Tulane University Middle American Research Institute.
Wrigley, E. A.
1977   Reflections on the history of the family. *Daedalus* 106:71–85.
Wu Leung, W. T., and M. Flores
1961   *Food composition table for use in Latin America.* Bethesda, Md.: Interdepartmental Committee on Nutrition for National Defense, National Institute of Health.
Xenophon
1970   *Xenophon's Socratic discourse: An interpretation of the Oeconomicus*, ed. Leo Strauss, trans. Carnes Lord. Ithaca, N.Y.: Cornell University Press.
Ximénez, Fray Francisco
1930   *Historia de la provincia de San Vicente de Chiapa y Guatemala.* Guatemala City: Biblioteca "Goathemala" de la Sociedad de Geografía e Historia.
Young, Kate, Carol Wolkowitz, and Roslyn McCullagh
1981   *Of marriage and the market: Women's subordination in international perspective.* London: CSE Books.
Zimmerman, Carle C., and Merle E. Frampton
1935   *Family and society: A study of the sociology of reconstruction.* New York: D. Van Norstrand.

Index

ABOUT THE AUTHOR

Richard R. Wilk is professor of anthropology at Indiana University at Bloomington. He has worked in archaeology and in applied anthropology, and has written extensively on the household and family. Among his recent works are *The Household Economy, Households* (co-edited with Robert McC. Netting and Eric Arnould), and *Archaeology of the Household* (co-edited with William Rathje).